I0793009

IMAGES
of America

ADAMS COUNTY

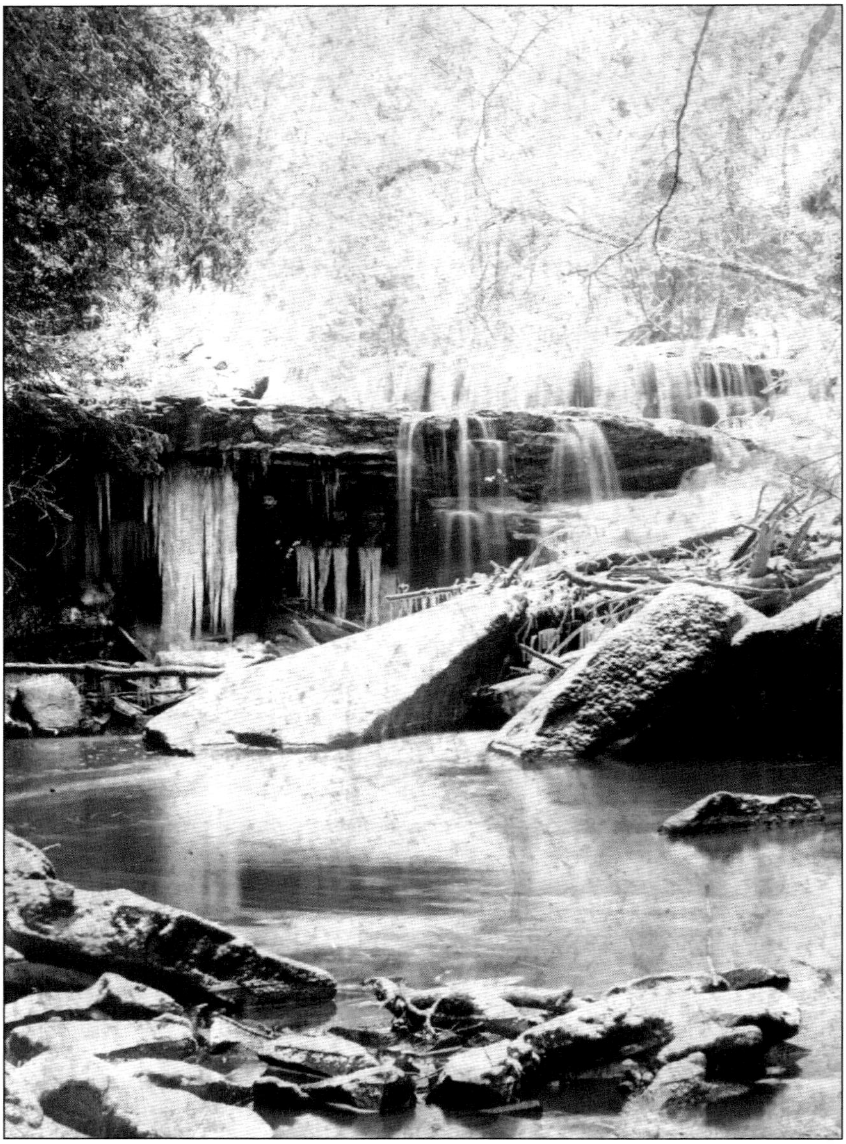

Cedar Falls is the largest waterfall in Adams County. Located in a spectacular gorge more than a mile upstream from the community of Cedar Mills, it is now part of the Richard and Lucile Durrell Edge of Appalachia Preserve System. Taken around 1900, this wintertime view is one of the earliest known photographs of this unique natural landmark. Notice the man standing under the ledge beside the large icicles. (Courtesy Valerie Young.)

On the Cover: In 1943, in the clubhouse of the Adams County Country Club in West Union, friends and coworkers of Eustice Stultz toast him as he prepares to enter the army. From left to right are Loran Grooms, George Watson, Ted Brodt, Eustice Stultz, and Ira Shell. Stultz served the remainder of World War II with the U.S. Army Air Corps in the South Pacific theater. Returning to West Union, he resumed his position at the village's post office, retiring in the early 1970s. (Courtesy Adams County Historical Society.)

IMAGES
of America

ADAMS COUNTY

Stephen Kelley

ARCADIA
PUBLISHING

ISBN 978-0-7385-8382-2

Published by Arcadia Publishing
Charleston, South Carolina

Printed in the United States of America

Library of Congress Control Number: 2010927422

For all general information contact Arcadia Publishing at:
Telephone 843-853-2070
Fax 843-853-0044
E-mail sales@arcadiapublishing.com
For customer service and orders:
Toll-Free 1-888-313-2665

Visit us on the Internet at www.arcadiapublishing.com

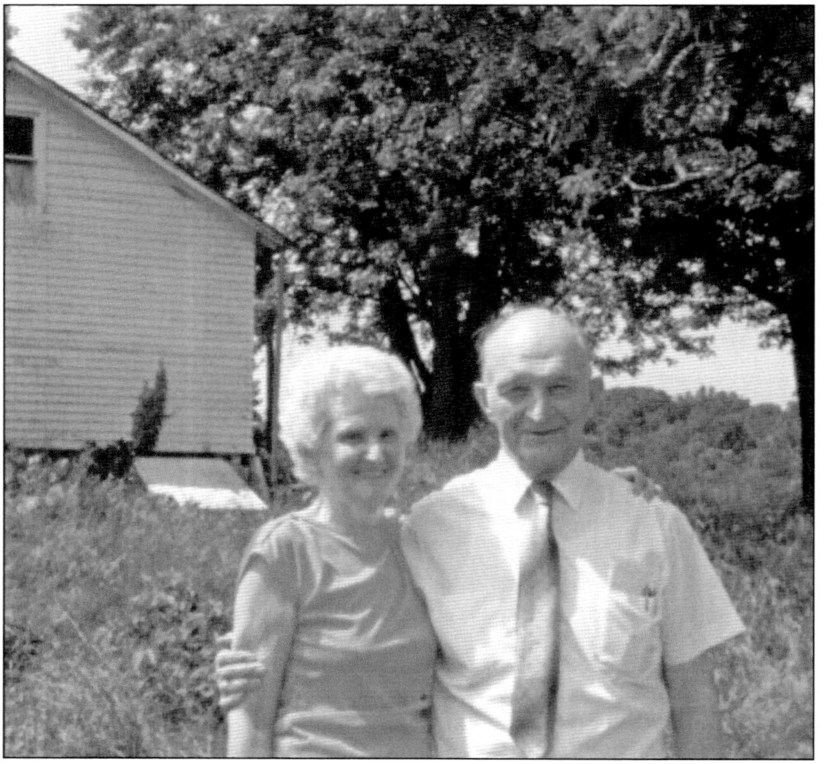

This book is dedicated to the memory of the author's parents, Byron S. and Almeda (Sue) Stamper Kelley. They are shown here in the summer of 1985 at the little three-room house in Scott Township, Adams County, where they had started housekeeping almost 40 years earlier. (Courtesy Rev. Dr. Susan Kay Kelley Roads.)

Contents

Acknowledgments

There were many individuals and organizations who provided photographs for this book. We especially want to recognize the Adams County Historical Society for giving us free rein to scour its archives, as well as the Adams County Genealogical Society for opening its files and photograph collections to us. The volunteers and members of both societies exhibited great interest in this project and were most helpful. A special thanks is given to Lois Kirschner Kidd, of the Manchester Historical Society, who generously offered vintage pictures from that organization's archives in addition to permitting us to use photographs from her personal collection.

Lester and Jean Wallis of Hillsboro, Ohio, have amassed a wealth of antique photographs over the past several decades. Longtime friends of the author, they too freely offered the use of their collection of Adams County photographs. Other individuals who provided several photographic images for this work include John and Carol Wickerham, William and Bessie J. Sininger and Valerie Young of West Union, and Mary Fulton and H. W. Johnson Jr. of Peebles. To all these and others who graciously provided photographs, as well as other support, we humbly thank you.

INTRODUCTION

Adams County, Ohio, was established by proclamation on July 10, 1797. The county is located in the south-central part of the state with the Ohio River as its southern boundary. It was named in honor of the incumbent president, John Adams. When first created, Adams County's boundaries encompassed approximately one-fifth of what was to become the state of Ohio. Its original northern boundary crossed through modern-day Marion County—more than 40 miles north of Columbus. Adams County was carved out of what was then known as the "Territory North West of the River Ohio," now referred to as the Old Northwest. It is the third-oldest county in Ohio, predating the formation of the state by more than five years.

The earliest identified humans to inhabit the Ohio Valley were the Paleo Indians. It is believed these peoples moved into the area about 11,000 years ago. One of the largest clusters of Paleo Indian encampment sites discovered in North America is near the Adams County community of Sandy Springs on the Ohio River. Subsequent prehistoric groups making their homes in Adams County included the Adena and Hopewell cultures, who left behind a number of burial mounds and earthen enclosures, a few of which may yet be seen. The Fort Ancient culture was the last of the prehistoric peoples to live here. They left one of the most intriguing and significant earthworks known in the New World—the Great Serpent Mound. This world-class monument of the past is preserved in Bratton Township in a park owned and operated by the Ohio Historical Society.

When the first whites began exploring this region, they found it well occupied by the Shawnee nation. They were among the most warlike of the eastern Native American tribes and put up a fierce resistance to the encroachment of white settlers. They relinquished their claims to southern Ohio only after a crushing defeat in 1794 at the Battle of Fallen Timbers.

The first permanent white settlement in Adams County was a fortified civilian community initially known as "Massie's Station," built on the banks of the Ohio River at Three Islands. Its founder, Nathaniel Massie (1763–1811), later became one of the largest landholders in Ohio and a prominent politician who helped pave the way for Ohio statehood. The little fort known as Massie's Station was built in the winter of 1790–1791. It gave rise to the village known today as Manchester, which ranks among the oldest towns in Ohio. One of the first "forters" to permanently settle outside Massie's Station was Thomas Kirker (1760–1837), an Irish immigrant who later served two terms as Ohio's second governor.

The first county seat was established at Manchester, but due to political differences, some of the county judges named Adamsville (located near present-day Rome) the county seat. A new seat of justice was platted at the mouth of Ohio Brush Creek in 1798. Named Washington, this pioneer log-cabin settlement served as the county seat until 1804.

In April 1803, only two months after Ohio was admitted to the Union, the new state's legislature passed an act that provided for the permanent establishment of a county seat for Adams County. Three commissioners were chosen to select the site for the new town. The land they chose was purchased, and in the spring of 1804, the lots were surveyed and sold at public auction. Thomas

Kirker, who was then serving as speaker of the Ohio Senate, named the new seat of justice West Union.

In 1796, Congress authorized the blazing of a road through the Northwest Territory from Wheeling, Virginia (now West Virginia), to Limestone (now Maysville), Kentucky. Work was begun in 1797 by Ebenezer Zane and his son-in-law John McIntire. This was the first official road blazed in the territory and became known as Zane's Trace. The trace passed through Adams County from the northeast to the southwest. Much of it followed an ancient buffalo trail and Native American path known by the Shawnee as Alanant-O-Wamiowee. Zane's Trace became the first mail road in Ohio and was a stagecoach route for several decades. Various historical figures traveled over this route through Adams County, including Gen. and Pres. Andrew Jackson, statesman and Sen. Henry Clay, Sen. Thomas Hart Benton, and the notorious Mexican general Santa Anna.

For several decades preceding the Civil War, there was much abolitionist activity in the county. Many residents, especially those of the various branches of the Presbyterian Church, became involved in the Underground Railroad. Many local ministers, such as William Williamson, John Graham, and Dyer Burgess, aided the antislavery movement throughout the region.

Following the outbreak of hostilities between the North and South in 1861, many companies of volunteers were raised in Adams County. Most of the 70th Ohio Regiment was composed of men from Adams and Brown Counties. They trained on the old fairgrounds—renamed Camp Hamer—on the south side of West Union before marching south to the battlefields. Confederate general John Hunt Morgan—the "Thunderbolt of the Confederacy"—and his raiders passed through the county in July 1863, creating much fear and havoc. Many Adams County homes, farms, and businesses were looted, and the raiders killed one civilian at Eckmansville during their incursion.

In 1910–1911, the county received much ongoing and unwanted national attention as almost 2,000 Adams County voters were disenfranchised when one of the nation's largest vote-buying scandals was exposed. Judge A. Z. Blair, who instigated the investigation, was hailed as a fearless fighter of political corruption by some but castigated by others as being among the worst politicians who had been buying votes. During this political turmoil, the courthouse, under somewhat questionable circumstances, burned to the ground.

In 1957, the county received much better national and even international publicity when it hosted the fifth World's Plowing Matches and Conservation Exposition. Fourteen nations participated in this historic four-day event that drew an estimated quarter-million visitors. A half century later, in 2007, the county celebrated the 50th anniversary of these contests of farming skills and agricultural exhibitions, inviting the former "Queen of the Furrows," Ann Lane Schaffer of Michigan, and the overall winner of the plowing contests, Willem DeLint of Holland, to return and reminisce about the original happenings of 50 years earlier.

Among the county's most notable native sons is John A. Cockerill, born in Locust Grove in 1845. He is known by some as the "Father of the New Journalism," editing several large newspapers during his career and cofounding the *Washington Post*.

One of the county's most noteworthy native daughters is Annie Turner Wittenmyer, born at Sandy Springs in 1827. Author of several books and hymns, she served as the first national president of the Women's Christian Temperance Union.

Another native daughter was sculptress Evelyn Longman Batchelder. Born on a farm near Winchester in 1874, she was the first female member of the National Academy of Design. She assisted Daniel Chester French in the creation of the Lincoln Memorial in Washington, D.C.

Yet another native daughter is novelist Julie Salamon, who grew up in the village of Seaman. She has authored five novels, two of which have been best sellers. Her book *The Christmas Tree* was made into a movie for television.

One

Before History

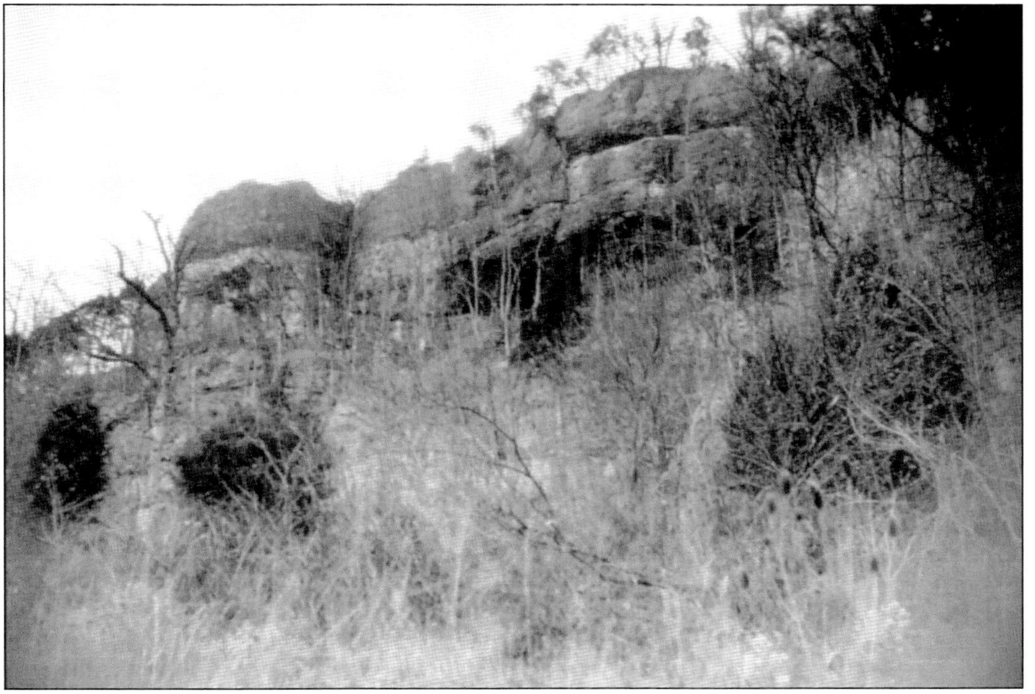

The Ohio chapter of the Nature Conservancy started acquiring land in Adams County in 1959. The conservancy targeted areas containing rare and endangered species of plants and animals. In 1960, the conservancy purchased Buzzard Roost Rock, a monolithic outcropping of dolomitic stone high above the scenic valley of Ohio Brush Creek. Shown here is the south face of that impressive formation, with Buzzard Roost Rock to the left. It was photographed on November 26, 1927, by Morten Carisle. (Courtesy Cincinnati Museum Center.)

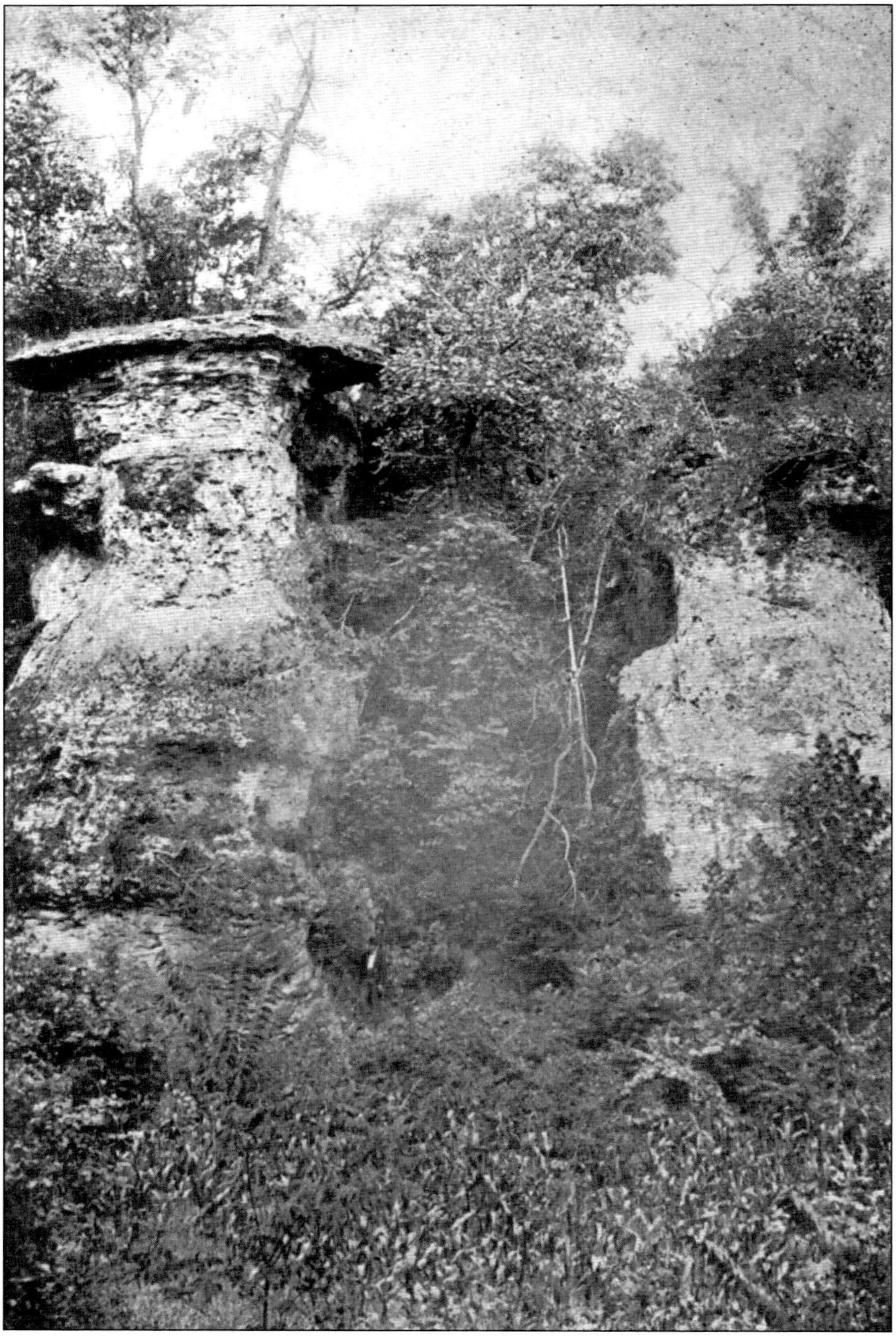

The Twin Rocks formation is found in the Edwin H. Davis State Memorial, an 88-acre nature preserve owned and administered by the Ohio Historical Society. Fashioned by nature from weathered dolomite, these columns tower over Cedar Fork in Meigs Township. The Davis Memorial contains prairie openings and rare plant life, in addition to fascinating rock outcroppings. This photograph was taken around 1898. (Courtesy Adams County Genealogical Society.)

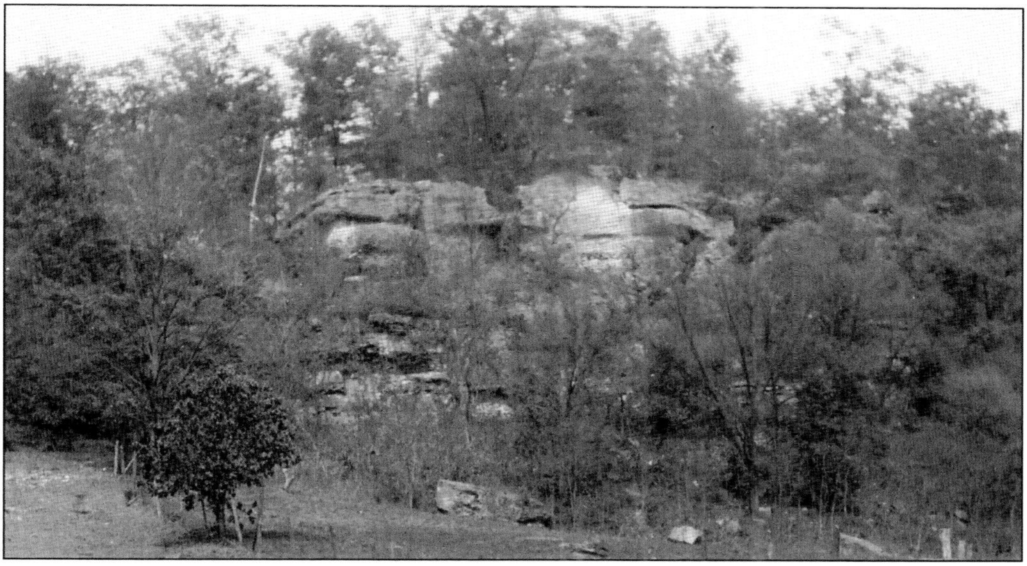

This natural ledge of stone overlooks the Ohio River near the village of Rome in Green Township. Six miles upstream between Sandy Springs and Rockville, similar stone ledges were quarried in great quantities from 1814 to 1909. Stone for the piers of the historic John A. Roebling Suspension Bridge in Cincinnati was cut in John C. Loughrey's quarry near Rockville. This postcard photograph was taken around 1909. (Courtesy Adams County Historical Society.)

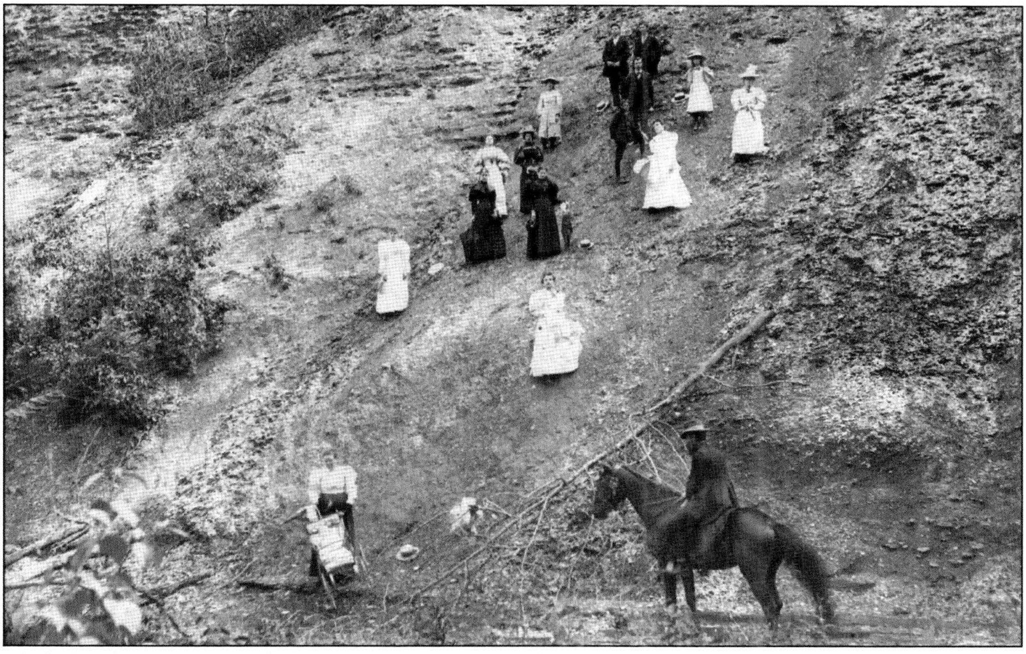

Shale banks are exposed along nearly the entire length of the eastern side of Adams County. Containing small amounts of oil, the concept of mining this shale was considered in the late 19th century but was rejected due to the cost of obtaining the oil. This group of young people poses for their picture on a shale bank near the village of Blue Creek in Jefferson Township around 1900. (Courtesy Adams County Historical Society.)

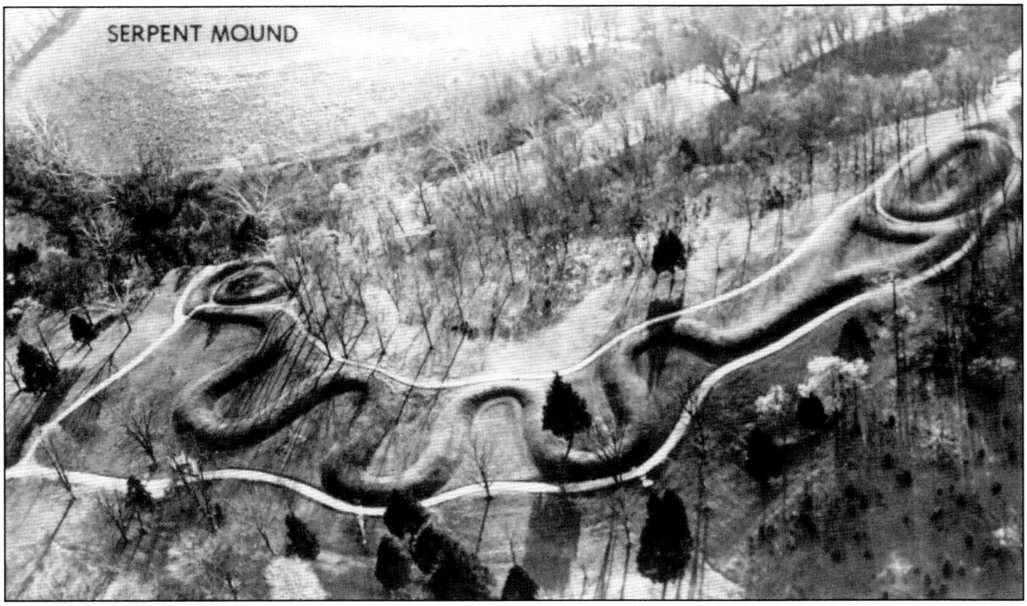

The Great Serpent Mound has evoked mystery since its discovery in 1847. Writhing along a high bluff overlooking the east fork of Ohio Brush Creek in Bratton Township, it was saved from the farmer's plow in 1886. Archaeologists have determined it was constructed by the prehistoric Fort Ancient culture around 1070 A.D. Diligent observers of celestial bodies, the Fort Ancient people built this earthwork with several solar alignments. (Courtesy Ohio Historical Society.)

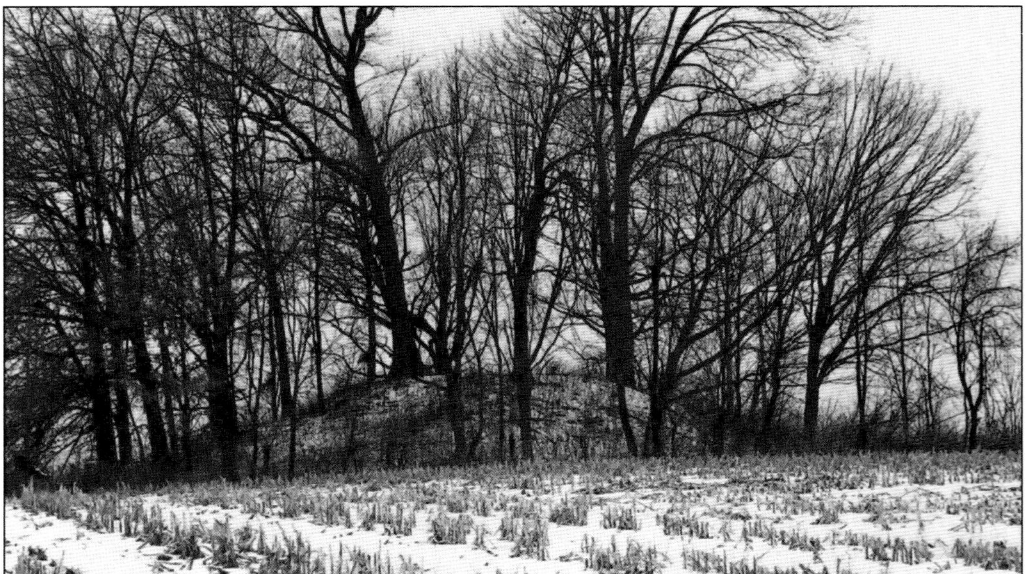

Located at the junction of State Route 136 and Winchester-Fincastle Road about a mile north of Winchester, this mound stands about 9 feet tall. It is believed to have been built by the prehistoric Adena culture about 2,600 years ago. As late as 1885, three circular earthworks—or sacred circles—were still in the immediate vicinity, but all trace of them is now gone due to aggressive agricultural practices. (Author's collection.)

Two

PIONEERS

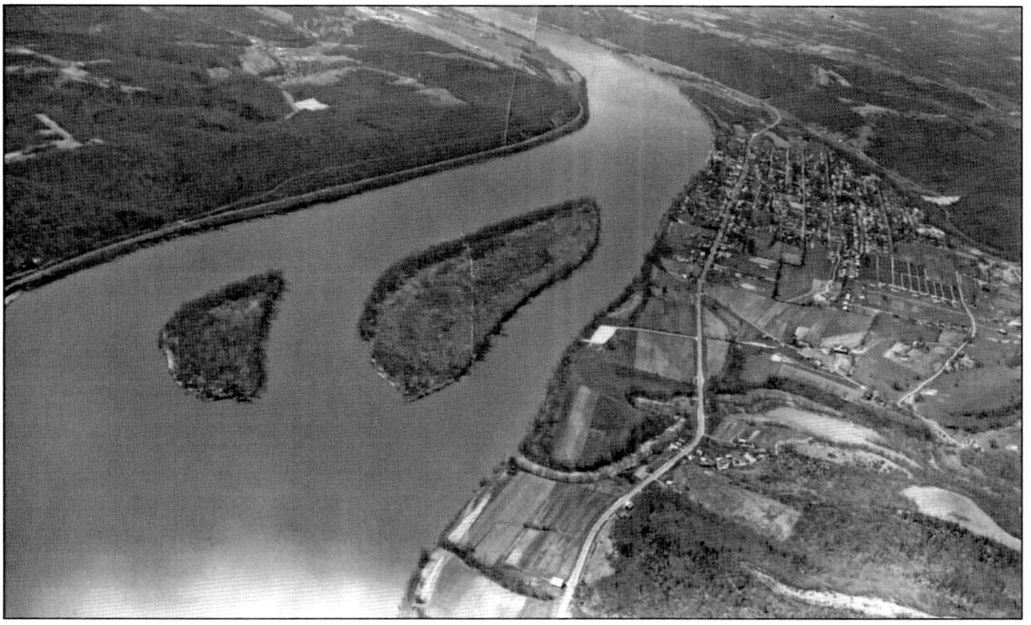

Manchester, the first permanent Euro-American settlement in the Virginia Military District and Adams County, was founded at Three Islands on the Ohio River. In this aerial view of Manchester taken by John Tom of Hillsboro, Ohio, around 1965, it is obvious that only two of the Ohio River islands have survived, with the third eroding away in the early 19th century. (Courtesy Lester and Jean Wallis.)

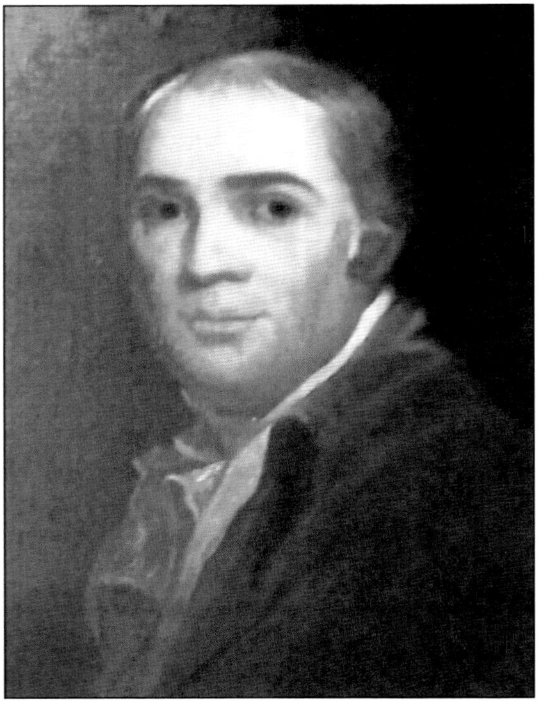

Nathaniel Massie (1763–1813) is considered the "Father of Adams County," spearheading the effort to found the first settlement here in the winter of 1790–1791. A native of Goochland County, Virginia, he grew wealthy as a land locator and surveyor in the Virginia Military District. He founded Chillicothe in 1796, which became the first capital of Ohio in 1803. (Courtesy Chillicothe and Ross County Public Library.)

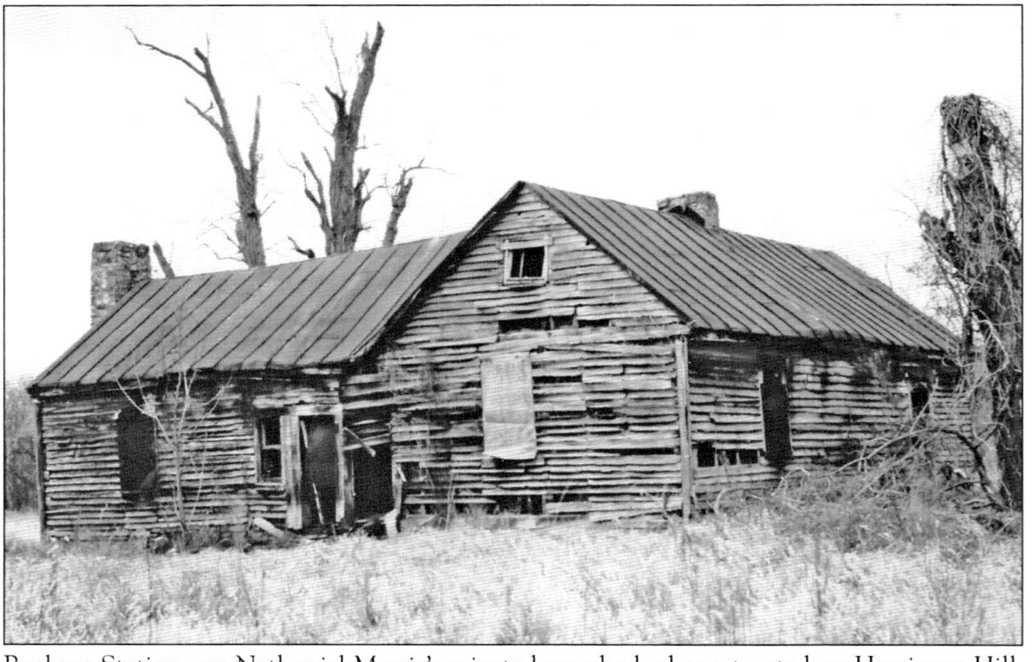

Buckeye Station was Nathaniel Massie's private home he had constructed on Hurricane Hill, about 4 miles east of Manchester. Erected in 1797, it was a frame structure and, by tradition, primarily built out of Buckeye trees, hence the name Buckeye Station. Sitting high on a ridge, it had a commanding view of the Ohio River. This image was taken about 1975. The old home no longer stands. (Author's collection.)

With the massive stone chimney on the west end of Buckeye Station as a backdrop, Russell Massie of Seaman (left), nephew Sonny Massie of Youngsville (right), and Sonny's son Harley Massie hold pictures of their ancestors, illustrating their direct descent from Nathaniel Massie, the original owner of Buckeye Station. This photograph was taken in 1976. (Author's collection.)

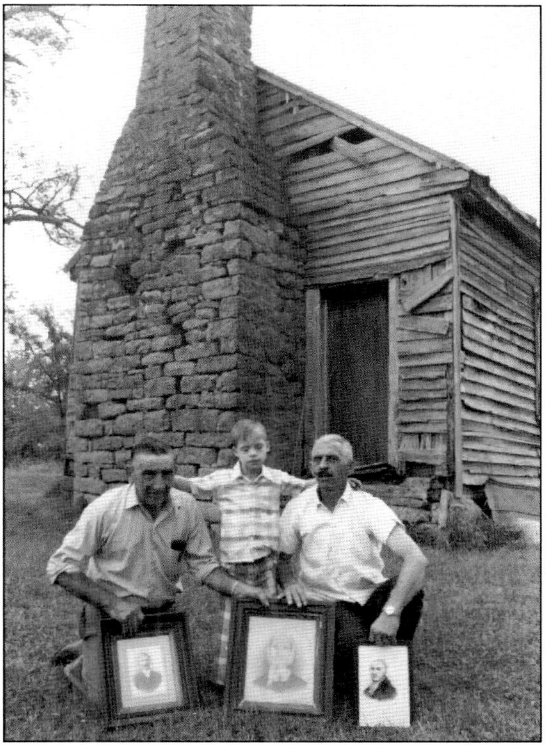

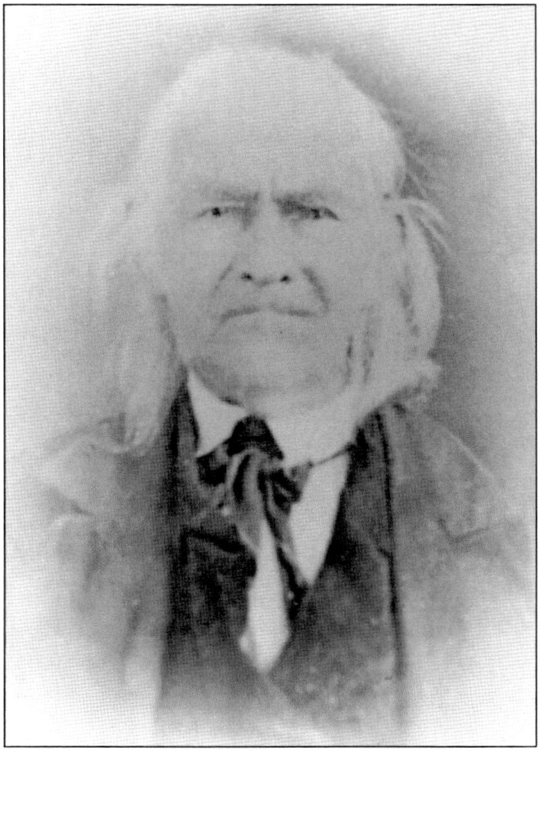

Israel Donalson (1767–1860) was among those who lived in the old fort at Manchester known as Massie's Station. Moving there by April 1, 1791, he roomed with Nathaniel Massie. Three weeks later, he was captured outside the fort by a war party of Shawnee Indians but managed to escape several days later. Donalson served as a delegate from Adams County to the Ohio Constitutional Convention in 1802. (Courtesy Ohio Historical Society.)

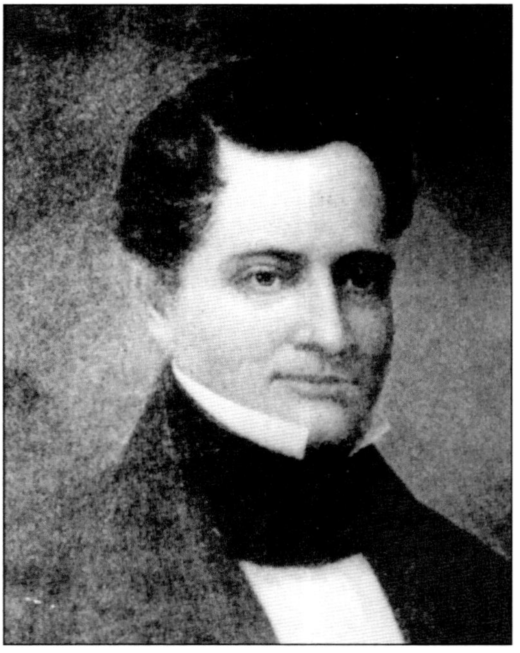

Irish immigrant Thomas Kirker (1760–1837), with his wife and children, moved to the little fort called Massie's Station in 1794. According to family tradition, he was the first to permanently leave the protection of the station and settle in the wilderness that became Adams County. After statehood, he served various terms in the Ohio House and Senate. He also served as the state's second governor in 1807–1808. (Courtesy Ohio Historical Society.)

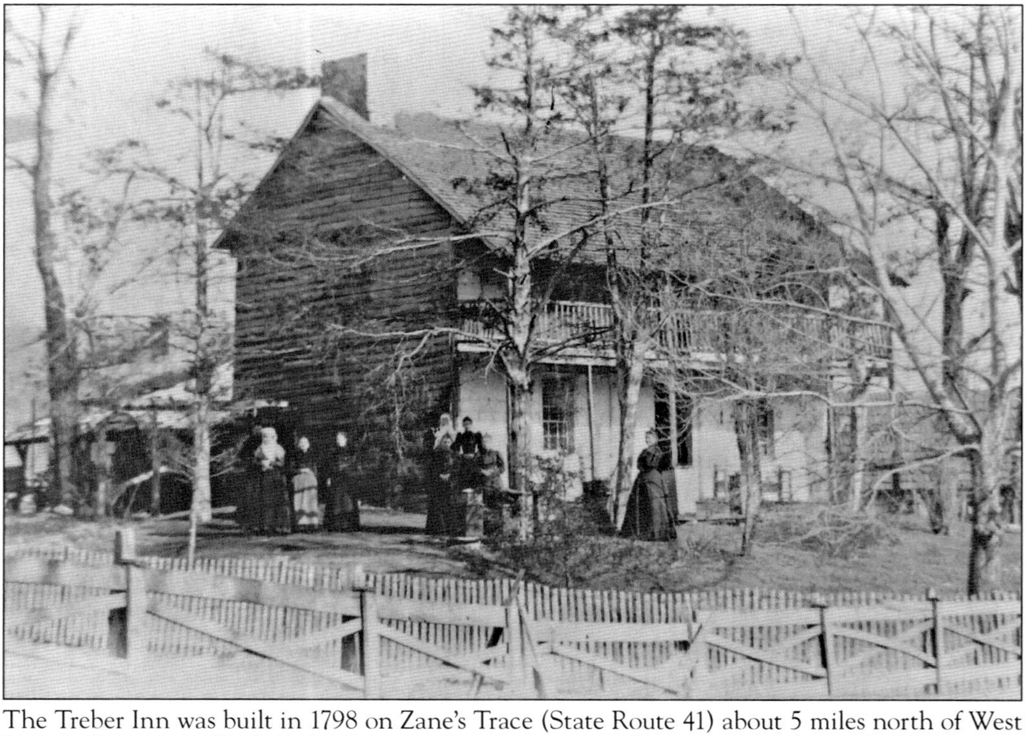

The Treber Inn was built in 1798 on Zane's Trace (State Route 41) about 5 miles north of West Union. Constructed by John Treber, a gunsmith, it was used as an inn for close to half a century. It is one of the oldest documented log buildings in Ohio and is listed on the National Register of Historic Places. This photograph was taken around 1895 by Lizzie Treber, the great-granddaughter of John Treber. (Courtesy William and Bessie J. Sininger.)

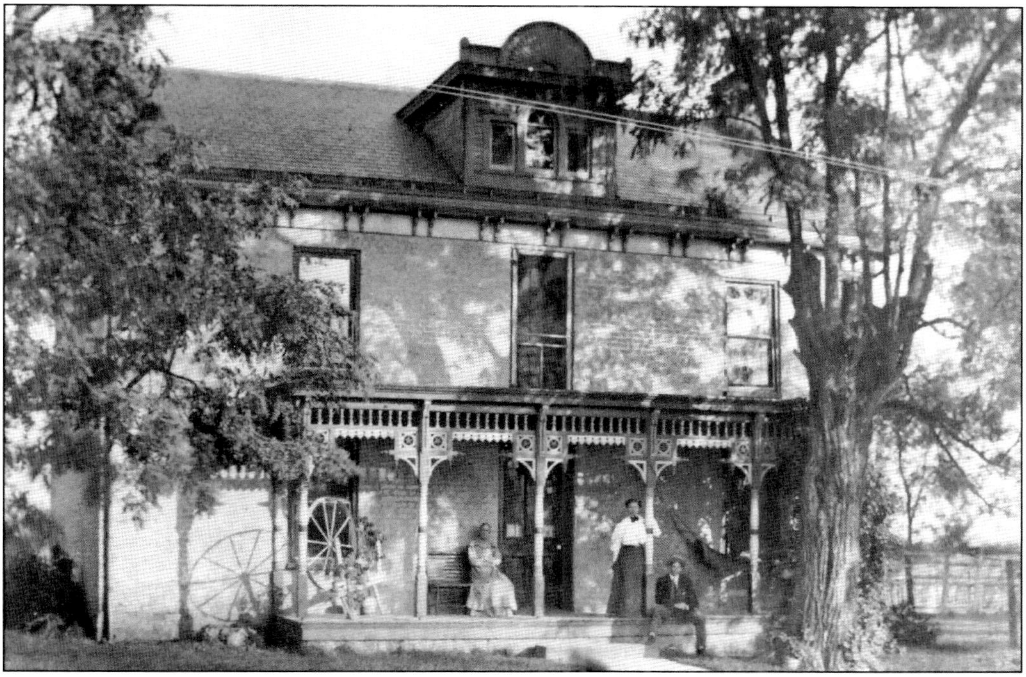

The Wickerham Inn was constructed on Zane's Trace in 1801–1802 by Peter Wickerham, a soldier of the American Revolution. It is located in Franklin Township between Peebles and Locust Grove and is listed on the National Register of Historic Places. It was entered by Morgan's Raiders on July 15, 1863, and several of the Confederate soldiers slept that night in the old brick structure. This image was taken around 1890. (Author's collection.)

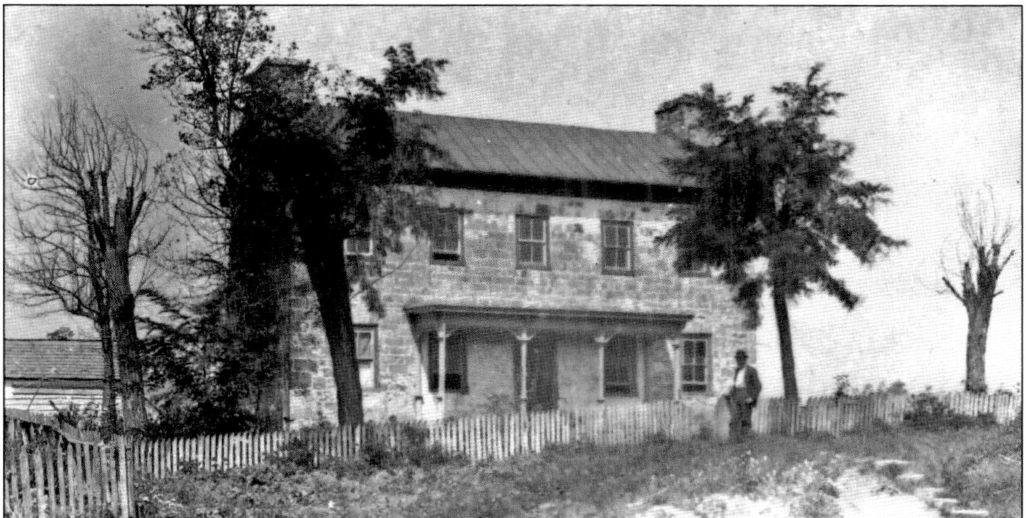

Andrew Ellison, one of the builders of Massie's Station, constructed this large stone house on Zane's Trace in Tiffin Township in 1798. Around 1806, a Mr. Allen began renting the home and operated a tavern here. A visitor in 1807 described it as a "handsome, roomy, well-finished house." It was torn down in 1886. This photograph was taken about 1885 by David I. Gardner. (Author's collection.)

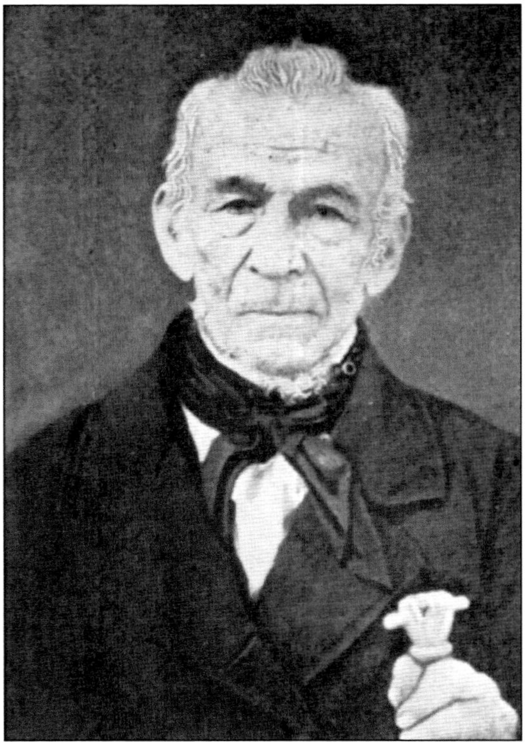

John Lodwick (1767–1861), another pioneer who lived at Massie's Station, moved there in 1794 with his family. He served four terms as county sheriff and, at age 55, served as a colonel of a local regiment during the War of 1812. While sheriff, at the opening of a new term of the court, he wore a cocked hat and carried a sword as he marched the judges from a nearby hotel to the courtroom while accompanied with martial music. (Courtesy Adams County Genealogical Society.)

This log home is among the oldest standing log structures in southern Ohio. Located a short distance east of the Sproull Bridge in Meigs Township, it was built around 1796 by Peter Shoemaker. It was purchased by Robert Sproull in 1825 and remained in the Sproull family for four generations. This photograph was taken around 1895 by Lizzie Treber, a great-granddaughter of Robert Sproull. (Courtesy William and Bessie J. Sininger.)

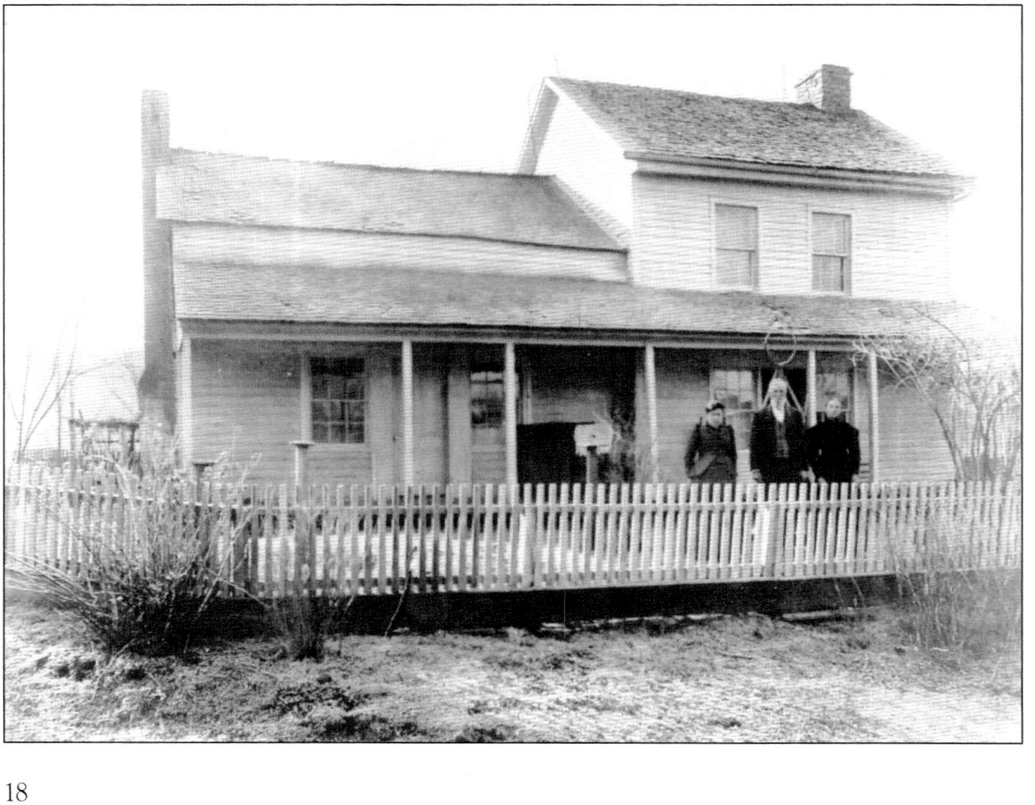

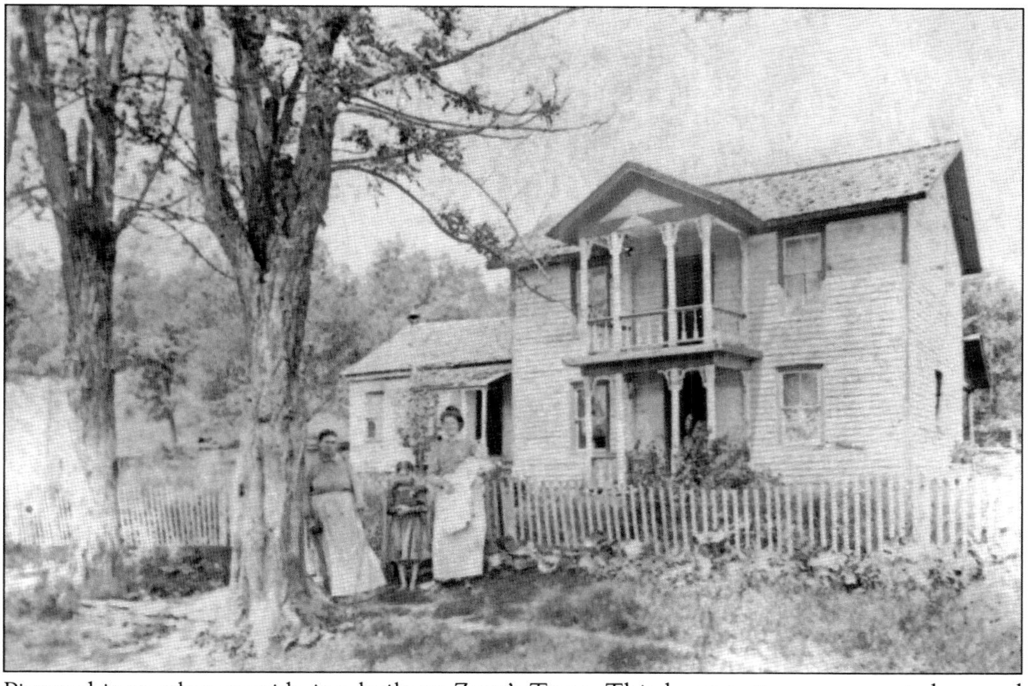

Pictured is another wayside inn built on Zane's Trace. This log structure was erected around 1810 and stands today on the west side of Ohio Route 41 a short distance south of the junction of Fawcett Road. The inn was built by Elizabeth and Samuel Jackman, who also operated a ferry across Ohio Brush Creek where the Sproull Bridge is today. This photograph was taken by J. E. Shriver about 1895. (Author's collection.)

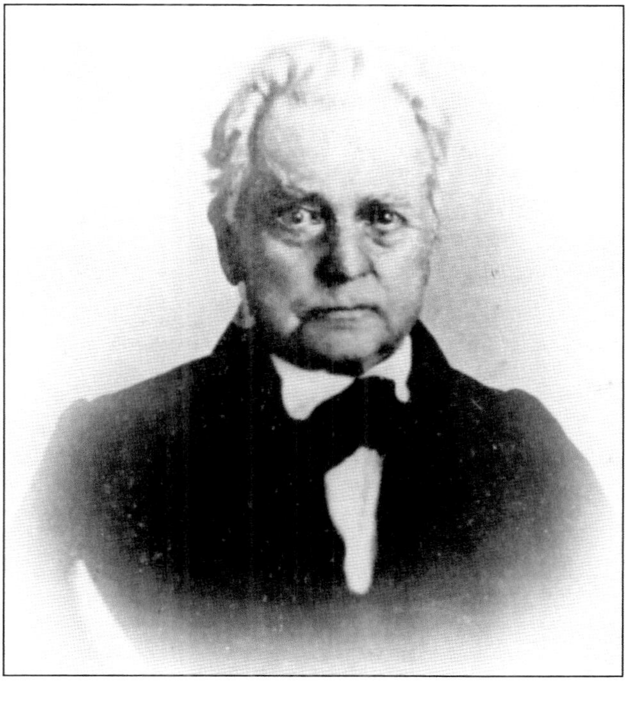

Joseph Darlinton (1765–1851) was a native of Winchester, Virginia. He moved to Adams County in 1797 and lived several years at the old county seat of Washington. He held numerous public offices, including representative to the Ohio Constitutional Convention, brigadier general in the Ohio militia, and county clerk of courts. Darlinton founded the village of Winchester in 1815. This daguerreotype of him was taken in 1851. (Courtesy Ohio Historical Society.)

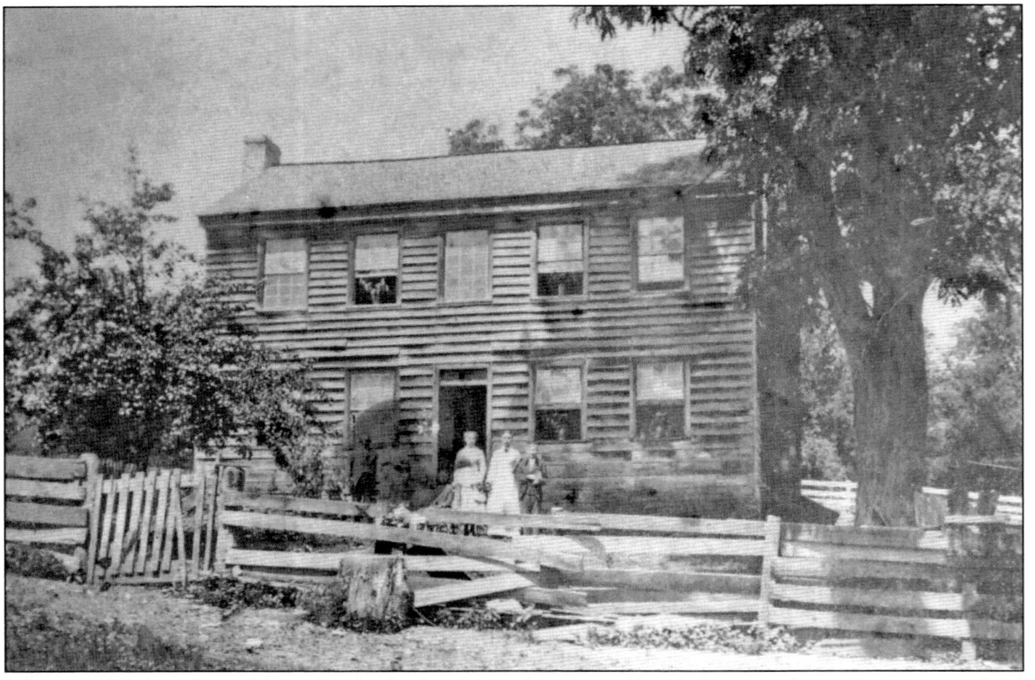

About 1835, Joseph and Jane Fry built this frame house on Zane's Trace a short distance south of the Fristoe Crossing of Ohio Brush Creek. In 1855, William and Mariah Jane McNeilan bought and converted the home to a wayside inn. The McNeilan Entertainment sign hung for only three years before the owners sold out and moved on. The house still stands today. This photograph was taken around 1876. (Courtesy Norman Butts.)

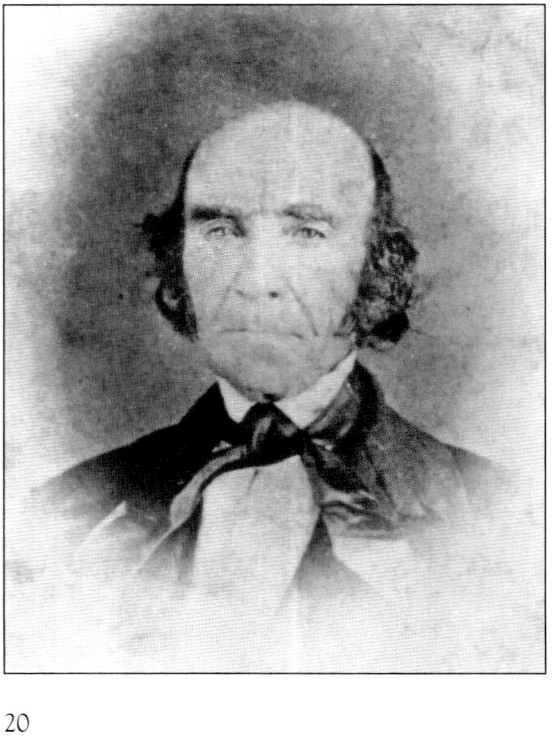

Robert Morrison (1782–1863) was an Irish immigrant. He moved to Adams County in 1803, buying land near the future site of Eckmansville. He served as a captain during the War of 1812 and was later made a brigadier general in the Ohio militia. He served four terms in the Ohio House. General Morrison is the great-great-grandfather of Marion Michael Morrison, better known as actor John Wayne. (Courtesy Ed Willman.)

Three

The Ohio River

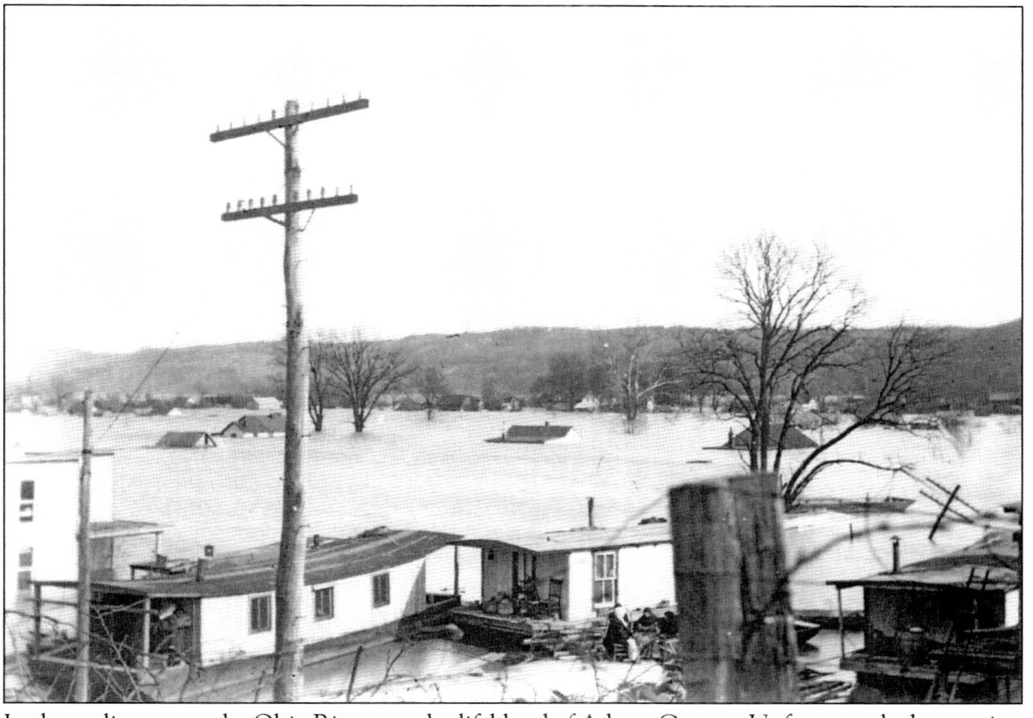

In the earliest years, the Ohio River was the lifeblood of Adams County. Unfortunately devastating floods swept away much of the wealth the river had brought. It is believed this view of the overflowing river in Manchester was taken during the great flood of 1913. This rare photograph shows shanty boats in the foreground, probably moored close to Sixth Street, before the water subsided. (Courtesy Lois Kidd.)

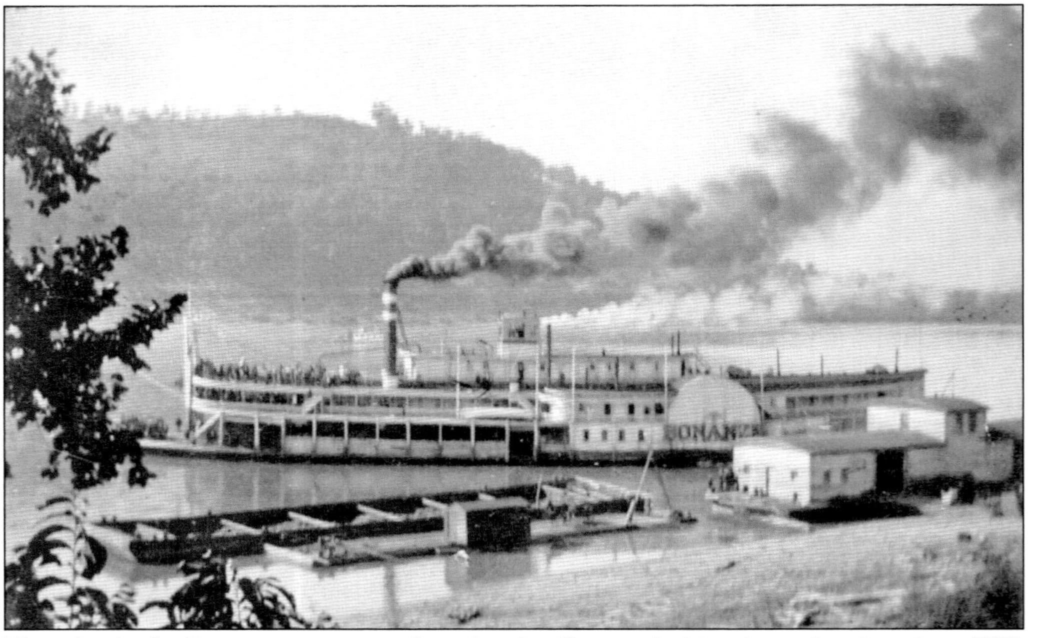

The side-wheeler *Bonanza* steams away from the wharf boat at the Manchester Landing about 1905. The *Bonanza* was built in 1885. It plied the waters of the Ohio and Mississippi Rivers for many years as a U.S. mail boat. It was dismantled in Cincinnati in May 1909. (Courtesy Manchester Historical Society.)

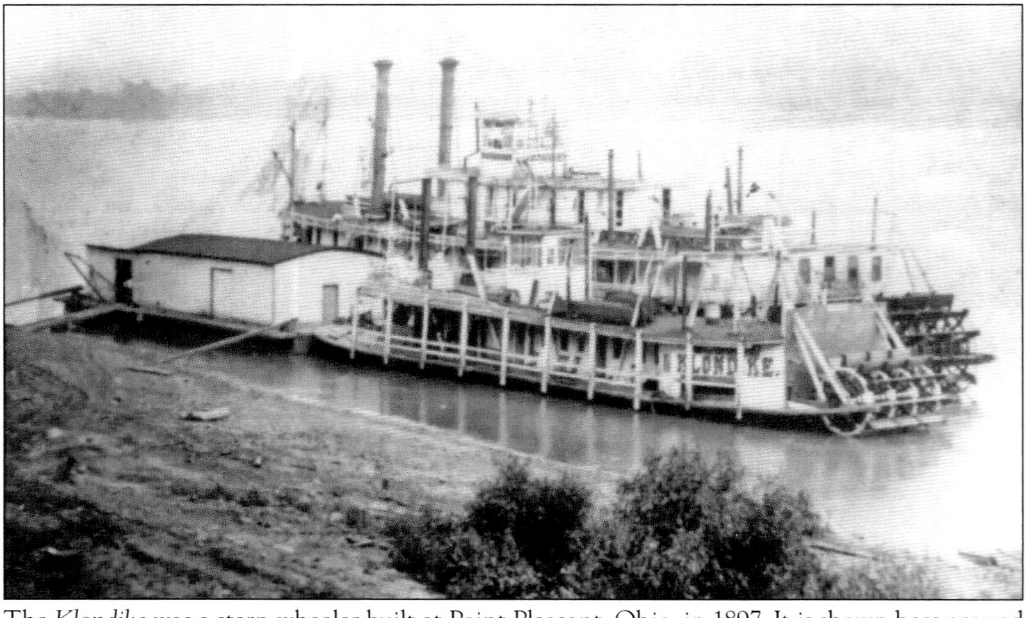

The *Klondike* was a stern-wheeler built at Point Pleasant, Ohio, in 1897. It is shown here around 1925 with the *Tacoma*, another stern-wheeler in the background, at the Manchester Landing. The history of the *Klondike* ended when it sank at Ashland, Kentucky, in later years. The *Tacoma* had been built in 1883 and remained in active service until burning on the Cincinnati riverfront in November 1922. (Courtesy Doris Lucas.)

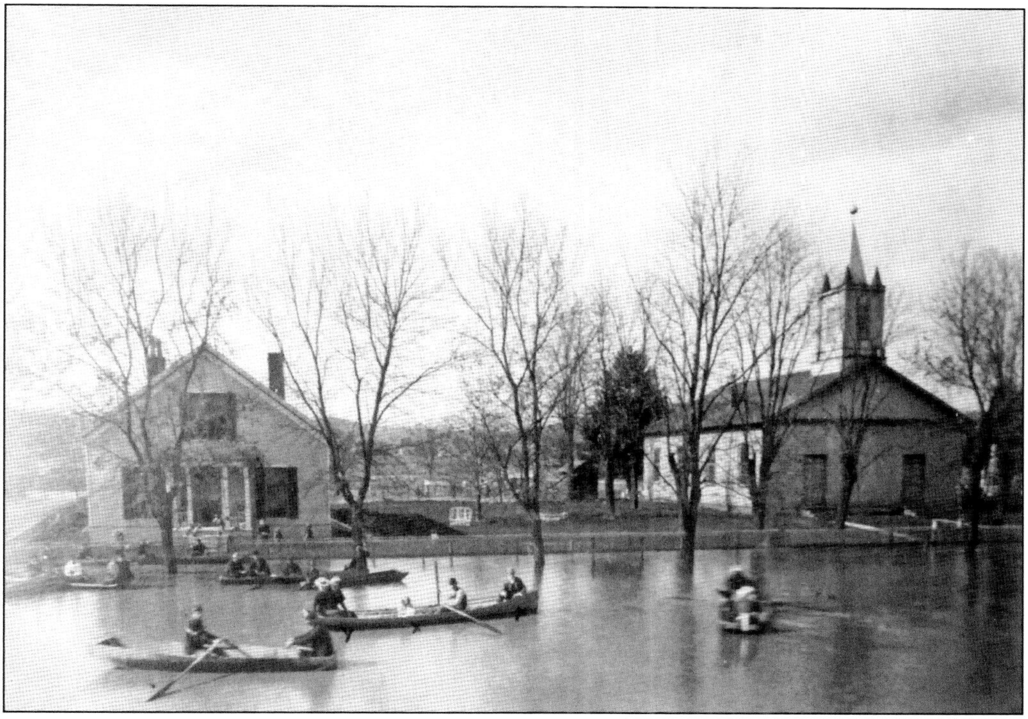

Here is a much-too-common view of boaters on Second Street in Manchester. It was the year 1897, when the Ohio River once again came calling. The old Presbyterian church (1845–1904) is seen on the right. (Author's collection.)

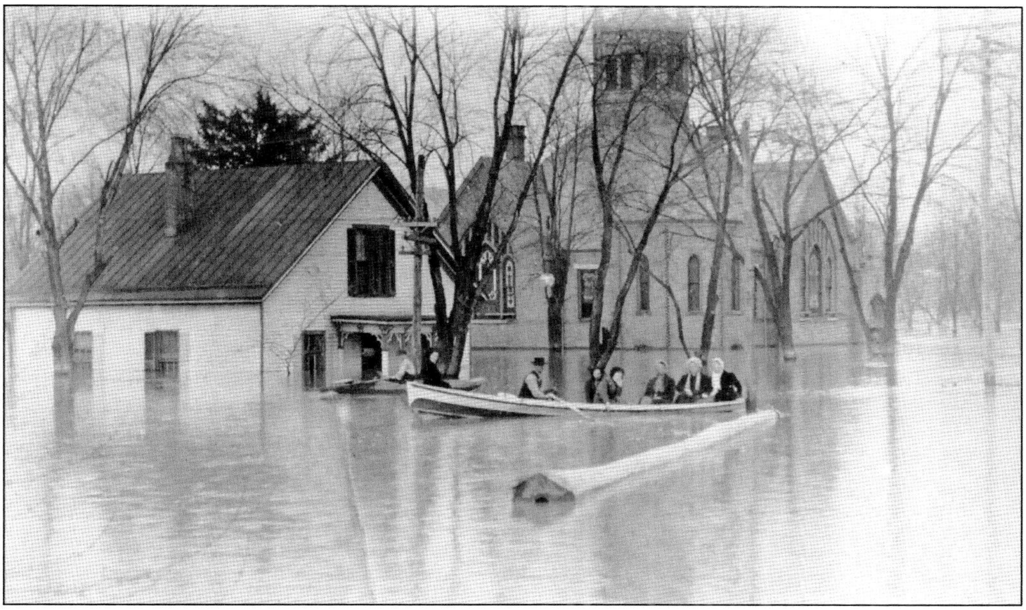

This photograph is approximately the same scene as above. This was taken 10 years later during the flood of 1907. The new Presbyterian church, built in 1904, was experiencing its first flood. (Author's collection.)

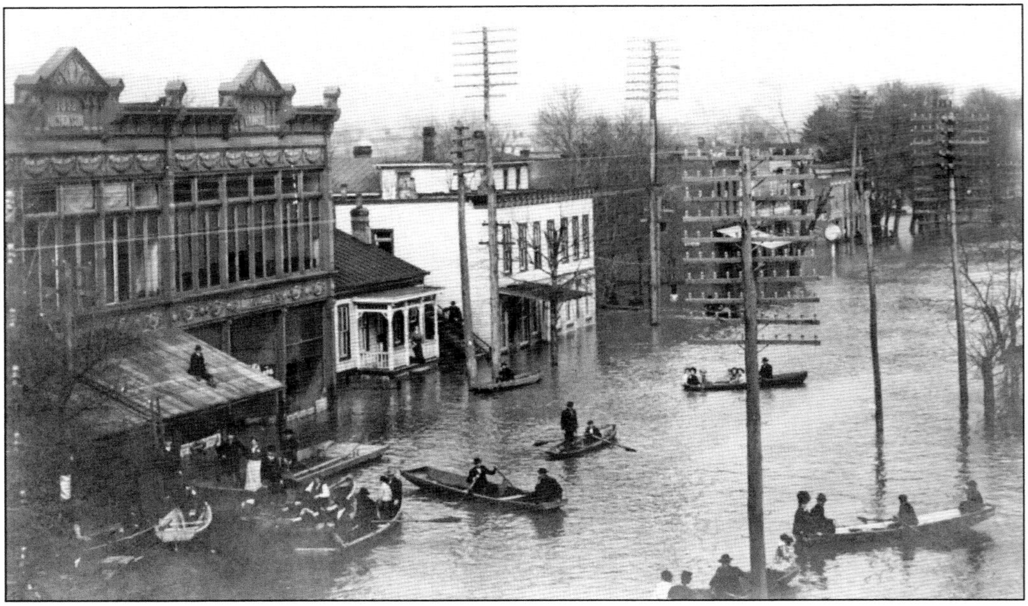

This is a picture postcard scene of the Manchester business district on Second Street during the Ohio River flood of 1907. The distinctive storefront of Vance's department store is plainly seen on the left. Numerous boaters seem to be taking in the scene. (Author's collection.)

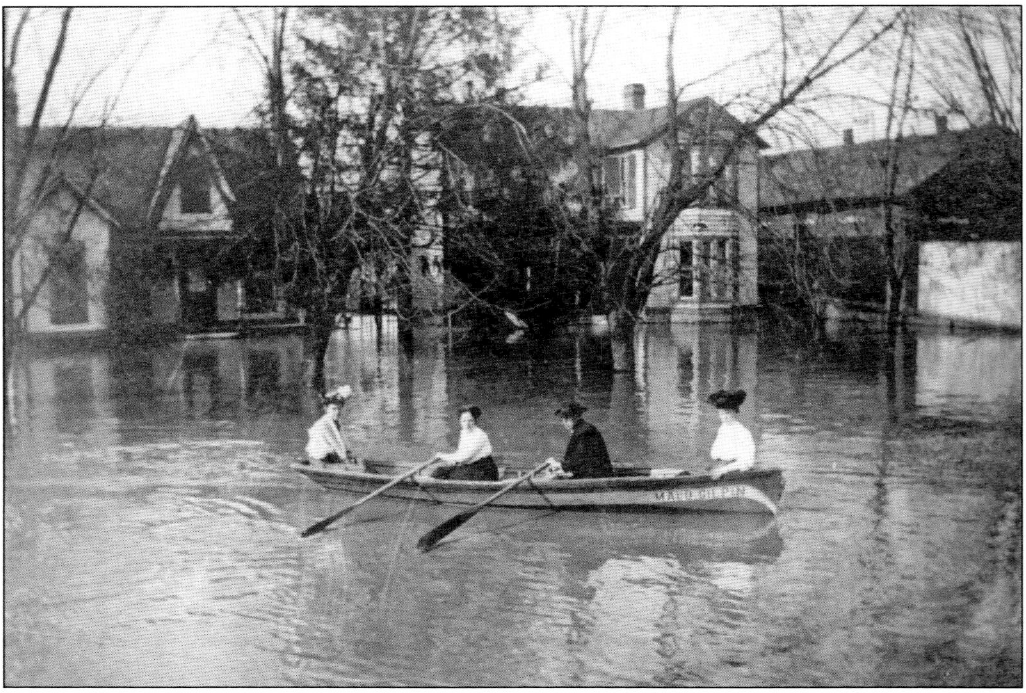

Four well-dressed young women are seen taking a leisurely boat ride on Manchester's Second Street during the 1907 flood. The name on their boat is *Maud Gilpin*. On the far right in the background can be seen the small brick village school built in 1855 that still stands today. (Author's collection.)

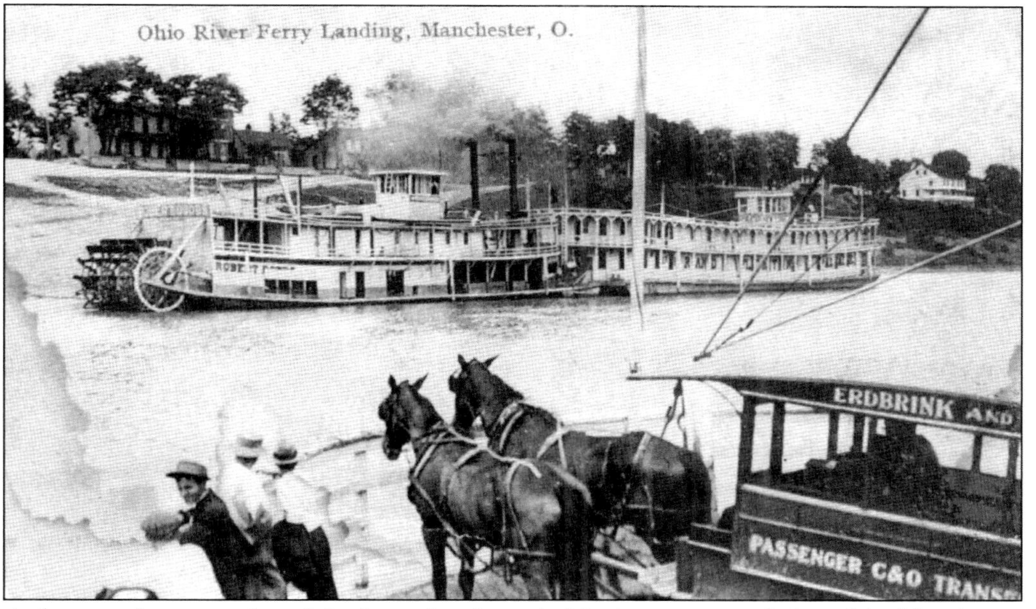

A photographer was on board the ferry when he took this picture-postcard view of the Manchester Landing from the river. On board the ferry was Edward Erdbrink's horse-drawn hack with which he transported passengers across the river to the South Manchester flag stop station on the Chesapeake and Ohio Railroad. (Courtesy Lois Kidd.)

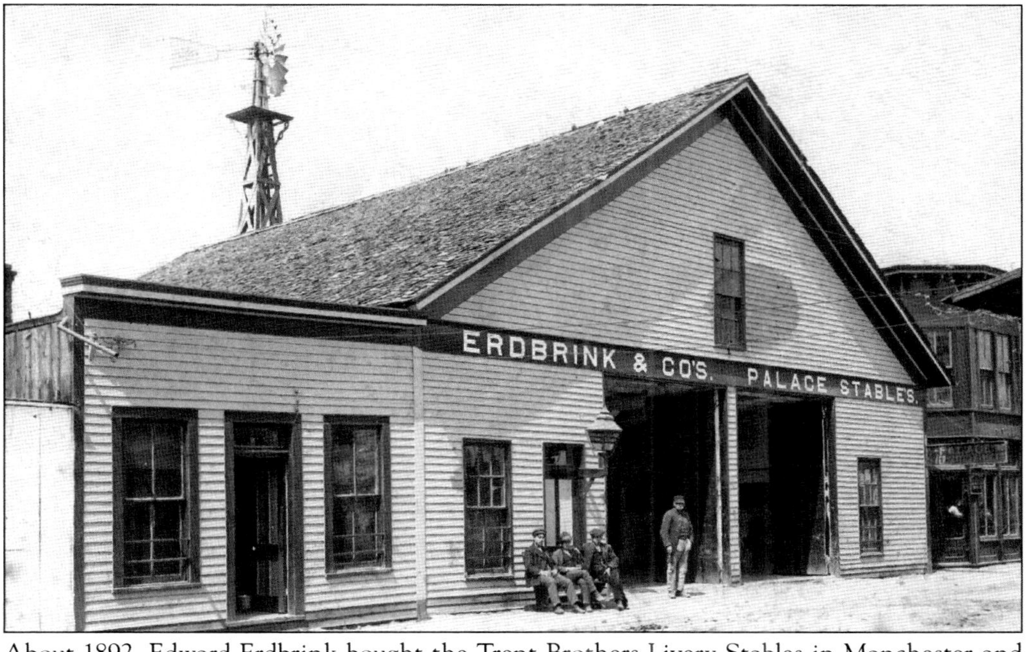

About 1892, Edward Erdbrink bought the Trent Brothers Livery Stables in Manchester and continued the business under his own name. Erdbrink and Company's Stables stood on the west side of Pike Street between Front and Second Streets. Here he rented horses and buggies, as well as providing hack services in the area and across the river by ferry. Erdbrink closed the business in 1918. (Author's collection.)

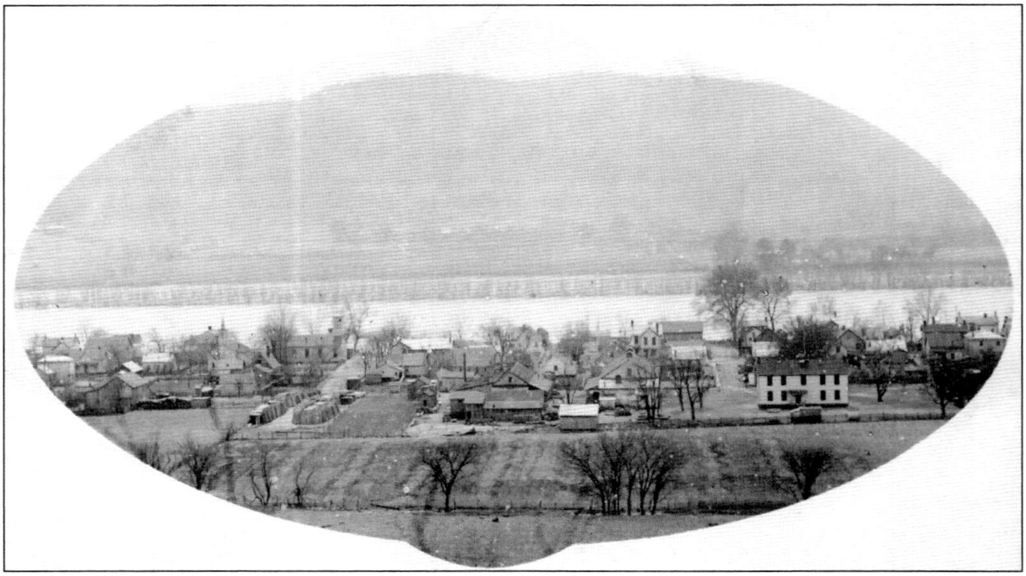

The Ohio River helped give birth to the tiny village of Rome. Founded in 1835 by William Stout, the river port became a shipping point for various wood products, including barrel staves, tan bark, hoop poles, and finished barrels. River barges were built near the public landing. This view was taken from the high hills overlooking the village around 1909. (Author's collection.)

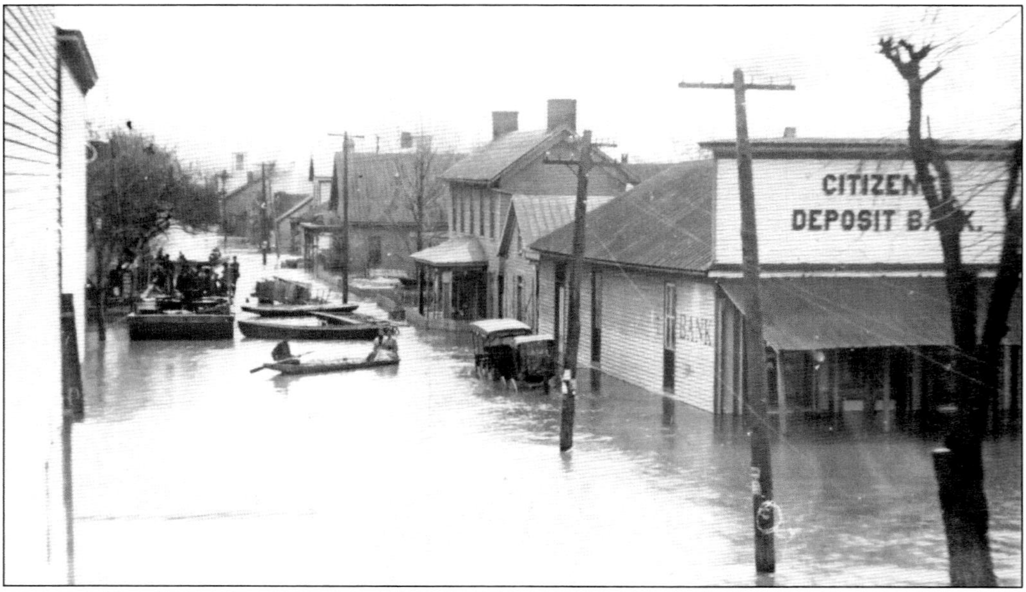

In 1913, the village of Rome boasted a financial institution known as the Citizens Deposit Bank. This postcard photograph shows it and the remainder of the village undergoing the rigors of the great flood of that year. The bank building was razed about 1954 but had a useful life, being utilized at various times as a dwelling, furniture store, service station, garage, bus stop, pool room, etc. (Courtesy David Piatt.)

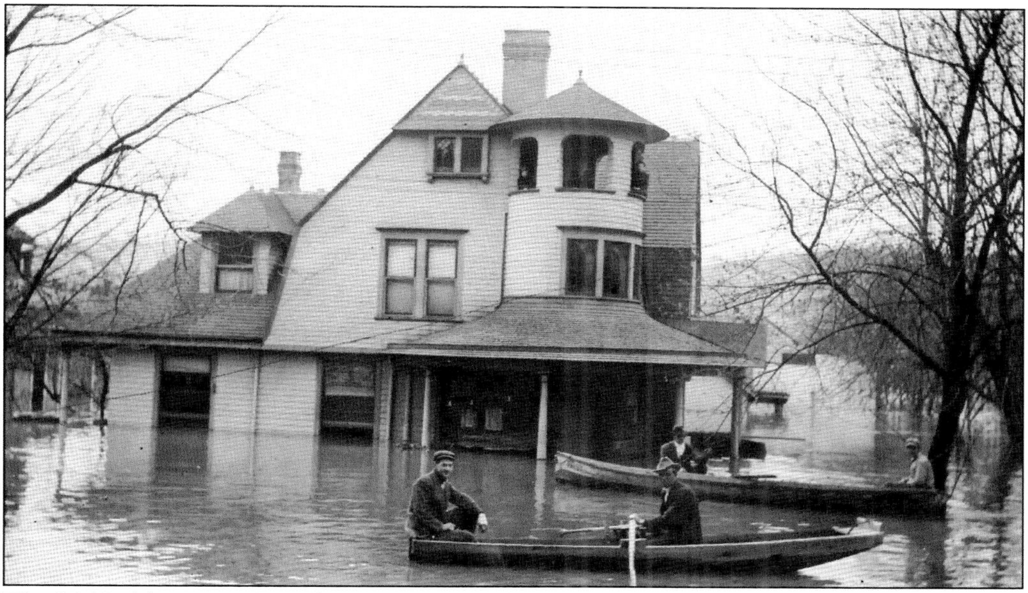

The McNeil home on Fourth Street in Manchester was of unusual design, being a hybrid of Queen Anne and shingle-style architecture. This attractive home fell victim to the 1913 flood and subsequent river inundations, something the owners evidently never planned on. (Courtesy Lois Kidd.)

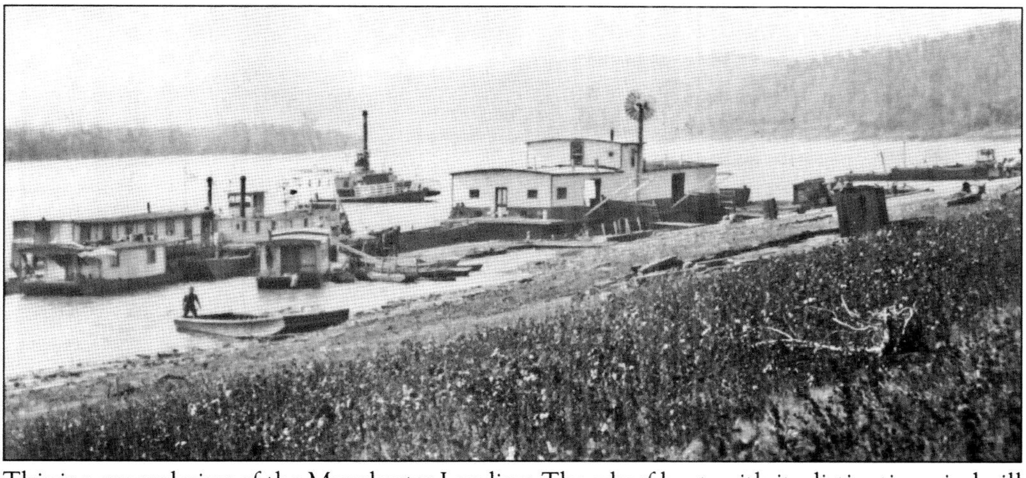

This is a general view of the Manchester Landing. The wharf boat, with its distinctive windmill spinning in the breeze, dominates the scene. The *W. H. Whiteman*, the village's ferryboat for about 40 years, is seen in the background approaching the landing. Several smaller watercraft are crowded together on the left. This photograph was taken in the era of 1900–1915. (Courtesy Doris Lucas.)

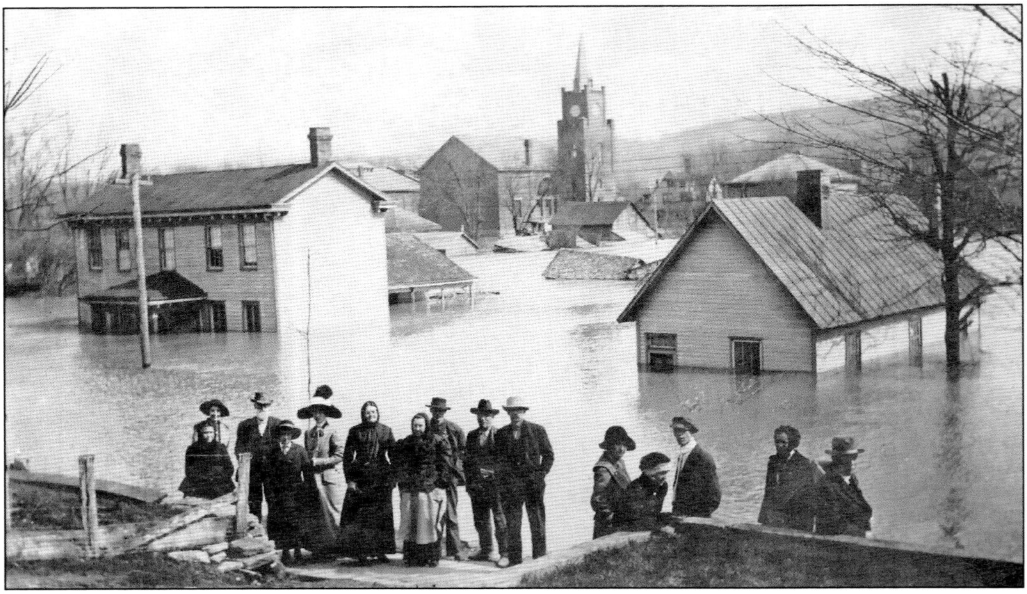

This picture postcard was taken during the 1913 flood; the photographer was probably standing on or near Sixth Street aiming towards the river. The waters were to rise several feet higher. The Manchester Opera House is seen in the middle background. (Author's collection.)

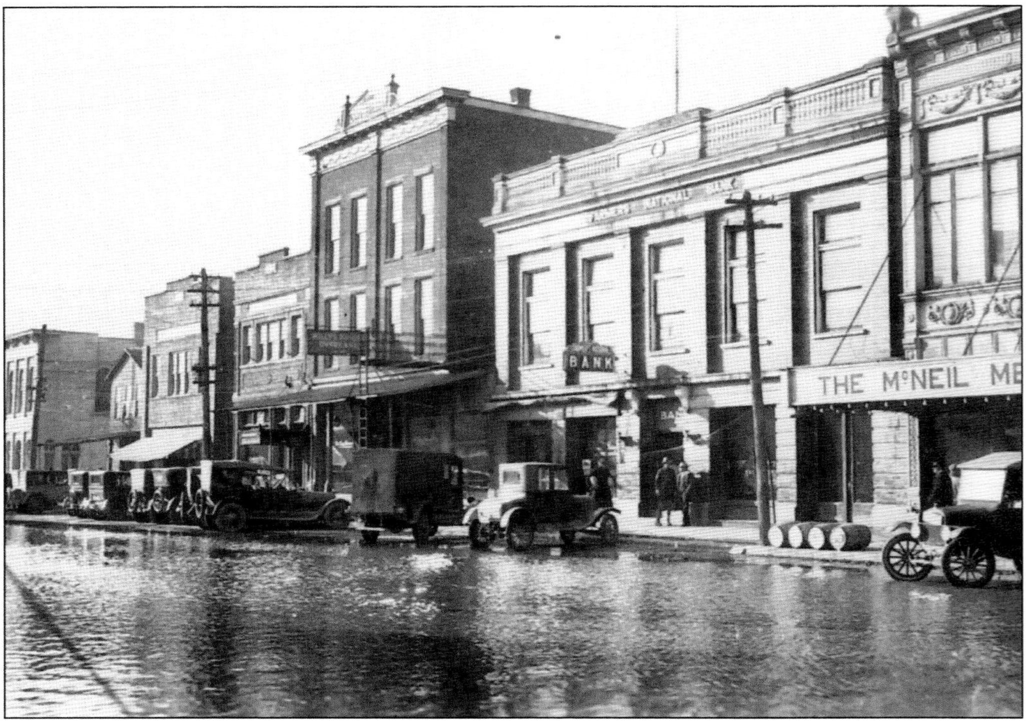

Fortunately for the residents of the Ohio Valley, the flood of 1927 did not rise too high. Here is a scene of Second Street at that time, showing how the water did not even reach the top of the curb on Manchester's main thoroughfare. (Courtesy John Parr.)

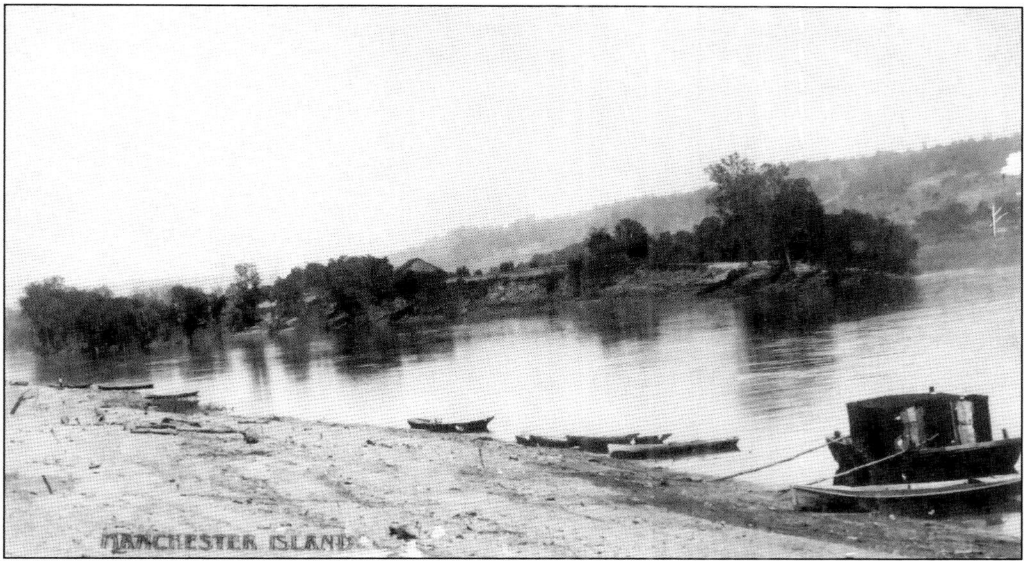

This is a c. 1909 postcard view of the big island at Manchester. It is said to embody 100 acres and was farmed for more than a century and a half. Frank Cooley of Manchester was one of the last to farm on the island. The two islands at Manchester are part of Lewis County, Kentucky, and are now part of the National Wildlife Refuge System. (Courtesy Lois Kidd.)

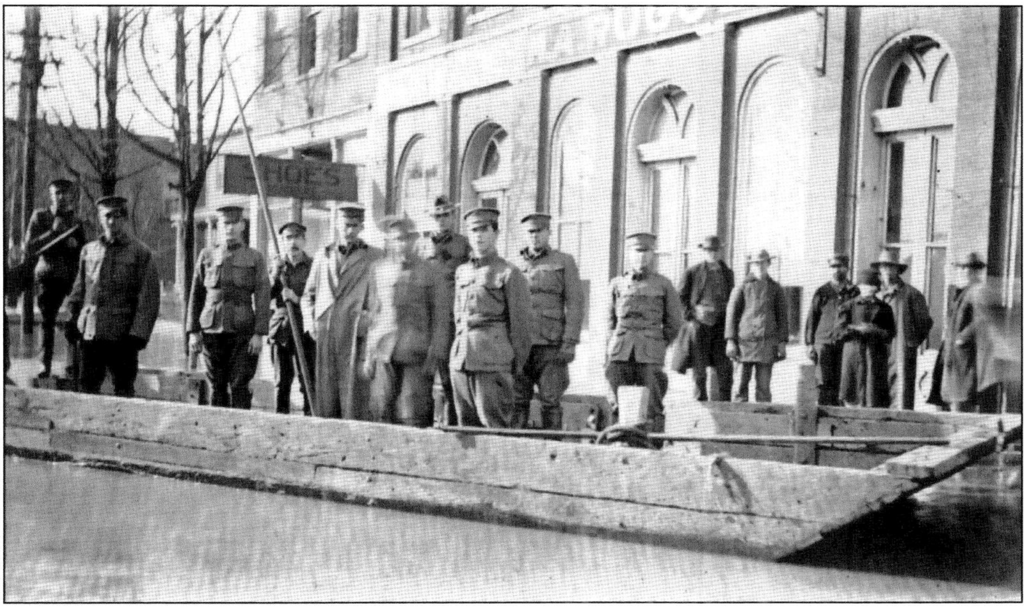

The National Guard was called out during the flood of 1927. Here are a few of the troops in a skiff on the north side of Second Street in Manchester between Pike and Pearl Streets. (Courtesy John Parr.)

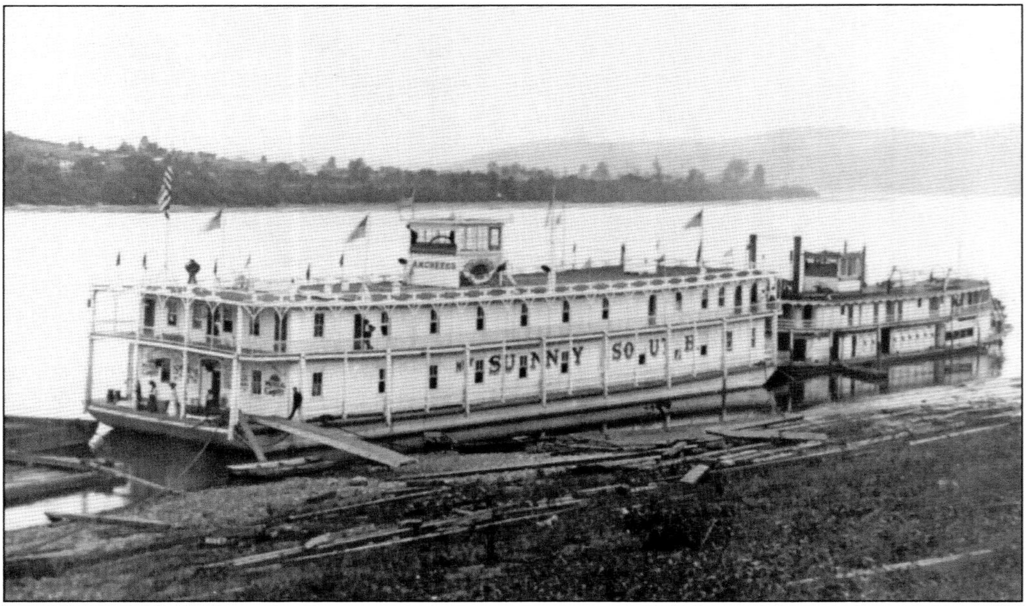

The *Sunny South* showboat is seen at the Manchester Landing about 1915. Boats such as this plied the inland waterways, offering entertainment on board in the form of stage shows featuring live musical comedies, drama, and whatever was then popular. Built in 1897 in Jeffersonville, Indiana, the *Sunny South* was first named *Electra*. It capsized on April 20, 1916, near Mobile, Alabama. (Courtesy Lois Kidd.)

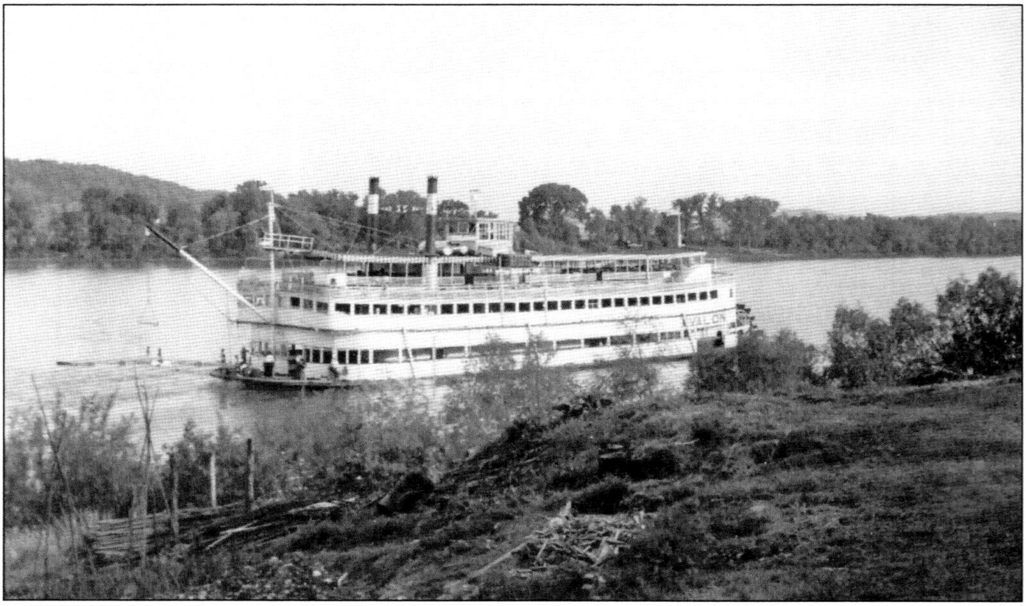

Here is the passenger ship *Avalon*, photographed about 1955. Built in 1915, it was first named *Idlewild* before being renamed *Avalon* in 1948. It was an excursion boat for several years and visited Manchester in 1961 for the senior high school prom. It was bought by the Jefferson County, Kentucky, Fiscal Court in 1962 and renamed *Belle of Louisville*—a name it still proudly bears today. (Courtesy Lois Kidd.)

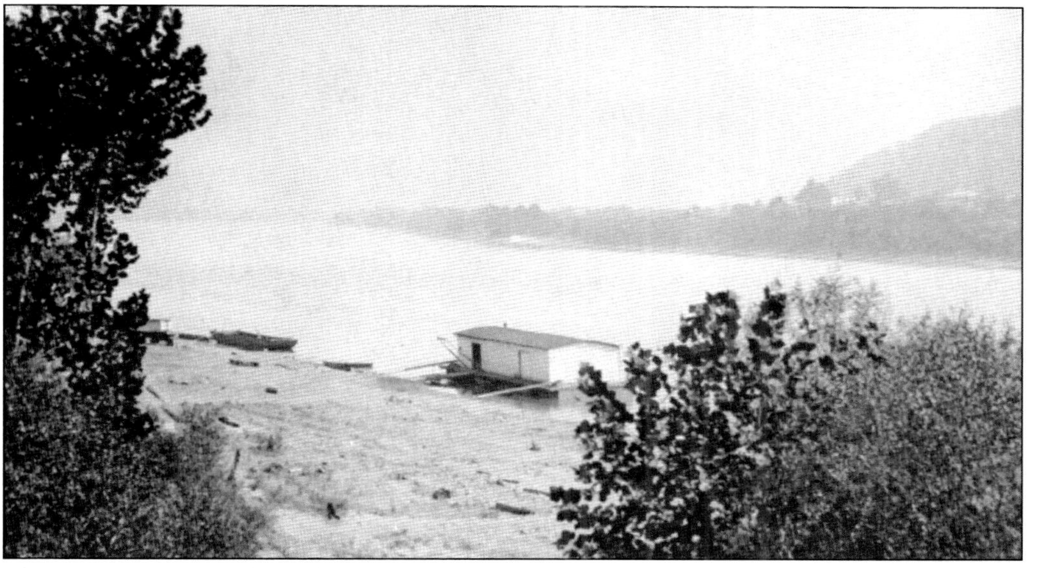

This was a common sight at the village of Rome for many decades. The wharf boat helped bring jobs and prosperity to the community. Although small, Rome had its share of riverboat men who lived here, and several businesses were dependent upon river commerce. (Author's collection.)

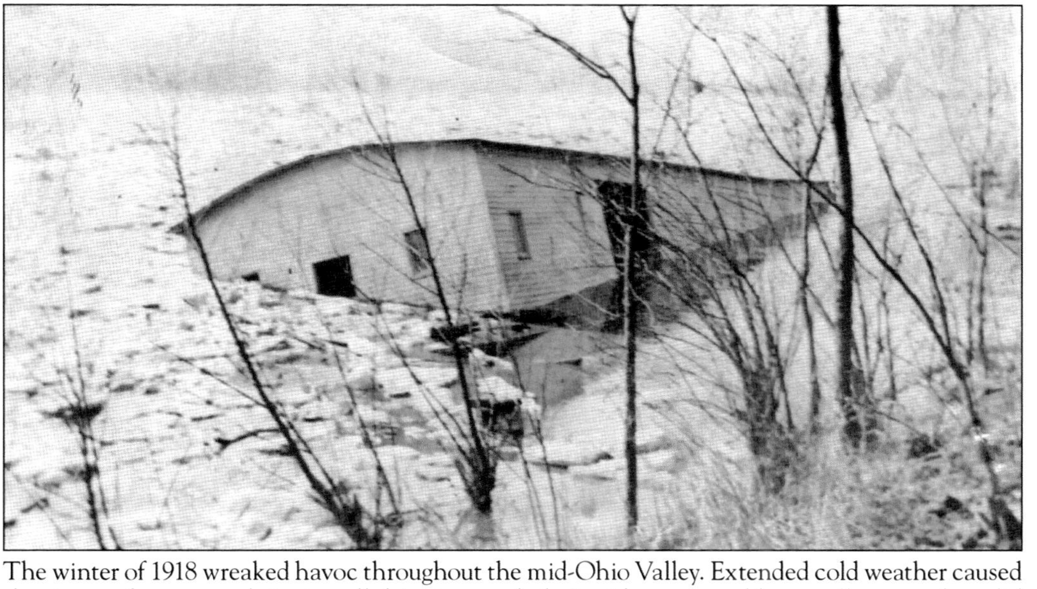

The winter of 1918 wreaked havoc throughout the mid-Ohio Valley. Extended cold weather caused the river to freeze over, bringing all shipping to a halt. Residents were able to walk across the solid surface of the river to the Kentucky shore and back. As the ice finally began to thaw, the floes crushed in the sides of the Rome wharf boat, sending it to the bottom. (Author's collection.)

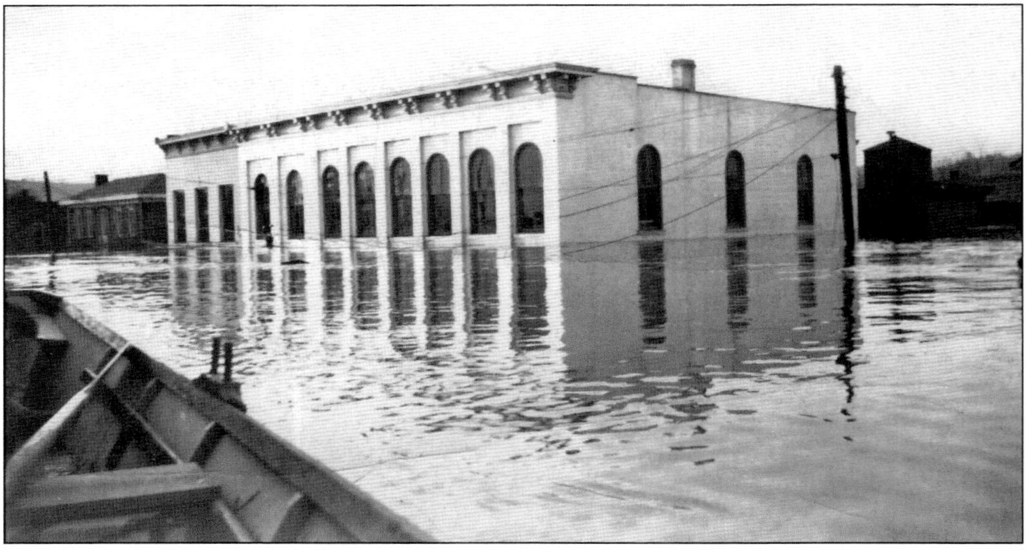

The flood of 1937 surpassed all previous inundations of the mid-Ohio Valley. The waters crested at an unheard of 79.9 feet in Manchester. This photograph shows the Kirker Hardware building on Second Street when there were 2.5 feet of water in the second floor. (Author's collection.)

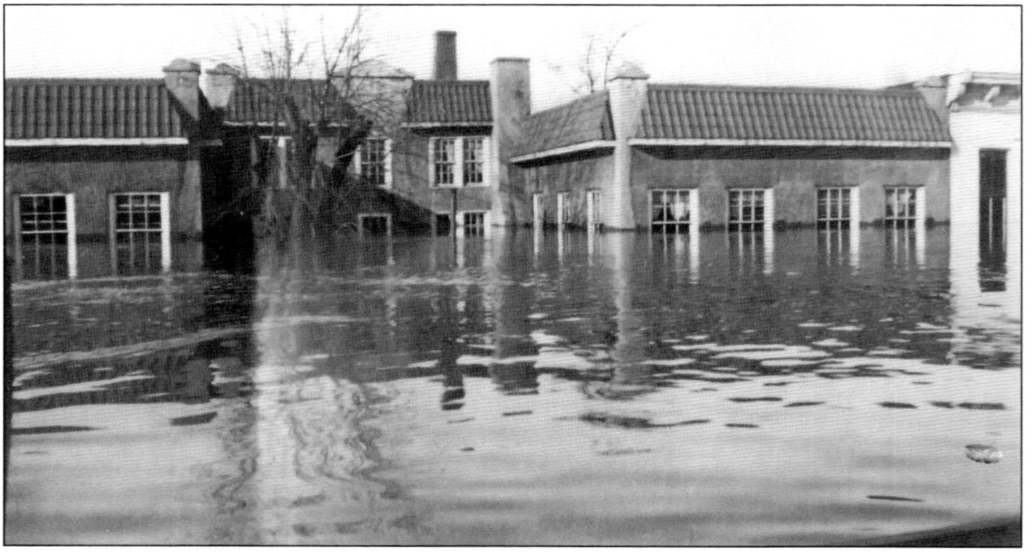

The Hotel Hester, another Manchester business, did not receive any mercy from the flood of 1945. Guests had to evacuate the structure and head for public shelters set up in the area's schools that were out of reach of the floodwaters. (Author's collection.)

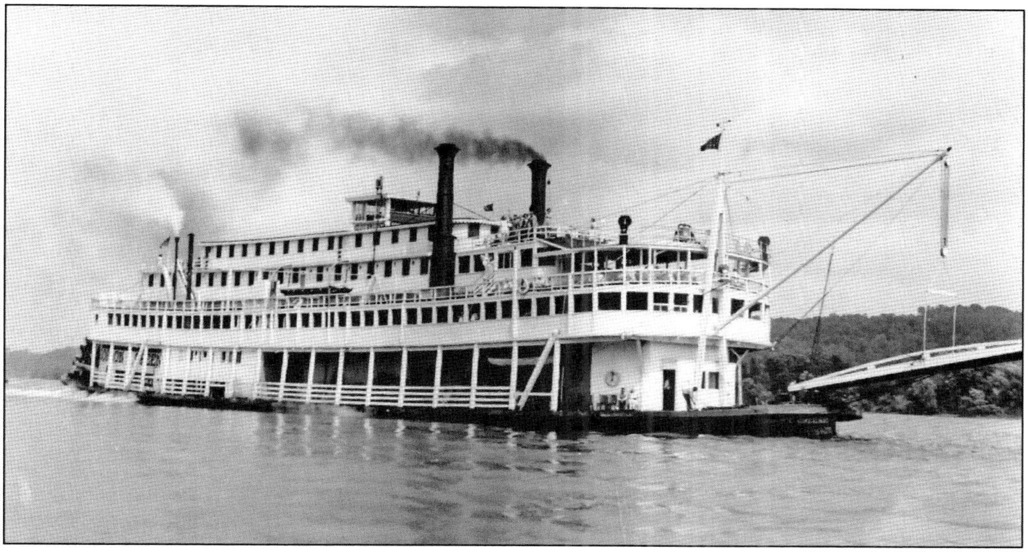

The *Gordon C. Greene*, a big stern-wheel passenger boat, was built in 1923 in Jeffersonville, Indiana, and was first named *Cape Girardeau.* This photograph was taken by Carl Kirschner of Manchester about 1953–1954 just a short distance above Wrightsville. The boat was featured in the movie *Gone with the Wind* in 1939. It sank in 1967 at St. Louis. (Courtesy Lois Kidd.)

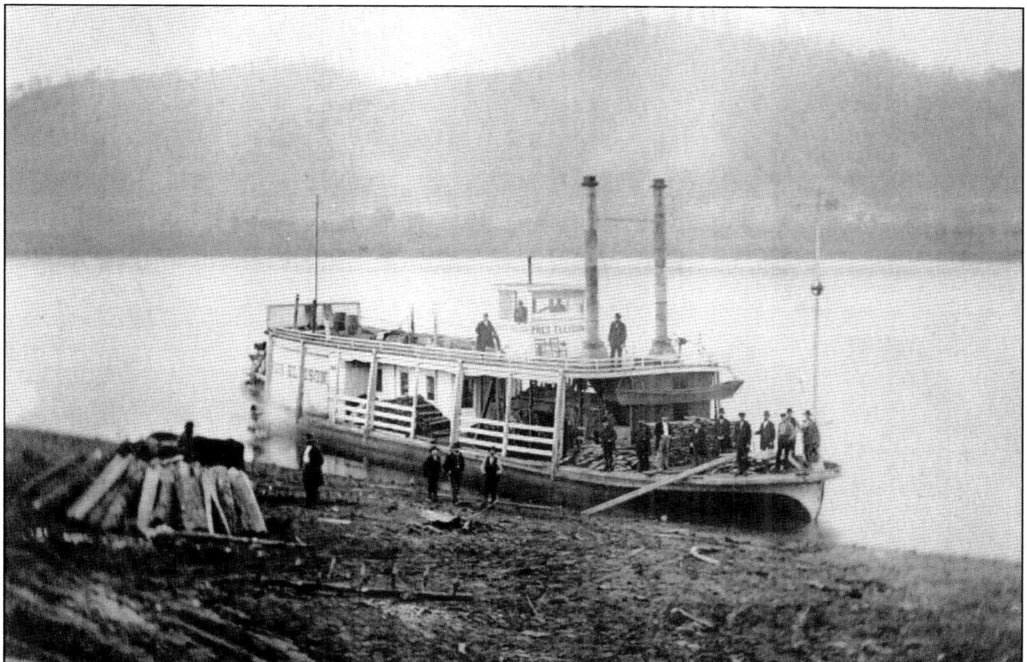

The *Pres Ellison* was built in Portsmouth, Ohio, in 1879. This packet boat was originally owned by Capt. George W. Edgington, a native of Manchester. He named his new boat after Pres Ellison of Manchester. Although it ran the Manchester–Maysville–Vanceburg trade for a short while, it was later based in Wheeling, West Virginia, for several years, running local routes. This photograph was taken at the Manchester Landing around 1900. (Courtesy Manchester Historical Society.)

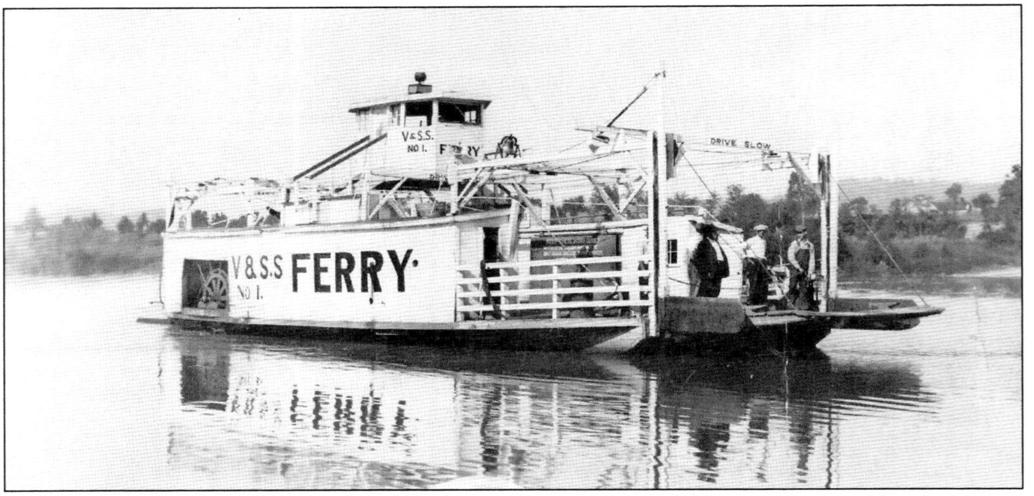

The Kenyon Ferry was located in Green Township and connected the community of Sandy Springs to the Kentucky village of Vanceburg on the south shore of the Ohio River. This ferry was owned and operated by the Kenyon family from 1810 until 1949, during which time several different vessels were used. This photograph was taken in 1933, when it was known as the Vanceburg and Sandy Springs Ferry. (Courtesy Adams County Historical Society.)

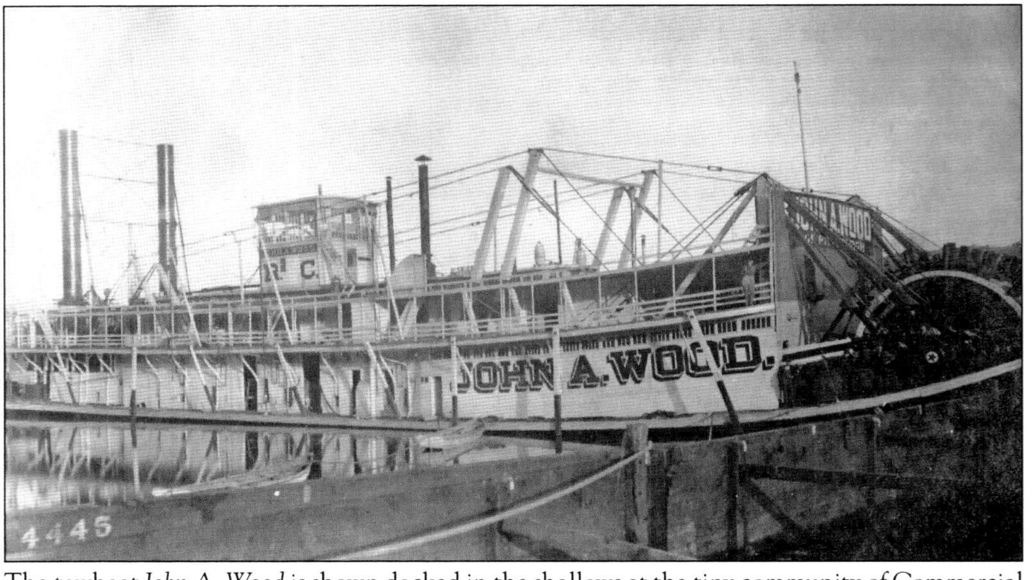

The towboat *John A. Wood* is shown docked in the shallows at the tiny community of Commercial Town in Green Township. This photograph was taken on November 16, 1910, by Second Mate Roscoe Kelley. The big stern-wheeler was forced to tie up at Commercial Town for almost four months due to a widespread drought that year, causing the Ohio River to drop to such a low level it was impossible to navigate. (Author's collection.)

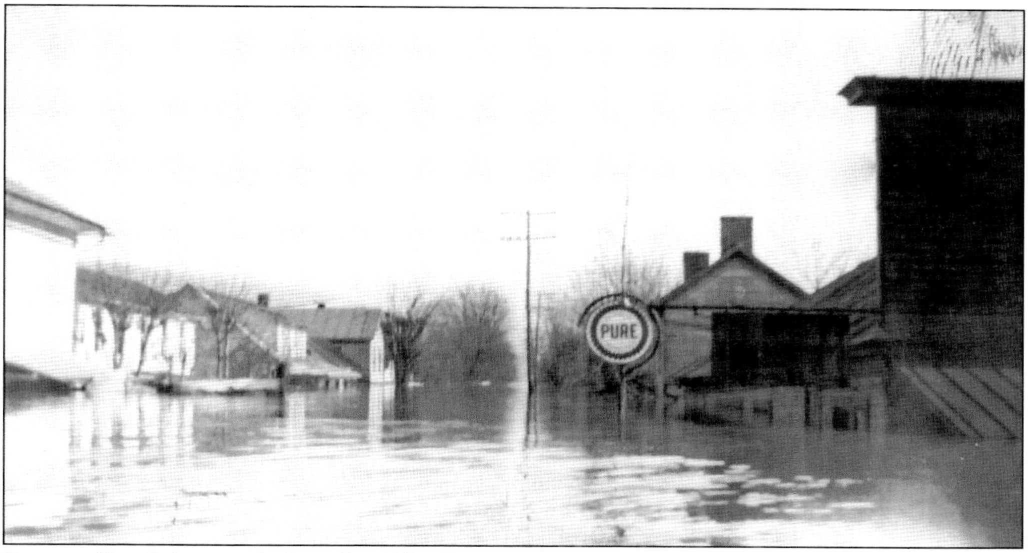

Rome suffered along with the other Ohio River communities during the disastrous flood of 1937. This snapshot was taken looking upstream on Second Street. The former Citizens Deposit Bank building is in the foreground on the right. (Author's collection.)

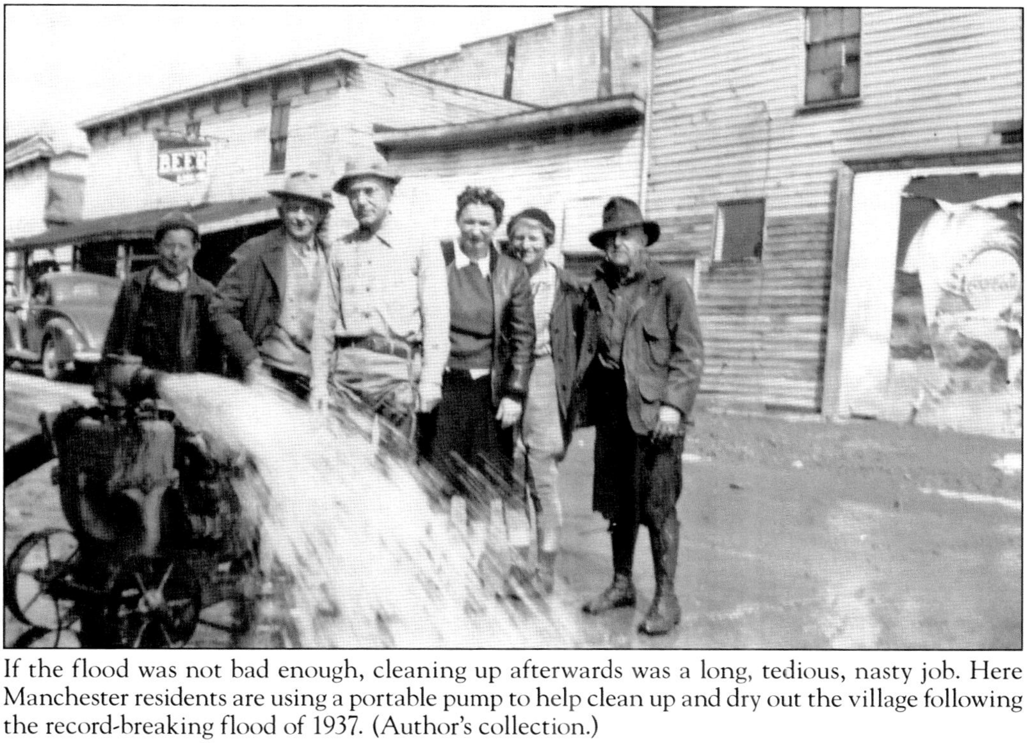

If the flood was not bad enough, cleaning up afterwards was a long, tedious, nasty job. Here Manchester residents are using a portable pump to help clean up and dry out the village following the record-breaking flood of 1937. (Author's collection.)

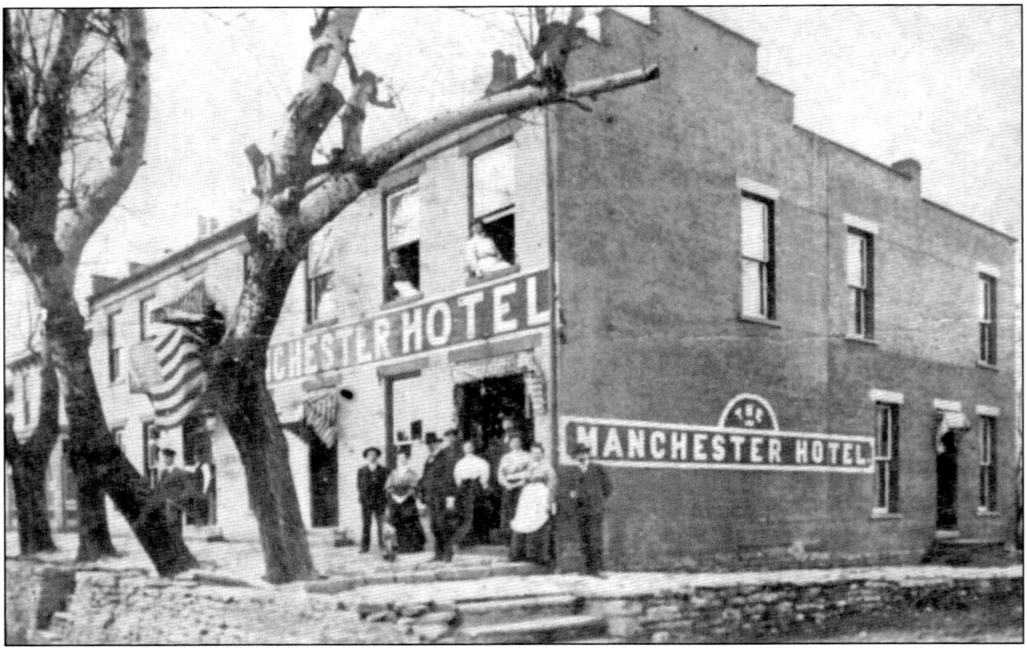

Riverfront communities with regular river traffic invariably had hotels near their landing to accommodate travelers. The Manchester Hotel was built in 1854 by M. V. Cropper. Following the Civil War, John McDaid operated it as the McDaid House. J. W. Lightbody owned it when this photograph was taken in 1906. The structure burned in January 1910 with John McDaid dying in the conflagration. (Author's collection.)

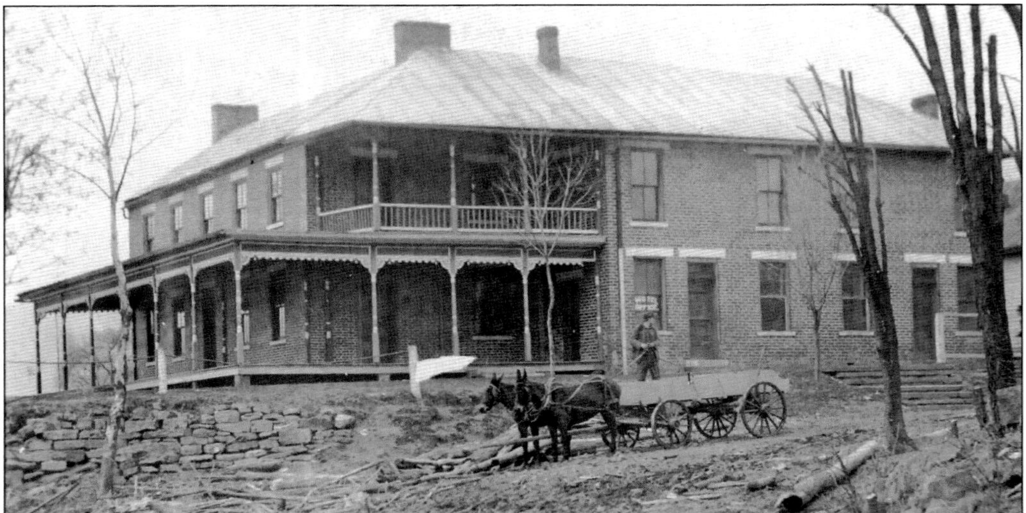

The Valley House was one of the largest structures ever built in Rome. Facing out over the Ohio River and sitting beside the public landing, it was constructed in 1837 by William Stout Jr., son of the village's founder. It was stated in *Historical Collections of Adams County Ohio, Volume II* that the Valley House was "an attractive stopping place for tourists . . . its beautiful view of the Ohio River and Kentucky's hills attracted many city vacationers." It burned in 1920. (Courtesy Adams County Historical Society.)

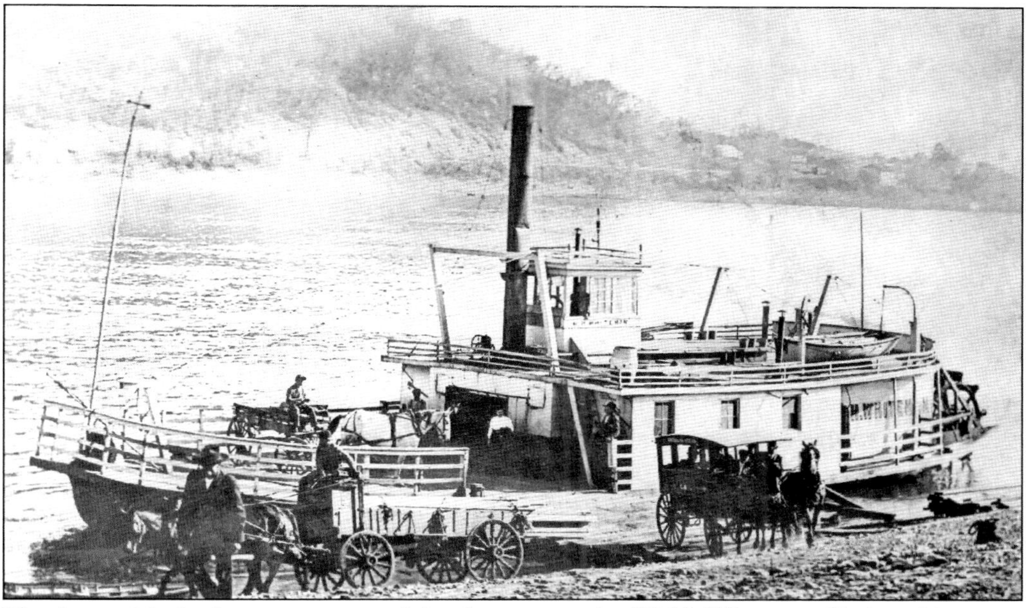

The ferry with the longest tenure at Manchester was the *W. H. Whiteman*. Built in Newport, Kentucky, in 1897, it was bought by Capt. Ernie P. Anshutz and Capt. H. C. Brown and brought to Manchester, where they also owned the wharf boat. After acquiring full ownership of the *Whiteman*, Anshutz sold it to Capt. Ernest Suiter, who operated the ferry until January 20, 1936, when it burned at the Manchester Landing. (Courtesy Adams County Historical Society.)

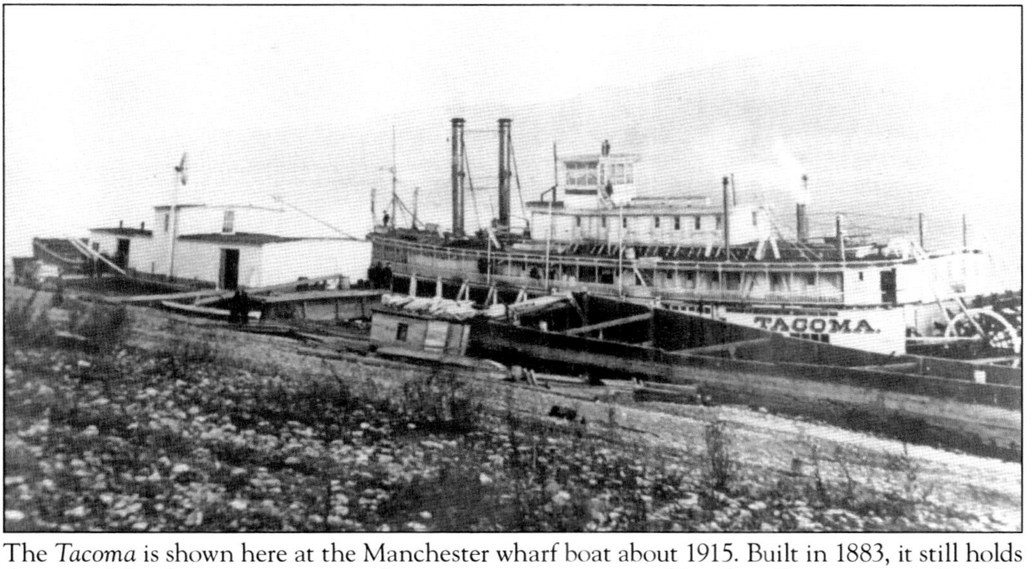

The *Tacoma* is shown here at the Manchester wharf boat about 1915. Built in 1883, it still holds the record for the most years served in continuous operation. Based in Cincinnati, it plied the waters of the Ohio River for a remarkable 39 years. It burned while moored on the Cincinnati levee on November 4, 1922, with three other boats, including the fabled *Island Queen*. (Courtesy Doris Lucas.)

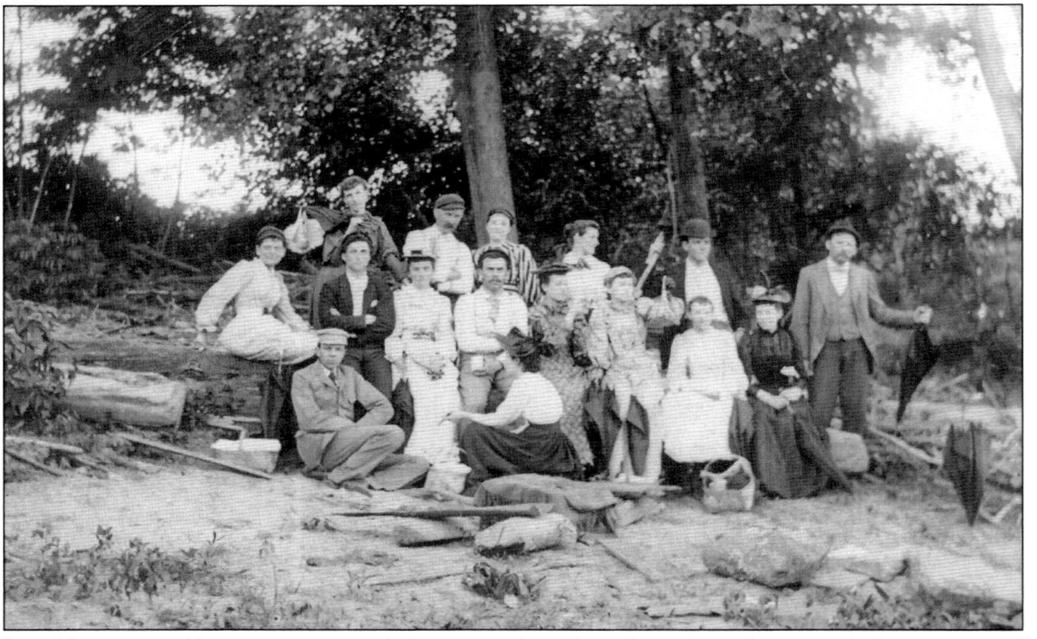

In addition to offering commercial shipping, the Ohio River has also provided recreational opportunities. This is a group of friends having a picnic on the big island at Manchester. Such outings on the islands were common. Notice how everyone, especially the women, was dressed up for this fun day. (Author's collection.)

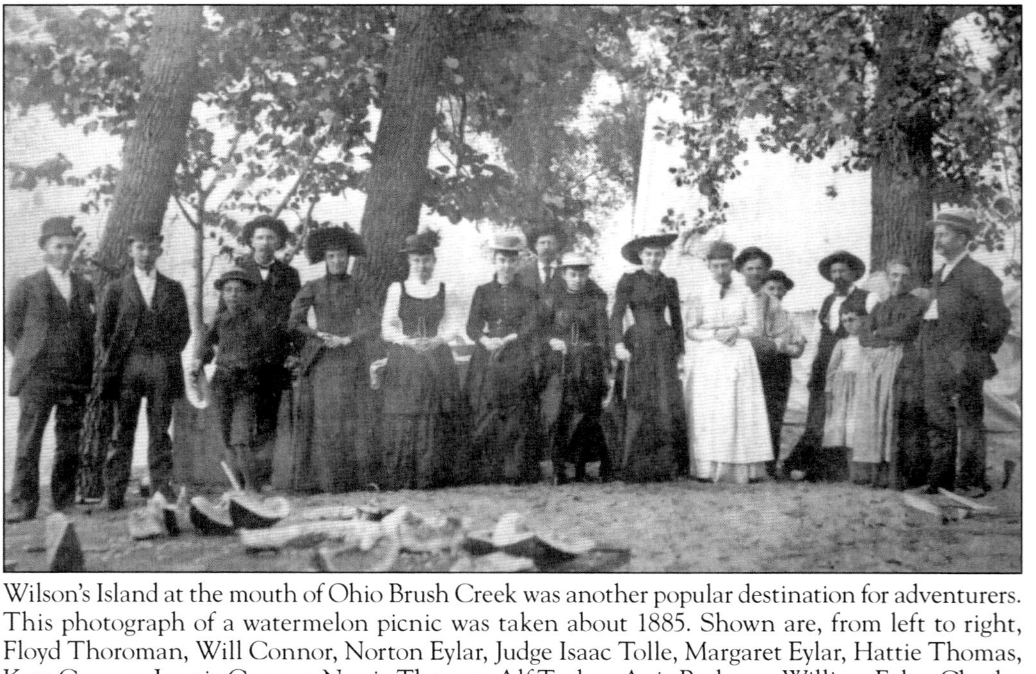

Wilson's Island at the mouth of Ohio Brush Creek was another popular destination for adventurers. This photograph of a watermelon picnic was taken about 1885. Shown are, from left to right, Floyd Thoroman, Will Connor, Norton Eylar, Judge Isaac Tolle, Margaret Eylar, Hattie Thomas, Kate Connor, Jennie Connor, Nettie Thomas, Alf Tucker, Axie Redman, William Eylar, Charles Thomas, Bill Cooper, Lottie Eylar, Ella Eylar, and Joseph Eylar, founder of the *People's Defender.* (Courtesy Valerie Young.)

Four

TIMBER AND AGRICULTURE

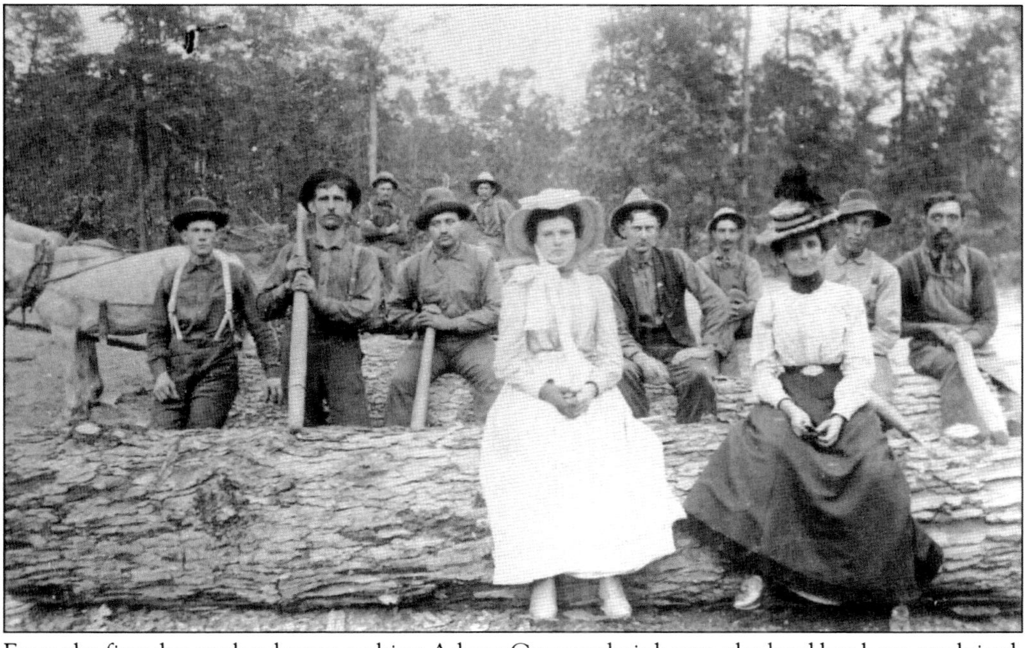

From the first day settlers began making Adams County their home, the land has been exploited. Trees were the first natural resource to feel the effects of civilization, and the timber industry in Adams County today is still a major source of employment. In this *c.* 1895 photograph taken by Lizzie Treber, two young women are paying a visit to a group of loggers in the Bentonville area. (Courtesy William and Bessie J. Sininger.)

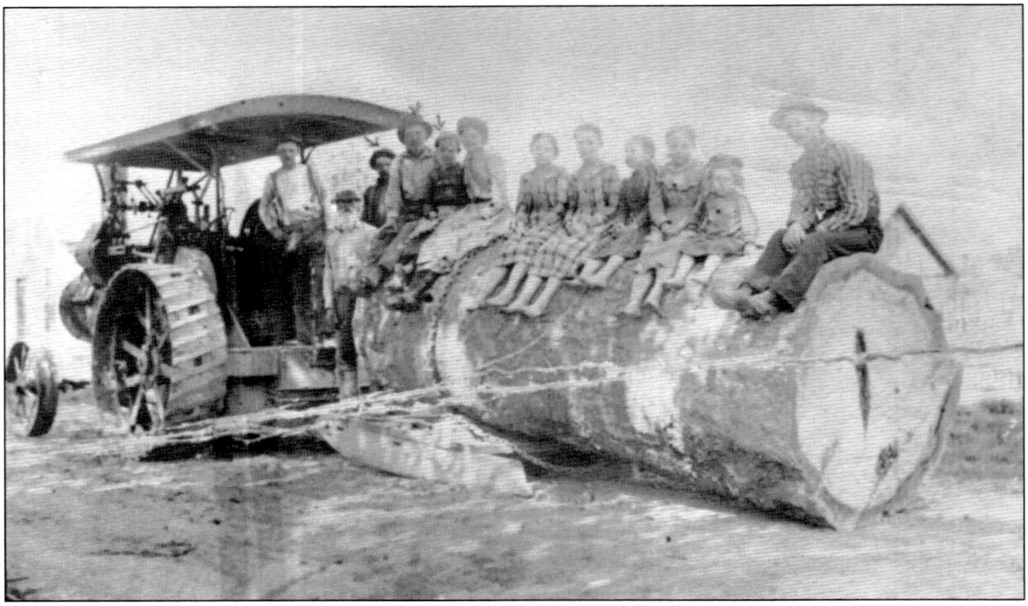

In less than a century, most of the hardwood forest that once covered Adams County was gone. Much of it was cut and burned to make way for cropland. By the beginning of the 20th century, when a really big tree was cut, it was newsworthy of a photographer's visit. Here in 1903 at Lawshe, Tom Smith had to use his steam engine to drag this 5-foot-diameter sycamore log. (Courtesy Adams County Historical Society.)

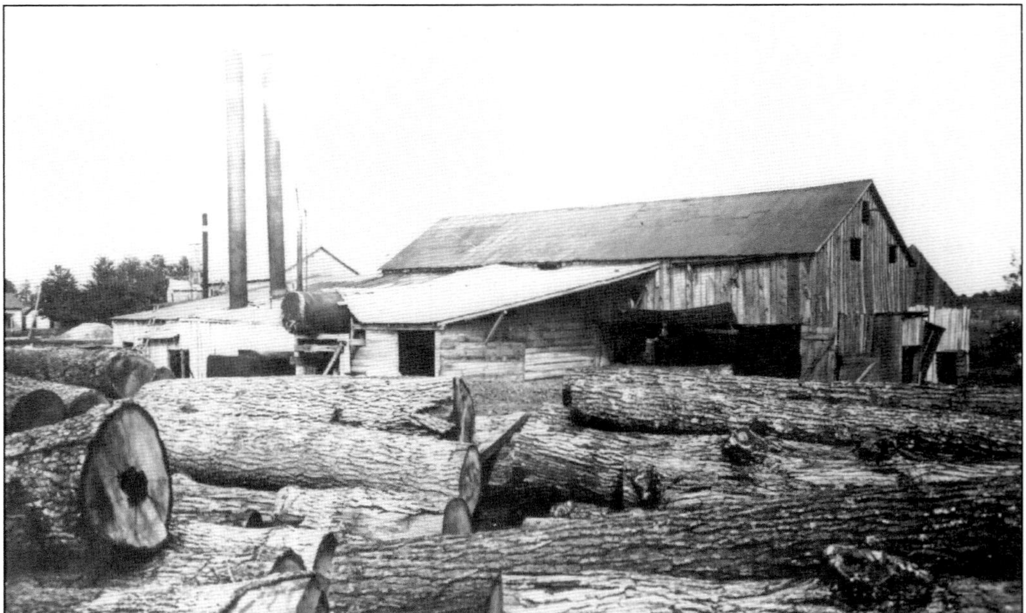

H. H. Mechlin started a lumber mill in Winchester in the 1890s. The company prospered, enabling Mechlin to build the biggest house in the village. This is a view of Mechlin's lumberyard with his mill in the background. (Courtesy Lester and Jean Wallis.)

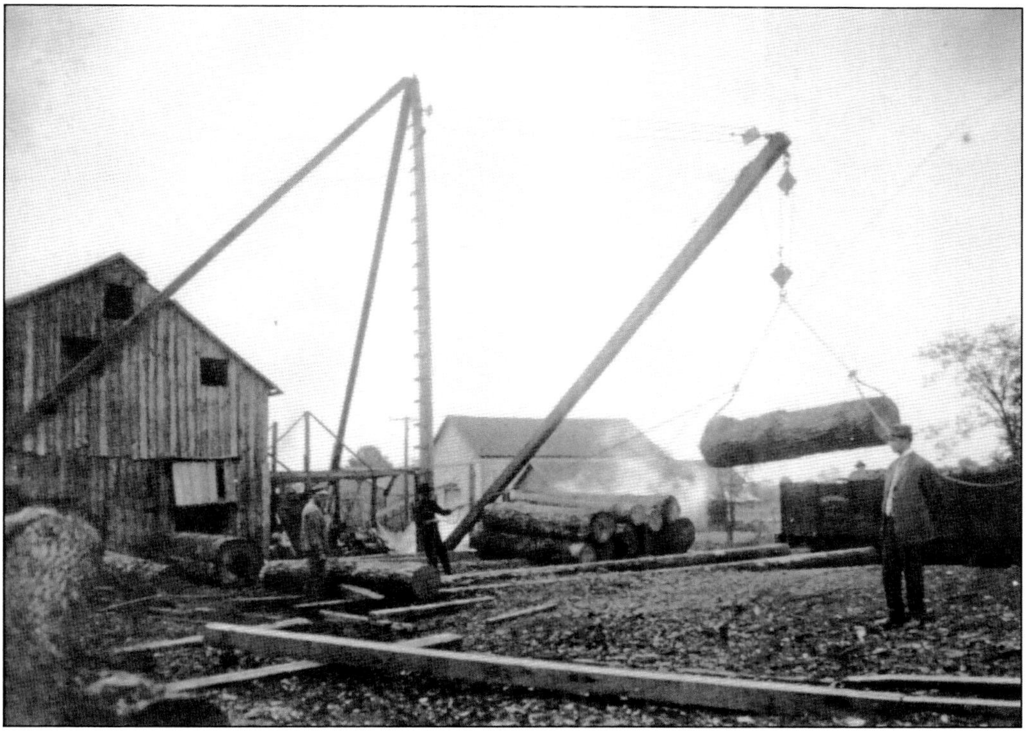

The boom of a derrick is being used at H. H. Mechlin's sawmill to lift and move heavy logs in the Winchester lumberyard about 1900. Mechlin, on the right, is observing the scene. (Author's collection.)

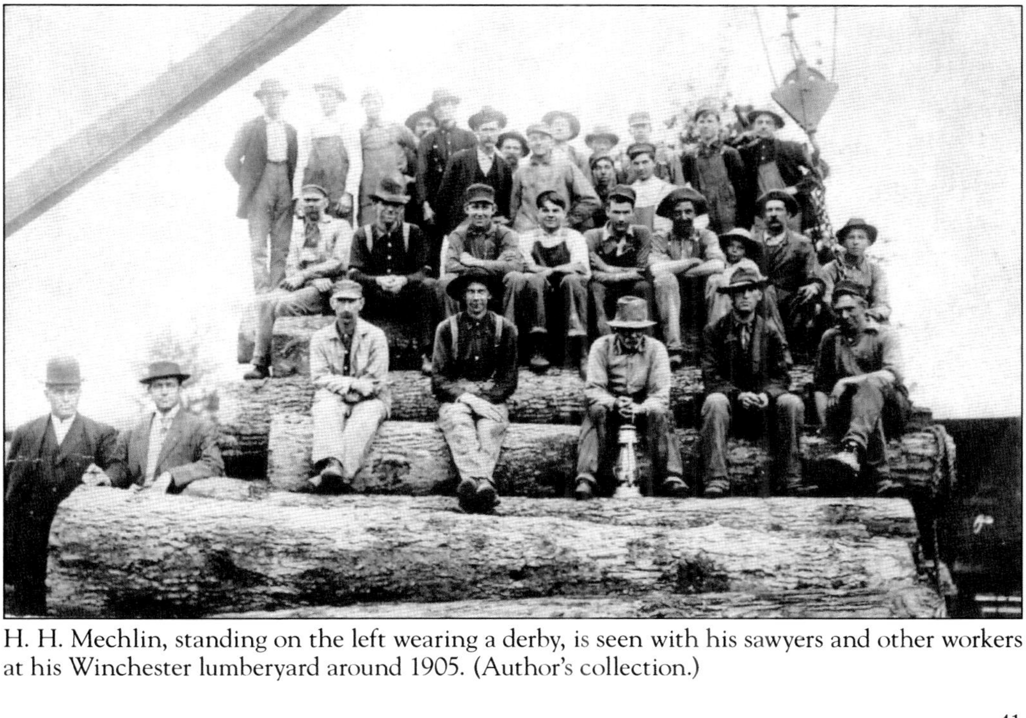

H. H. Mechlin, standing on the left wearing a derby, is seen with his sawyers and other workers at his Winchester lumberyard around 1905. (Author's collection.)

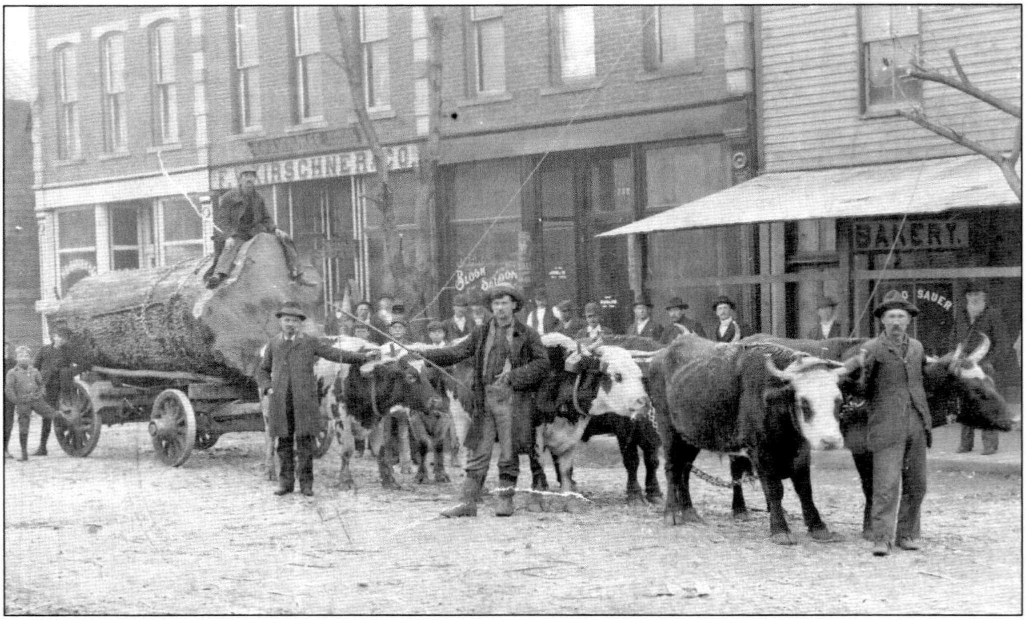

It took three yoke of oxen to haul this very large log through downtown Manchester about 1895. It is believed the log was being transported to the Ohio Valley Furniture Company, located on Front Street, a short distance from where this picture was taken. Standing close to the butt end of the log in a dress hat and overcoat is Lyman P. Stivers, a Manchester businessman and former county sheriff. (Author's collection.)

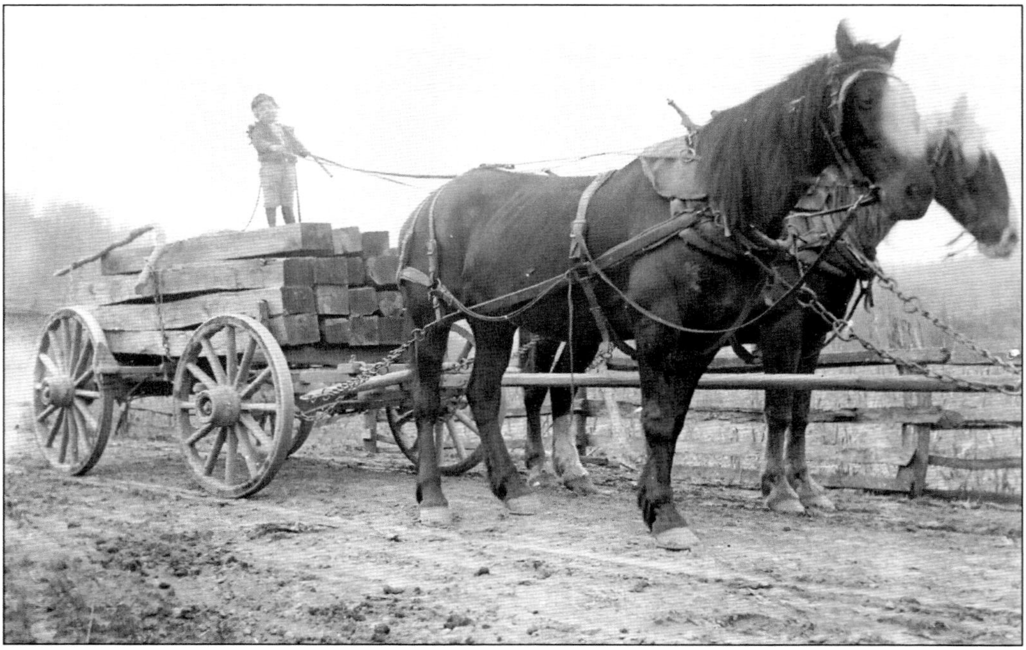

A very young John Meyers, who lived near Peach Mountain, stands on a wagonload of newly cut railroad ties heading for market about 1905. This photograph was taken by Winifred Johnson Holmes. (Courtesy Adams County Historical Society.)

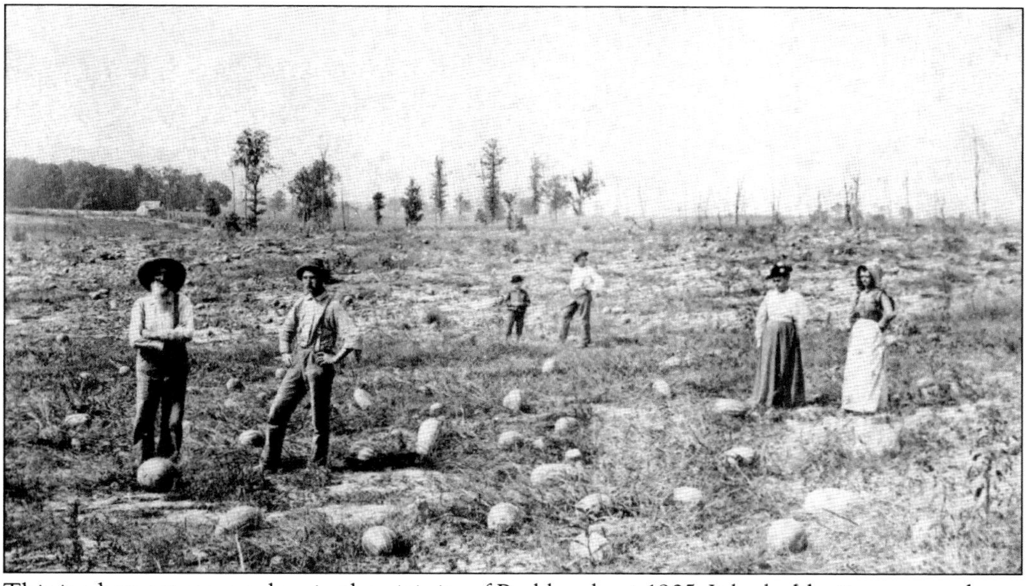

This is a harvest scene taken in the vicinity of Peebles about 1905. It looks like it was a good year for melons. The fruit and vegetable market played an important role in the county's commercial development at that time. (Author's collection.)

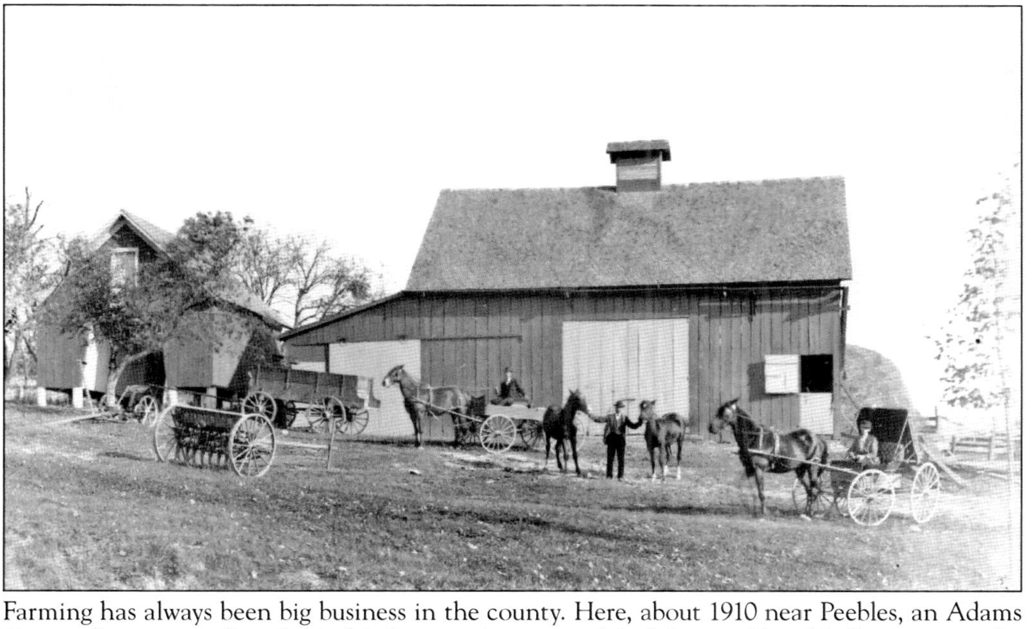

Farming has always been big business in the county. Here, about 1910 near Peebles, an Adams County farmer proudly exhibits his farm equipment and draft horses. David I. Gardner was the photographer. (Author's collection.)

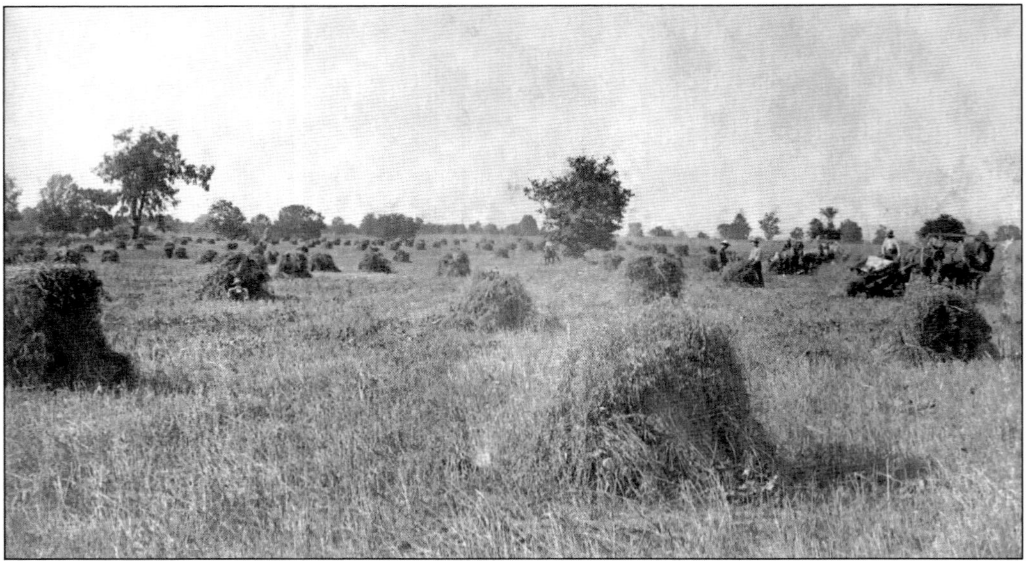

Before farm machinery was mechanized, most of the labor was performed by hand. Here is a wheat field in the Peebles area, where the newly cut wheat was tied into shocks by farm laborers in preparation for threshing. Amish fields in Adams County look very much like this today. (Author's collection.)

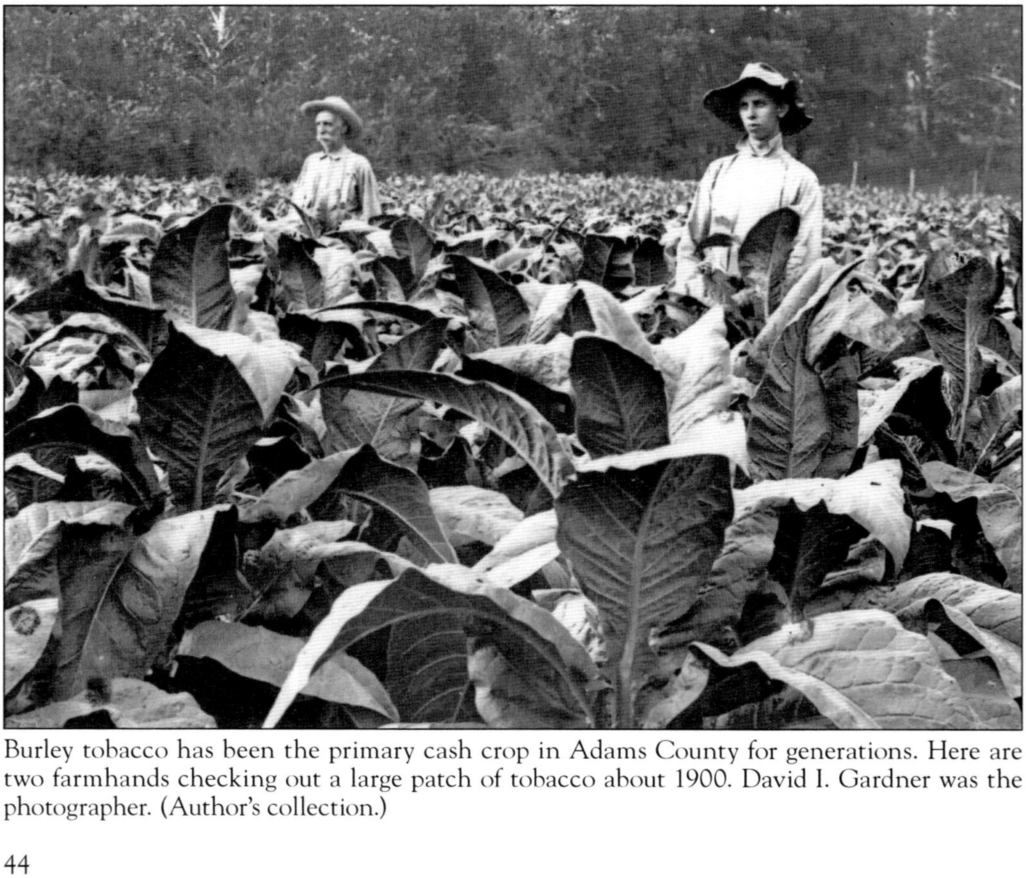

Burley tobacco has been the primary cash crop in Adams County for generations. Here are two farmhands checking out a large patch of tobacco about 1900. David I. Gardner was the photographer. (Author's collection.)

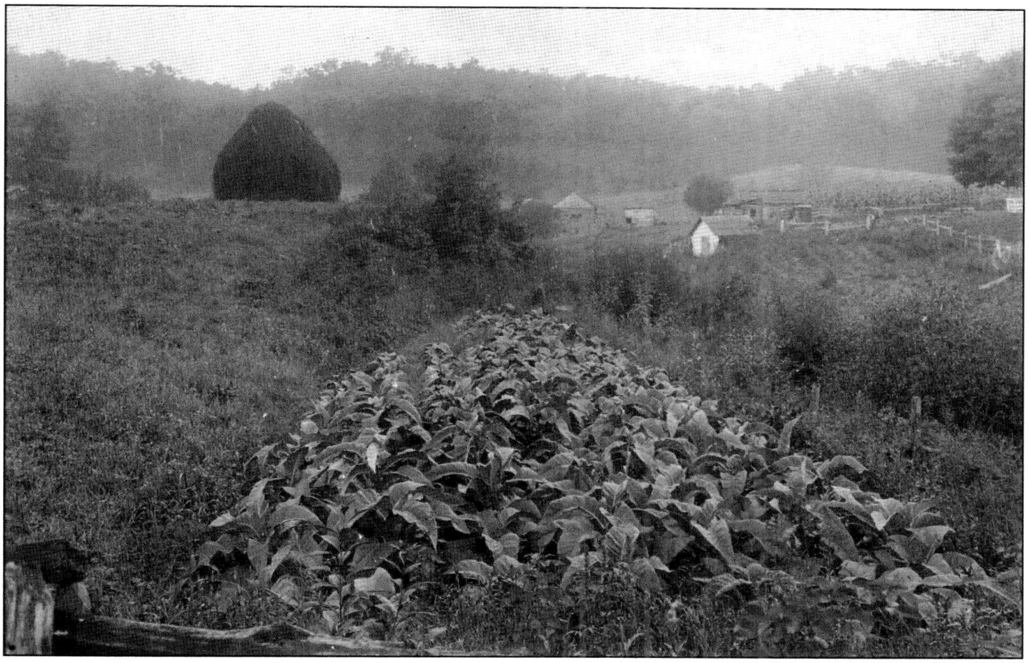

In August 1891, members of the Columbus Camera Club toured the northeastern corner of Adams County. One member, Prof. J. N. Bradford, photographed this small patch of tobacco between Locust Grove and Sinking Spring beside old Zane's Trace. Notice the tall haystack in the left background. (Courtesy Lester and Jean Wallis.)

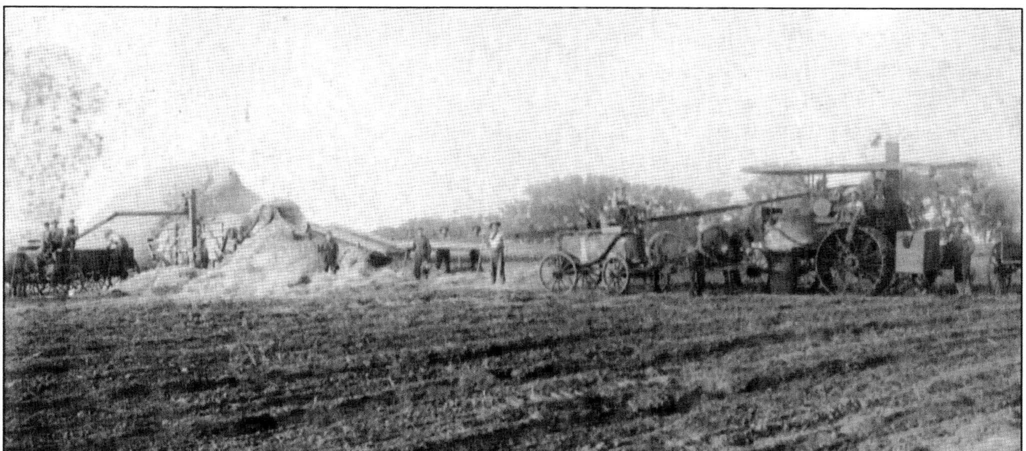

Threshing day was always a major event on the farm. Friends and neighbors would gather to help with the harvest. The men and boys worked in the fields, while the women and girls prepared a bountiful repast for the noonday meal. Here is a typical harvest scene of wheat being threshed in the vicinity of Peebles around 1915, complete with steam engine, thresher, water wagon, and grain wagons. (Courtesy Adams County Historical Society.)

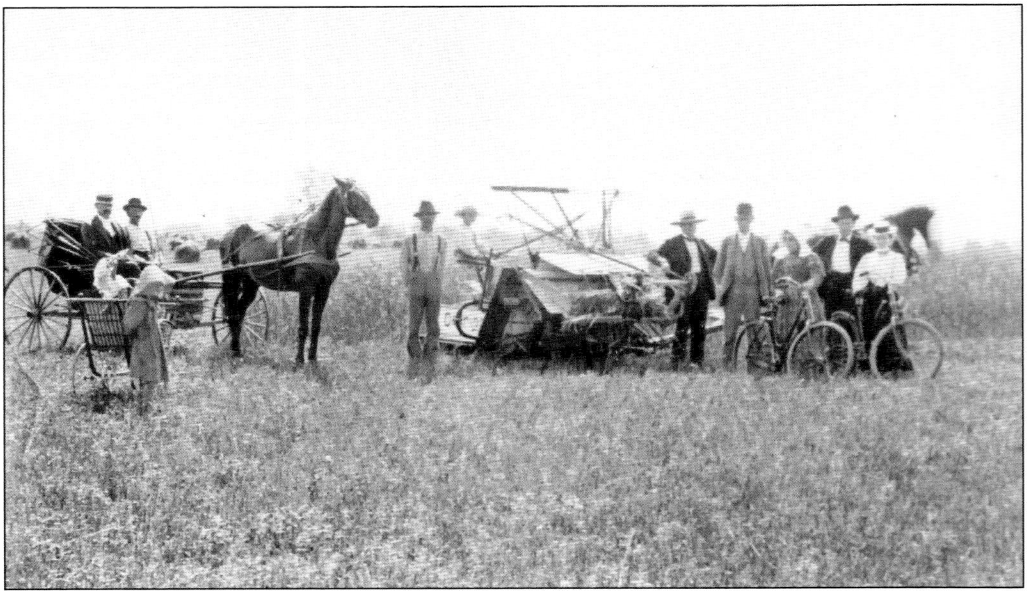

A farmer in the Winchester area is checking out his new horse-drawn reaper about 1890. It will mean less backbreaking work for his family and farm hands. Notice the two women who have ridden bicycles into the field. (Author's collection.)

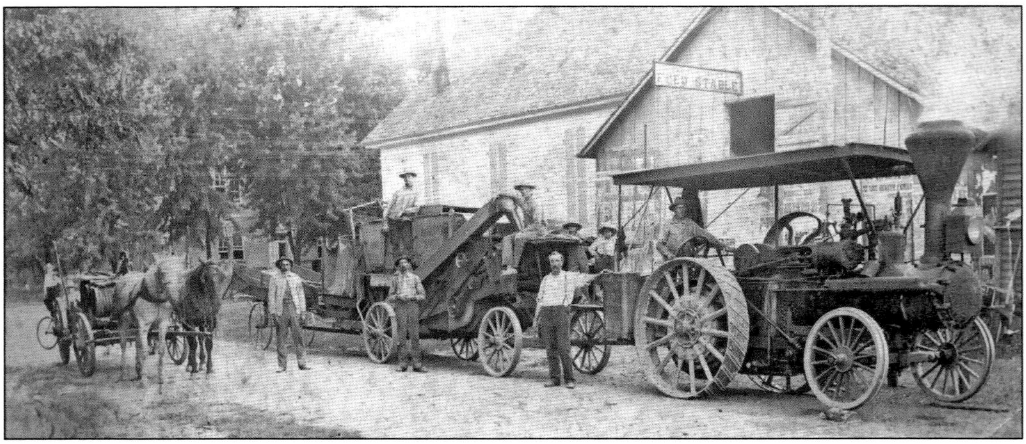

The owner of this threshing outfit is posing for the photographer on Market Street in West Union about 1905. The equipment is parked in front of the Palace Hotel Feed Stable. The east side of the Christian Union Church is seen behind the thresher. The water wagon is parked on the far left of the photograph, and the courthouse is seen beyond the trees. (Courtesy Adams County Historical Society.)

Five

Faith and the Underground Railroad

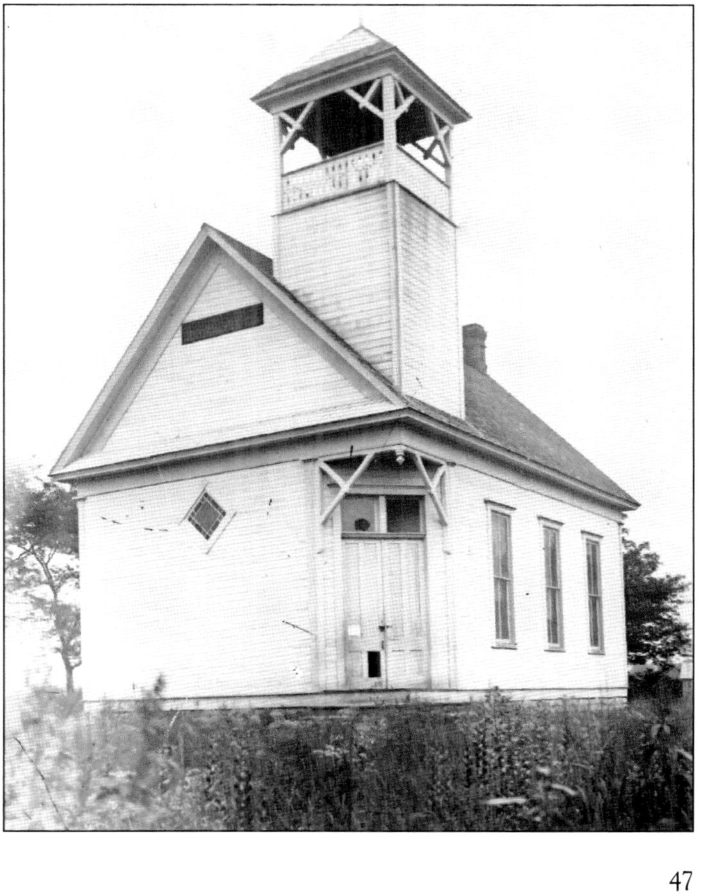

This is the only known photograph of the old Tranquillity United Presbyterian Church. Erected in 1853, this view of the structure was taken about 1895 by an unknown photographer. The little church sat adjacent to the Tranquillity Cemetery and overlooked the George's Creek Valley. Lightning struck this house of worship in 1903, resulting in its total destruction. Today the Tranquillity Community Church sits on the site. (Courtesy Lester and Jean Wallis.)

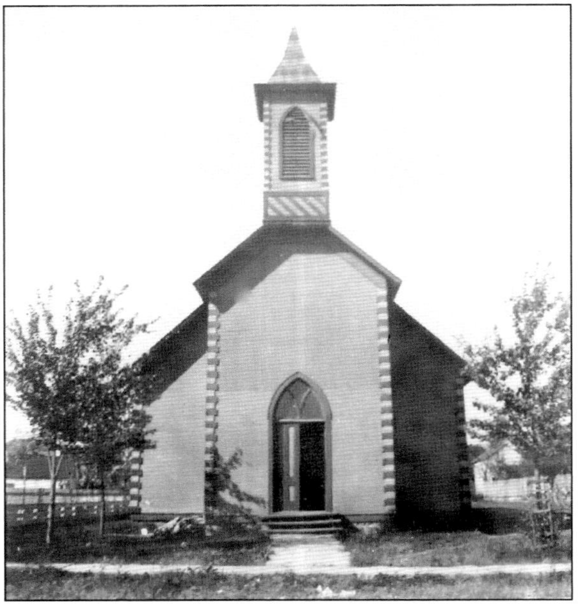

The village of Peebles was founded in 1883. It quickly grew, and soon the need for churches became apparent. In 1887, a United Presbyterian congregation that had organized in the village acquired land on north Main Street and started construction on a house of worship. This is a photograph of that structure taken around 1888 by Jennie McAdow Broomhall. It was razed several years later (see below). (Courtesy Lester and Jean Wallis.)

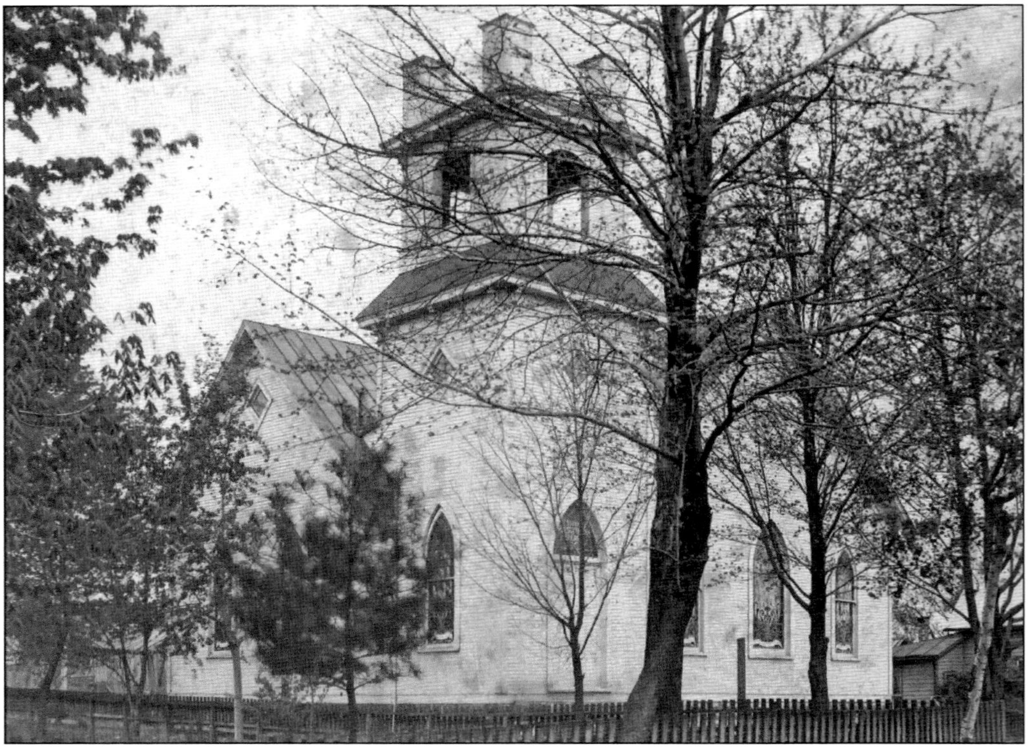

After constructing their first church in 1887, members of the Peebles United Presbyterian congregation continued to expand, eventually outgrowing the church. In 1907, they tore down their house of worship and erected a much larger Gothic Revival–style structure on the same site. It is shown here as it appeared about 1910. In later years, the congregation faltered, and in 1930 the church closed its doors. The building was razed in 1977. (Courtesy John and Carol Wickerham.)

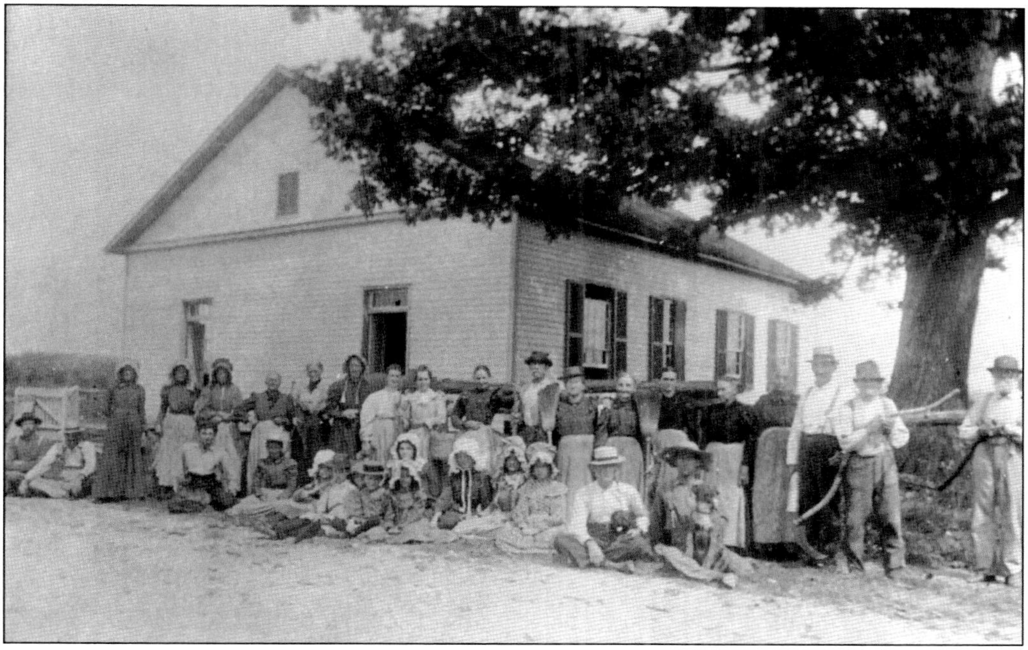

The Union Church, to this day, sits on the south edge of Bentonville. This structure was completed in 1854, replacing a small brick church that had been built on the same site in 1832. The church was originally affiliated with the Christian church but joined the Christian Union denomination following World War I. This photograph was taken by Lizzie Treber about 1900. (Courtesy William and Bessie J. Sininger.)

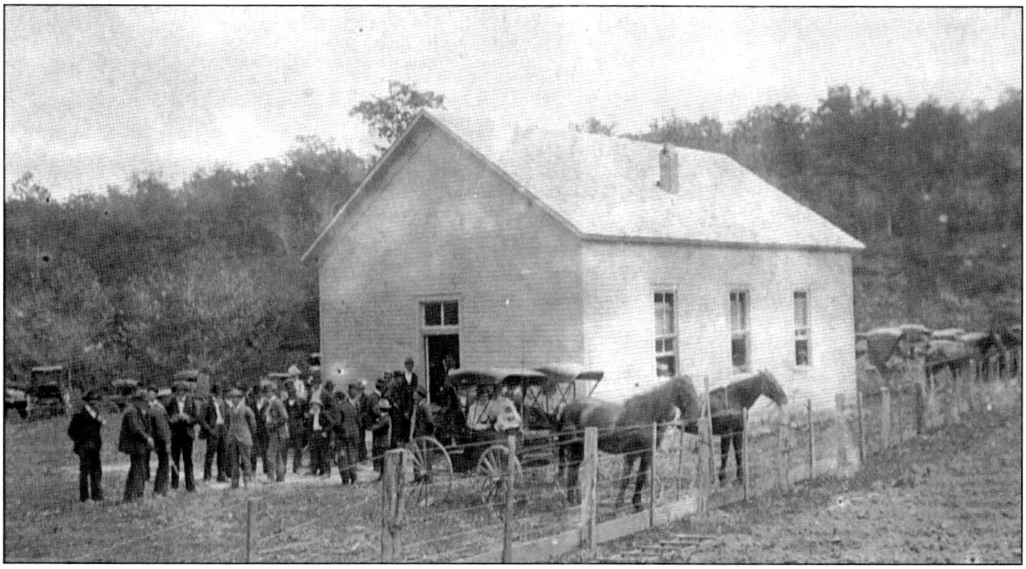

This little church faithfully served its congregation from 1900 until 1966. Sitting 2 miles north of West Union on State Route 41, it was the Lick Fork Church of the United Brethren in Christ. The congregation built a larger structure in West Union and moved there in 1966. This photograph was taken by Lizzie Treber. It is believed she took the photograph in 1900 at the church's dedication. (Courtesy William and Bessie J. Sininger.)

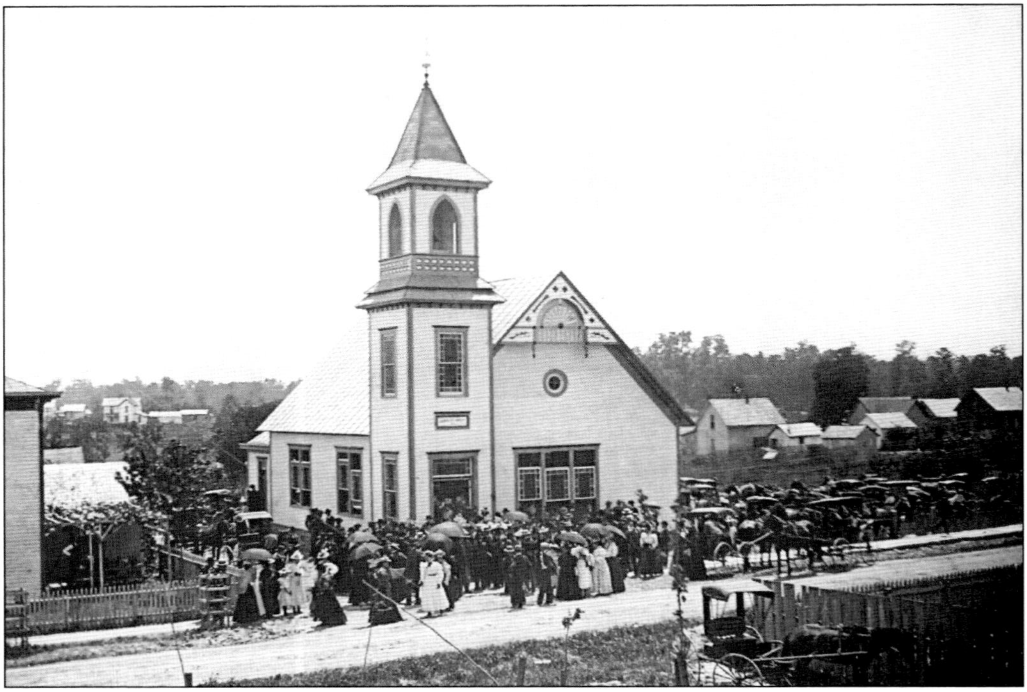

This was the Peebles Church of Christ on Vine Street. Photographer David I. Gardner took this photograph on June 5, 1898, at the church's dedication. In recent years, the congregation built a larger house of worship in a different part of town and sold this structure. (Courtesy H. W. Johnson Jr.)

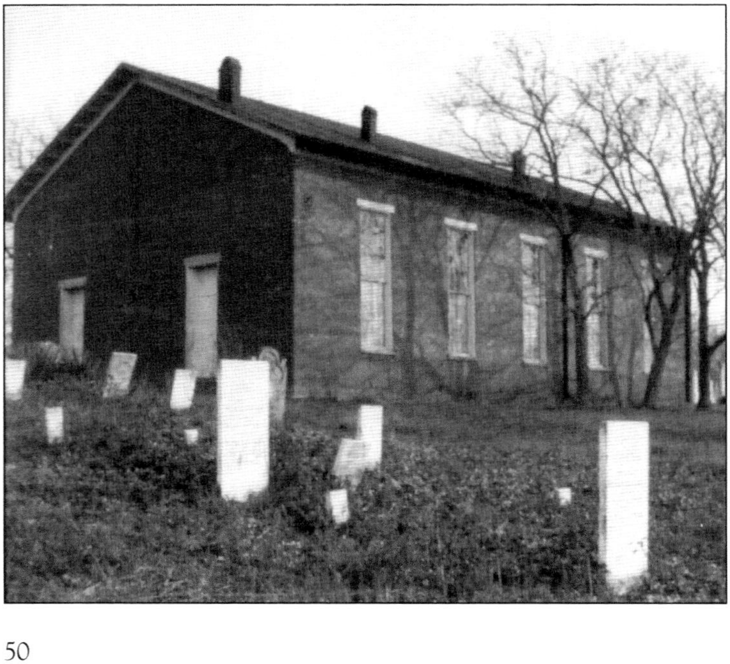

The village of Cherry Fork was originally known as North Liberty. The area was a hotbed of abolitionist activity, and members of the Cherry Fork Associate Reformed Presbyterian Church were very involved in the Underground Railroad movement. Their brick church, shown here, was constructed in 1854 in the community cemetery. It remained in use until 1907 when replaced by a larger structure built in the village. (Author's collection.)

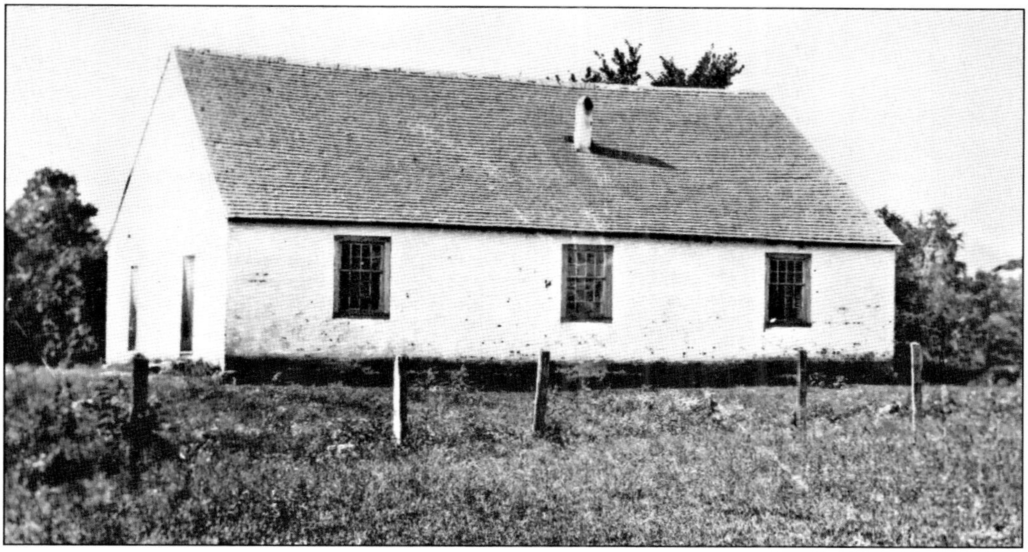

Among the earliest pioneers to settle in Adams County were the Covenanters. A very rigid religious sect, they completed this brick church in 1840 on present-day Nichols Ridge Road in Scott Township. It was named Bethel Meeting House. Due to divisions that occurred in the congregation, the church was used for only 16 years, closing in 1856–1857. This photograph of Bethel Meeting House was taken by Finley Black about 1858. (Courtesy Lester and Jean Wallis.)

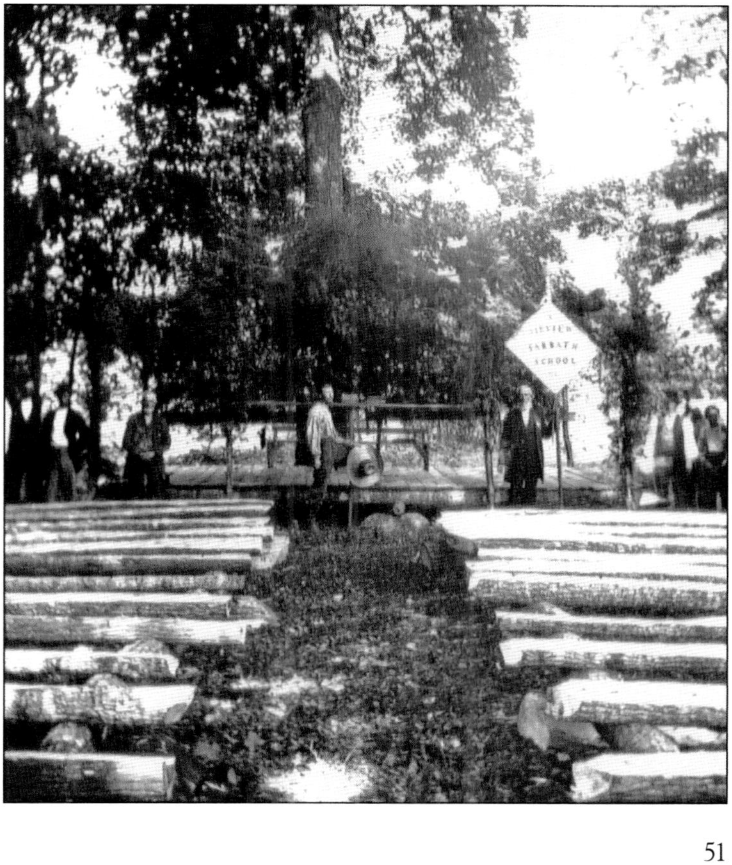

In the tiny community of Fairview in Liberty Township, a congregation of the German Methodist Episcopal Church was organized prior to the Civil War. In the early years, services were conducted in the German tongue. This *c.* 1890 stereo view was taken of an outdoor worship area adjacent to the church utilizing split-log pews facing a small, raised platform. A sign reads, "Fairview Sabbath School." (Courtesy Lester and Jean Wallis.)

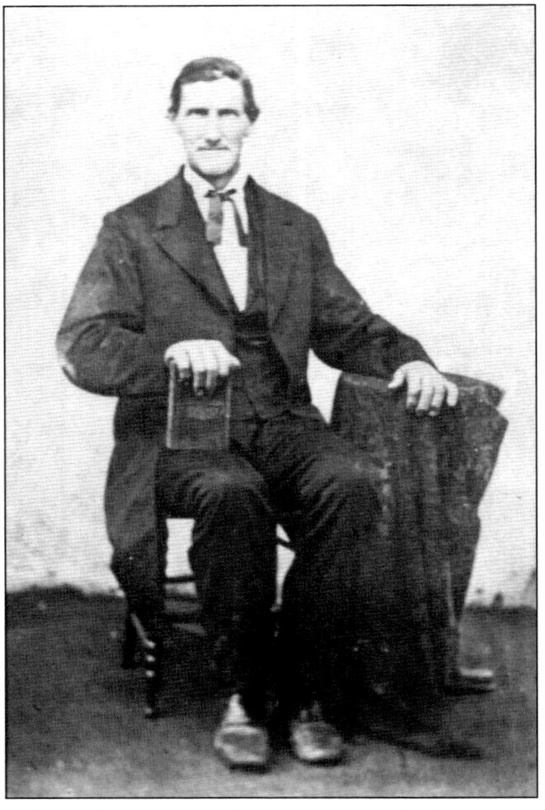

Jesse Wamsley (1813–1887) began preaching at age 14. He became a Methodist Circuit Rider at age 28. During the Civil War, he was persuaded to join the Christian Union denomination that was made up of former Methodists who opposed their church's stand on the war. He became a leader in the Christian Union cause, preaching for that church for 23 years after preaching 37 years for the Methodists. (Author's collection.)

The Mineral Springs Chapel was built across the road from the big Mineral Springs Hotel in 1874. Affiliated with the Presbyterians, it was locally called the "Little Brown Church in the Vale" due to its paint color and setting. A few years after the resort failed, the church also closed. Many of those who had attended the church had been resort patrons. The presbytery sold the church building in 1963. It no longer stands. (Author's collection.)

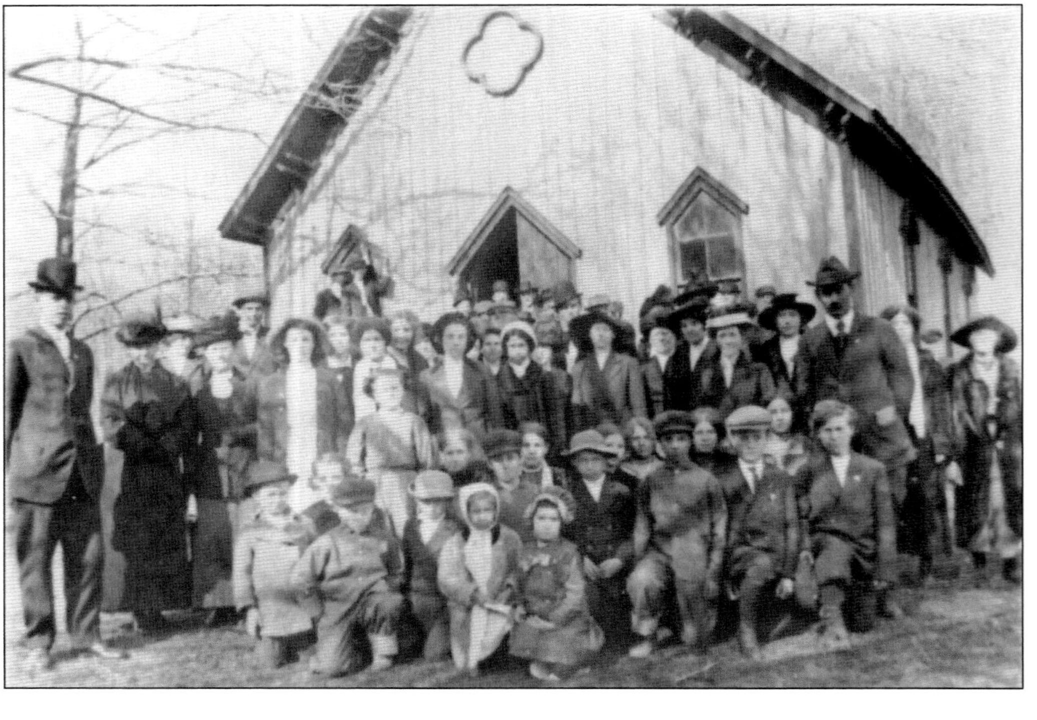

The Peebles Methodist Episcopal congregation was organized in 1886. The church structure shown here was built on Vine Street in 1887. A parsonage was completed beside it in 1895. The church grew as the population of the village also expanded. Not long after the beginning of the 20th century, the congregation decided to enlarge and remodel their church (see below). This photograph was taken around 1895 by Jennie McAdow Broomhall. (Courtesy Lester and Jean Wallis.)

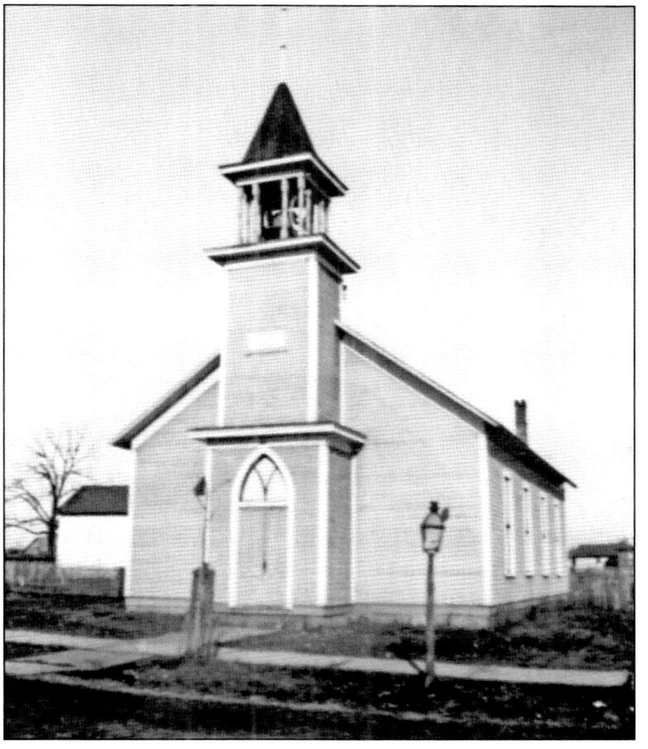

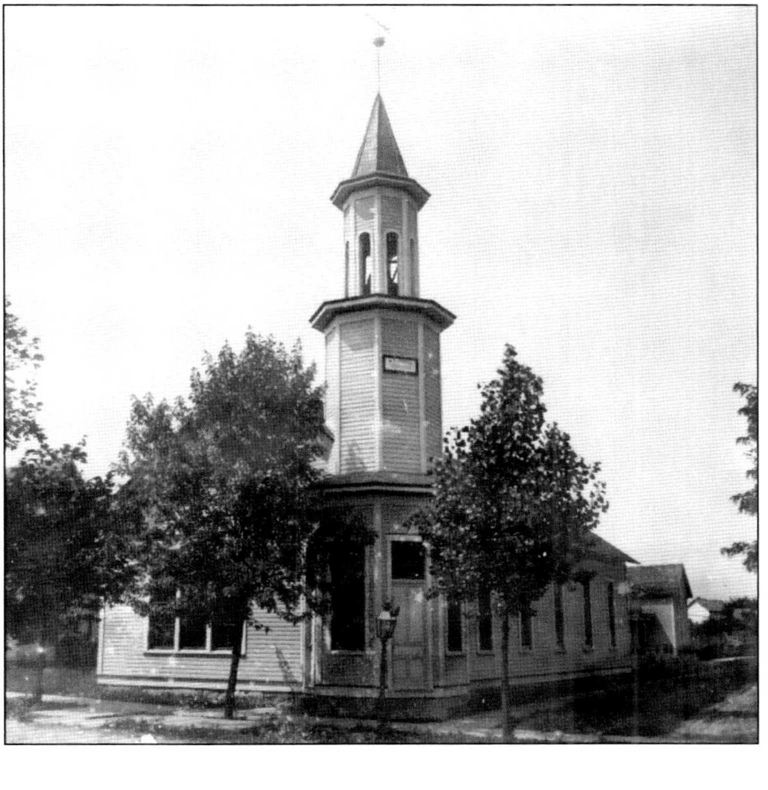

In July 1905, Peebles photographer Jennie McAdow Broomhall took this view of the newly remodeled and enlarged Peebles Methodist Episcopal Church. Its tall bell tower was placed on the corner of the church, with the main entrance facing outward from the base of the tower at a 45-degree angle. The church retained this appearance until major remodeling took place in 1935. (Courtesy Lester and Jean Wallis.)

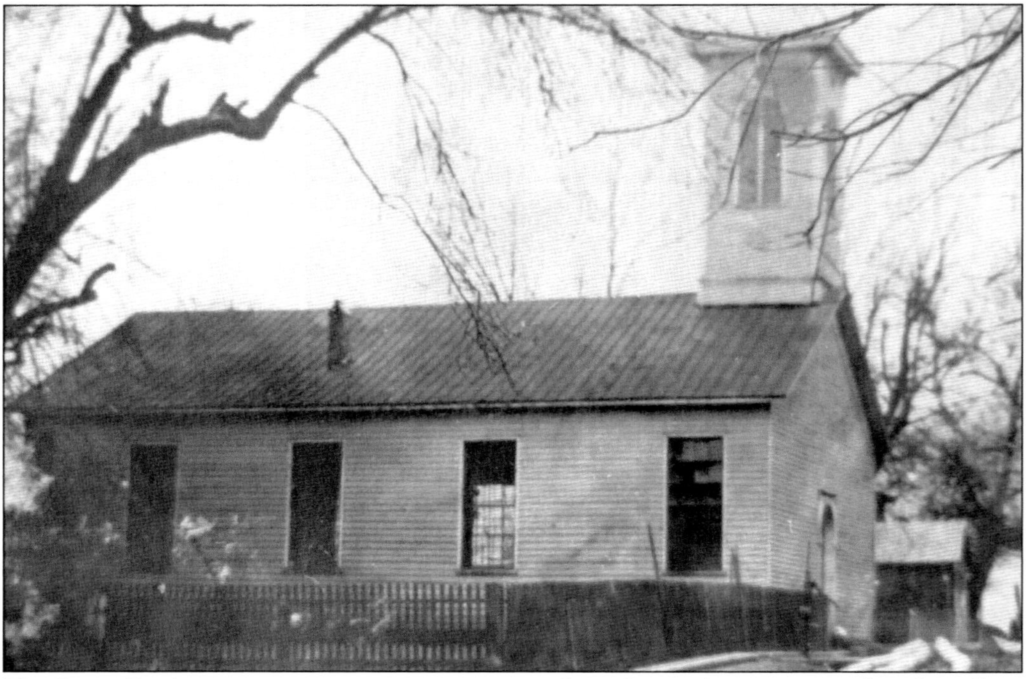

The Rome Presbyterian congregation was organized in 1844, only nine years after the village was founded. It is unknown when the church was constructed, but it was probably standing by 1850. Following World War I, membership in the congregation began significantly decreasing in numbers. Despite efforts to save the church, this trend continued, and it closed a final time after World War II. The church was razed in 1949. (Author's collection.)

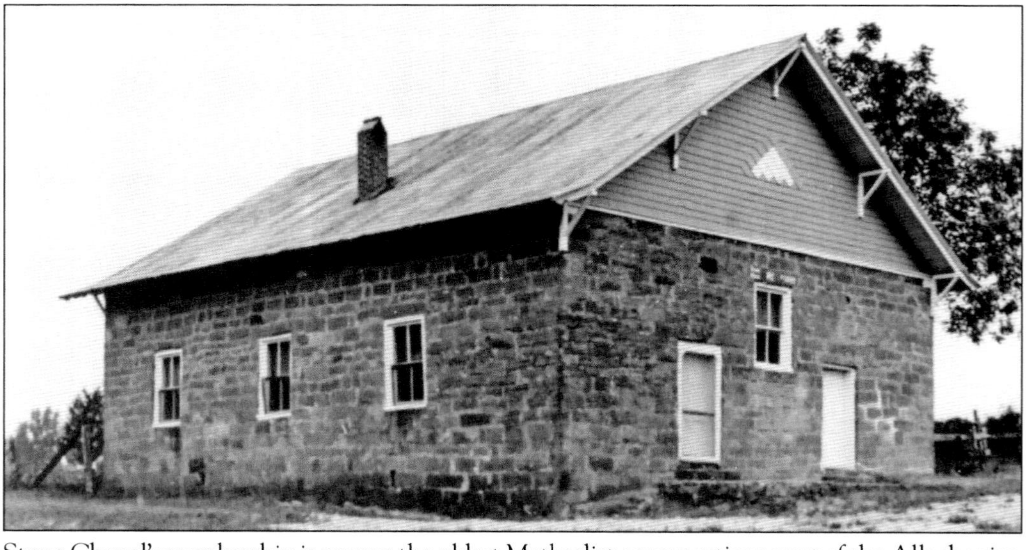

Stone Chapel's membership is among the oldest Methodist congregations west of the Alleghenies. It was organized in 1797 and built its first church structure in 1802, known as Fields Meeting House on Ohio Brush Creek. It was not until 1835–1836 that Stone Chapel was constructed under the supervision of Maxwell Gaddis. The congregation is very active to this day. This photograph of the church was taken around 1940. (Author's collection.)

The United Presbyterian church on Wheat Ridge Road was built in 1881–1882 and named Unity. In time, a tiny crossroads community grew up around the church and took the same name. The church was destroyed by fire on April 29, 1934. The Great Depression then had a firm grip on the nation's economy, and the church was never rebuilt. This photograph was taken by Finley Black about 1883. (Courtesy Adams County Historical Society.)

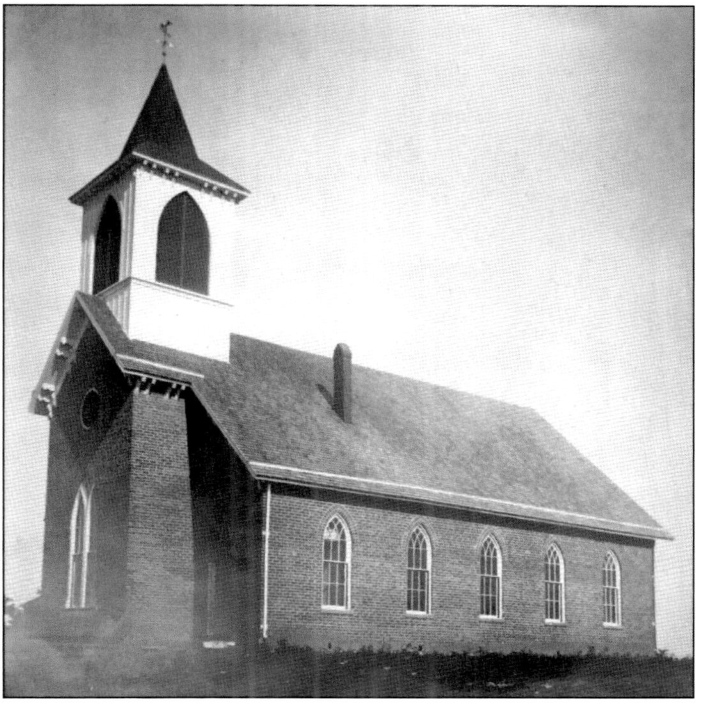

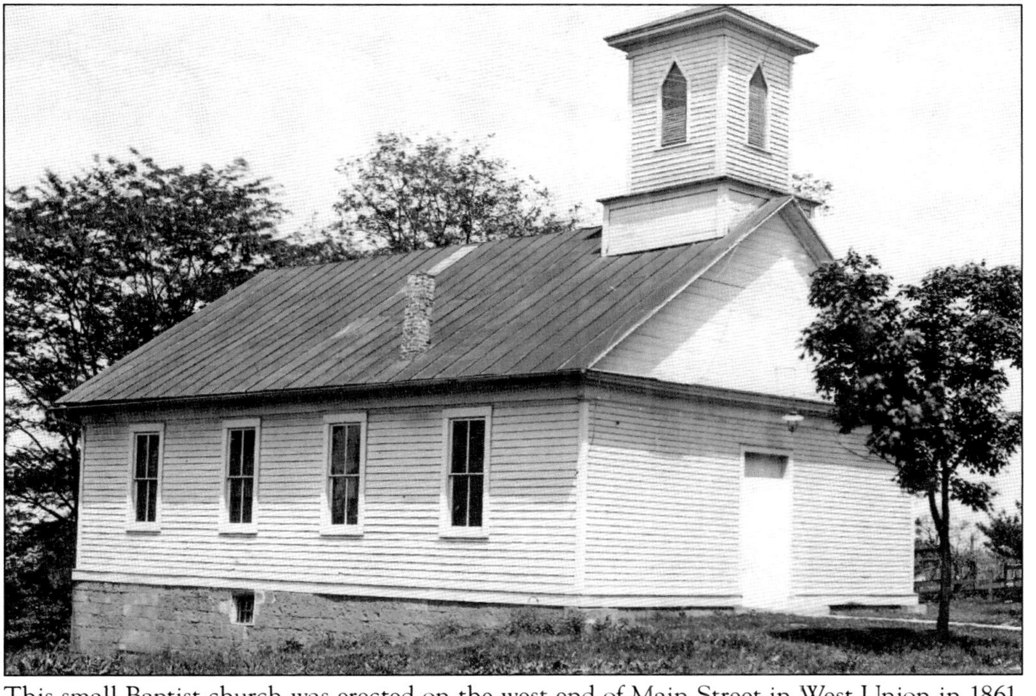

This small Baptist church was erected on the west end of Main Street in West Union in 1861. It replaced an earlier structure that had been flattened by a tremendous windstorm that swept through southern Ohio in May of that year. This 1861 structure was used until razed in 1911 for construction of the present brick church. (Author's collection.)

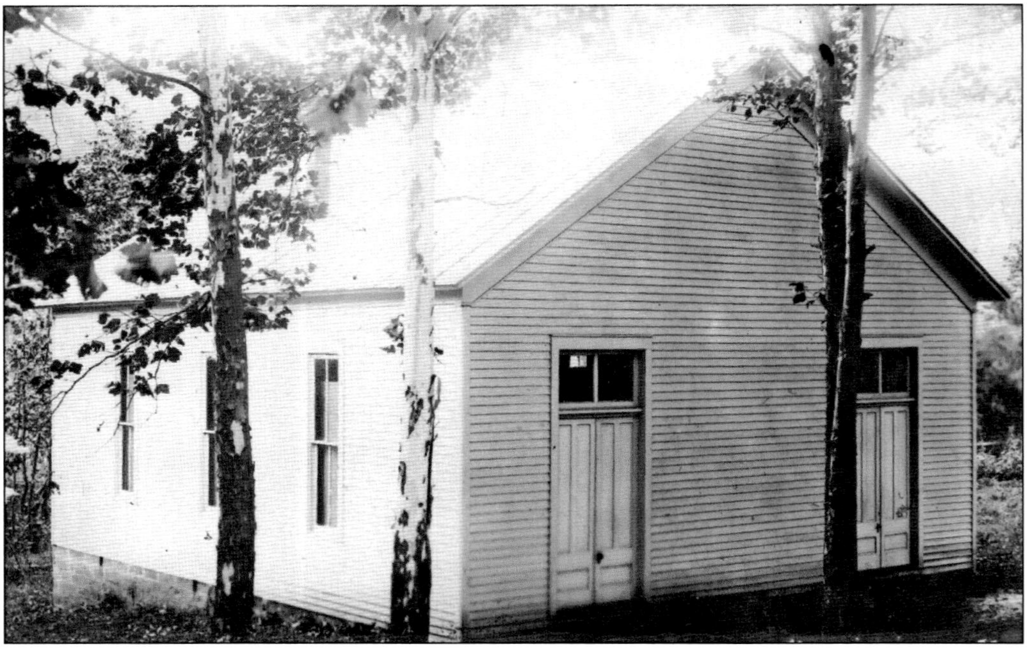

Here is a *c.* 1910 picture postcard view of the Cedar Mills Methodist Episcopal Church that was built in 1893. Notice the two front doors, a typical feature of many early Methodist and Presbyterian churches that required the sexes to be separated during worship services—one side reserved for women, the other for men. The Methodists closed this church in 1971. It has been used for a community church since that time. (Author's collection.)

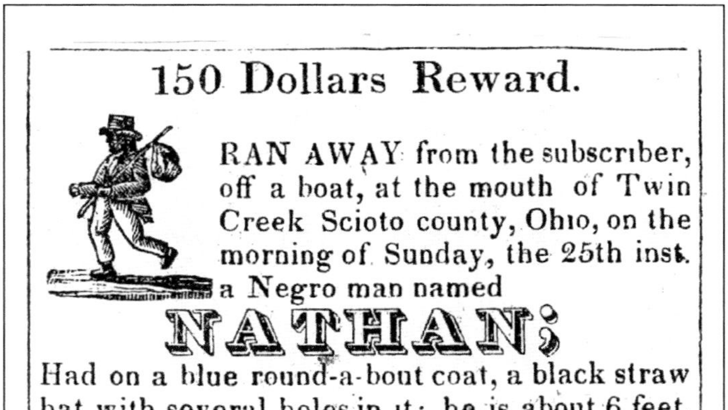

150 Dollars Reward.

RAN AWAY from the subscriber, off a boat, at the mouth of Twin Creek Scioto county, Ohio, on the morning of Sunday, the 25th inst. a Negro man named

NATHAN;

Had on a blue round-a-bout coat, a black straw hat with several holes in it: he is about 6 feet, one or two inches high; is a very good cook, and has been a Sailor; is supposed to be about 28 or 30 years of age.

The above reward and all reasonable charges will be paid to any person who will deliver him to the subrscriber at Parish St. James, Acadia county, Louisiana. J. B. ORY.

September 26, 1825. 16-18

This newspaper notice of a slave who escaped from a riverboat near Portsmouth, Ohio, was printed in the *Village Register*, a weekly newspaper published in West Union. This advertisement, placed in the paper in September 1825, indicates the desire for freedom held by those in bondage and the desire of their owners to keep them in slavery. (Courtesy Adams County Historical Society.)

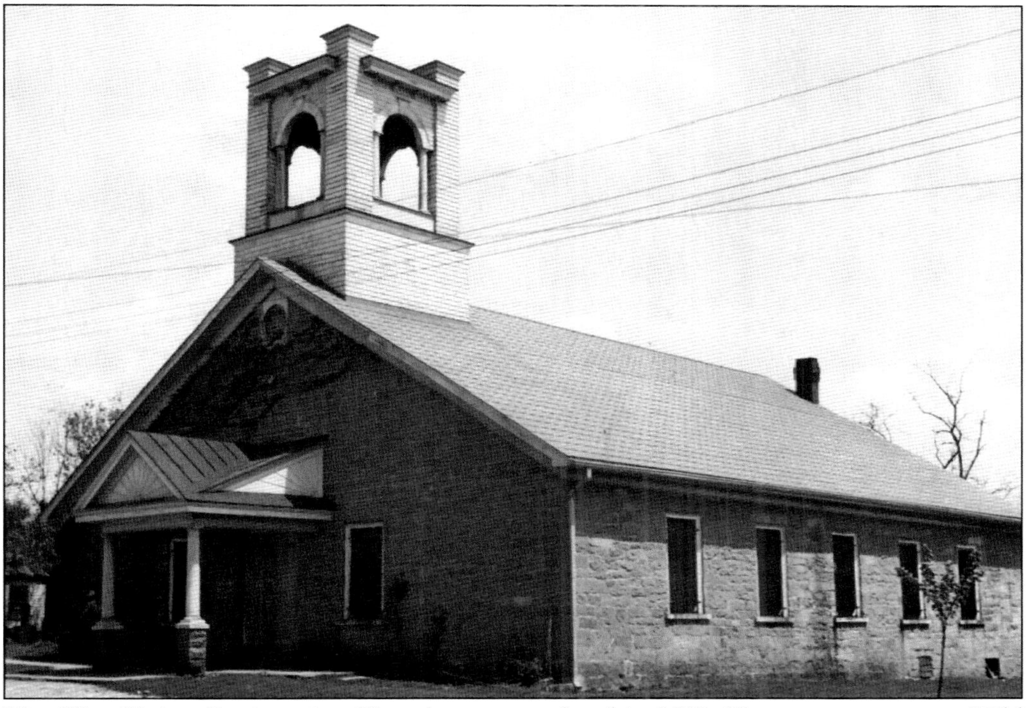

The West Union Presbyterian Church was completed in 1810. The stonemason was "Old Stonehammer" Thomas Metcalf of Kentucky. He later served as the 10th governor of Kentucky. Many members of this church were ardent abolitionists and were involved in the Underground Railroad. The church is listed on the National Register of Historic Places. This photograph was taken about 1915. (Author's collection.)

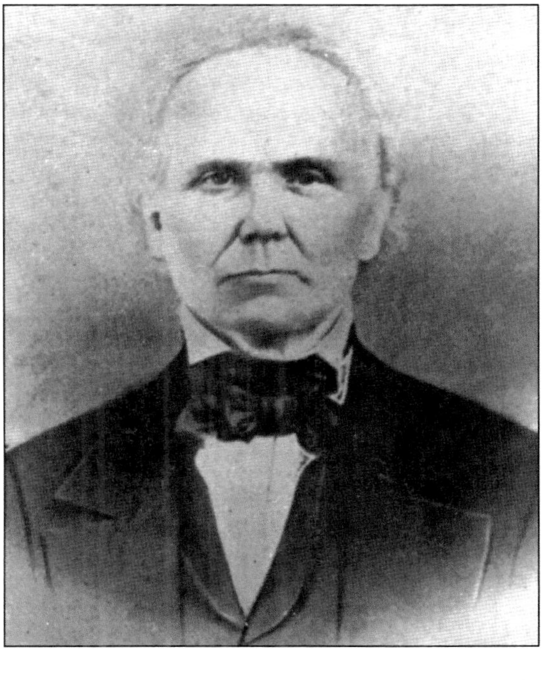

Dyer Burgess (1784–1872) was pastor of the West Union Presbyterian Church from 1820 to 1829. He was a fiery abolitionist who encouraged his congregation to assist fleeing slaves in their attempt to find freedom in Canada. His home was a frequent target of rocks and rotten eggs from those in the area who sympathized with the South and the institution of slavery. (Courtesy Adams County Genealogical Society.)

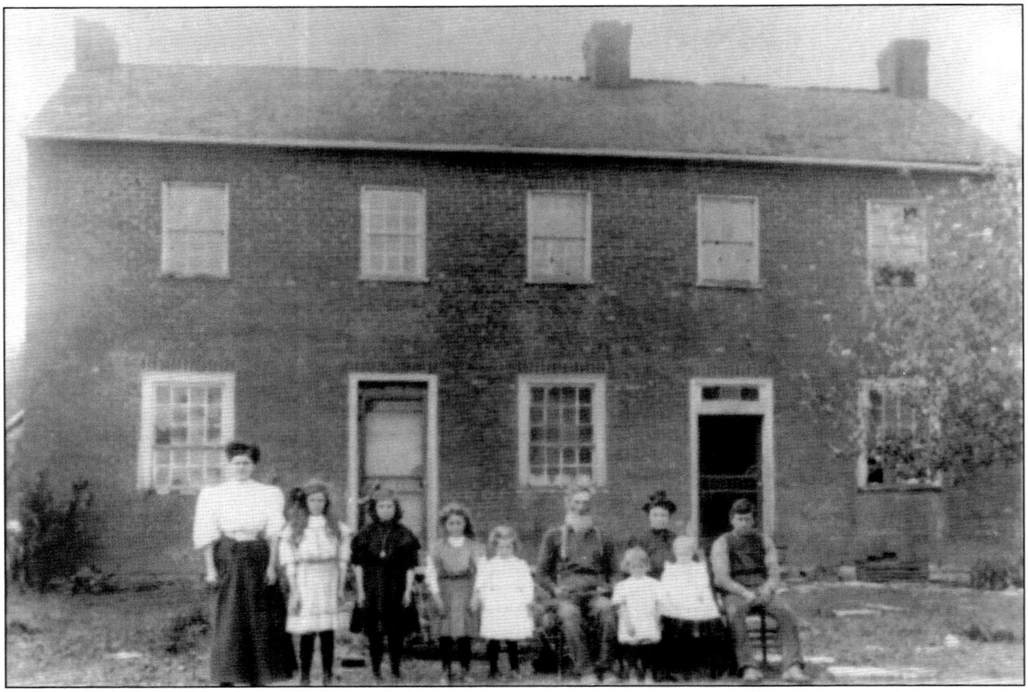

The Gen. William McIntire home on Graces Run in Wayne Township was a well-known station on the Underground Railroad. Family tradition relates that upon one occasion when slaves were hidden in the house, the general's wife, Patsey, single-handedly, with a bucket of boiling water, held off a party of Kentucky slave hunters until help came. This photograph was taken around 1909 when it was owned by the Elmer Wickerham family. (Courtesy Adams County Historical Society.)

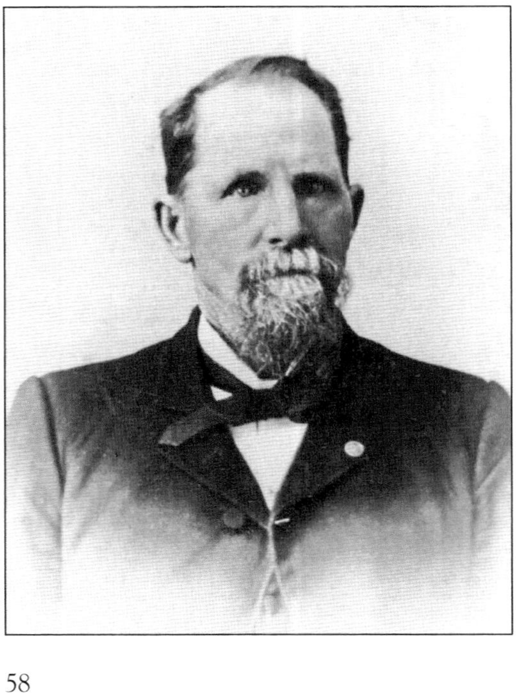

William H. Snedaker (1835–1929) began conducting slaves on the Underground Railroad when he was 17. He guided slaves from his parents' home in Decatur (Brown County) to Gen. William McIntire's home on Graces Run. In the 11 years he led slaves from station to station, he never lost a single passenger, nor was he ever caught. (Courtesy Carolyn Charles.)

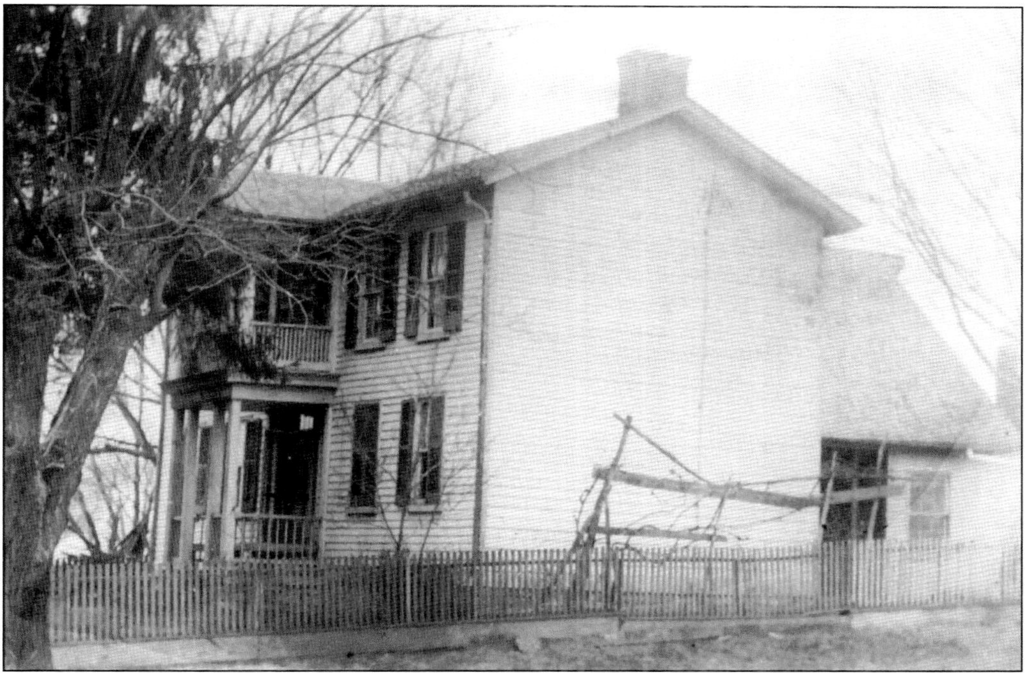

Nathaniel and Mary Ann Thompson Patton built this home overlooking Graces Run in Oliver Township about 1850. They were members of the Associate Reformed Presbyterian church and were abolitionists. They used their home and resources in giving shelter and aid to runaway slaves. This view of the Patton home was taken around 1909. (Author's collection.)

Nathaniel (1826–1908) and Mary Ann Thompson Patton (1827–1909) used their home as a station on the Underground Railroad. Their farm received unwanted visitors when Morgan's Raiders rode down Graces Run Road on July 15, 1863. (Author's collection.)

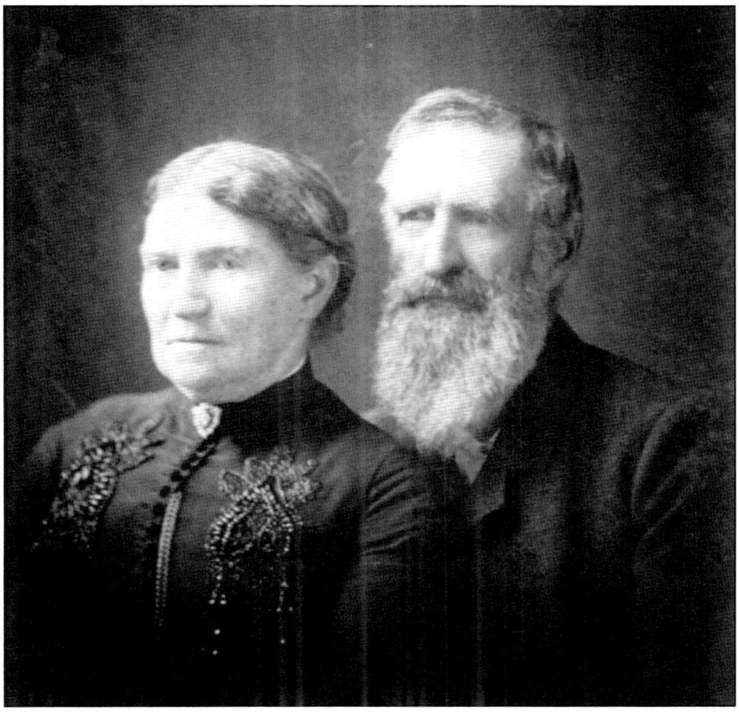

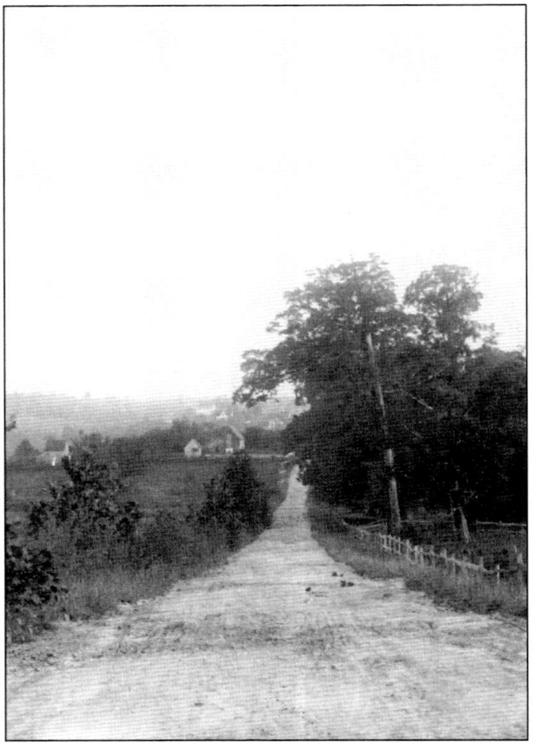

Zane's Trace, later renamed Maysville and Zanesville Turnpike, became a route on the Underground Railroad. This section of the road was photographed in August 1891 by P. Smythe, a member of the Columbus Camera Club who was touring Adams County. This view shows a section of the road between Locust Grove and Sinking Spring in neighboring Highland County. (Courtesy Lester and Jean Wallis.)

Here is a *c.* 1910 view of the south side of the Wickerham Tavern. Tradition says the tavern was a station on the Underground Railroad. It was visited by Morgan's Raiders in July 1863. Shown here are the children of Jacob and Annabel Cannon Wickerham: from left to right are Walter, Irene, George, and Minnie, who is mowing the lawn. The inn remained in the Wickerham family for over 170 years. (Courtesy Lester and Jean Wallis.)

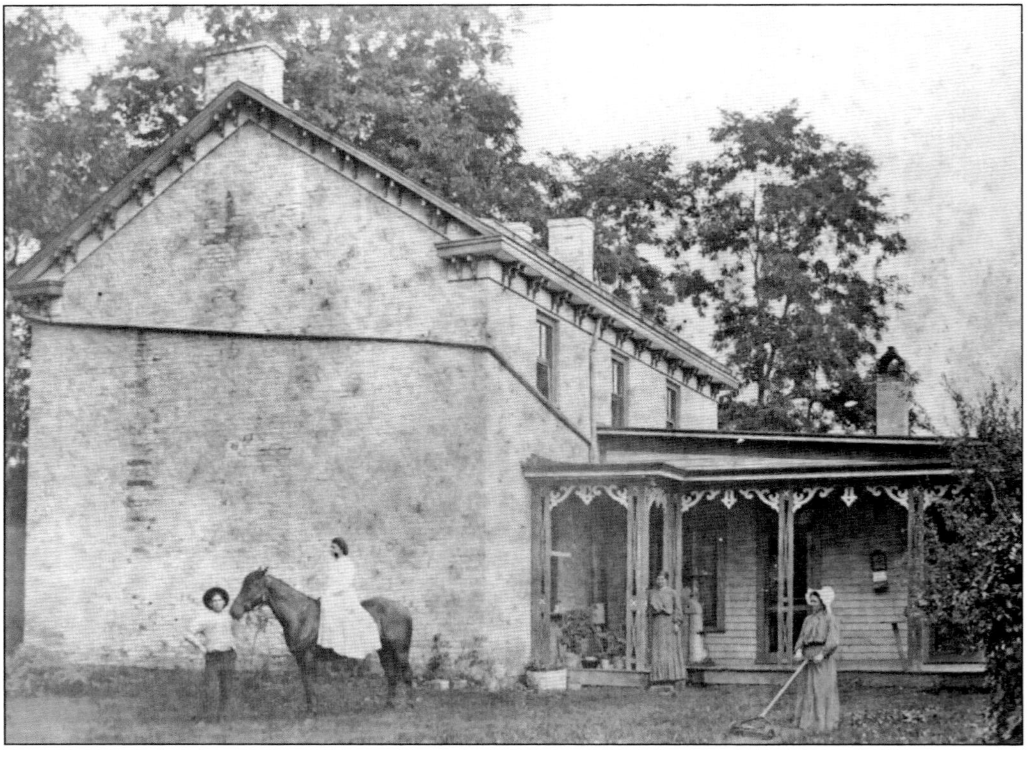

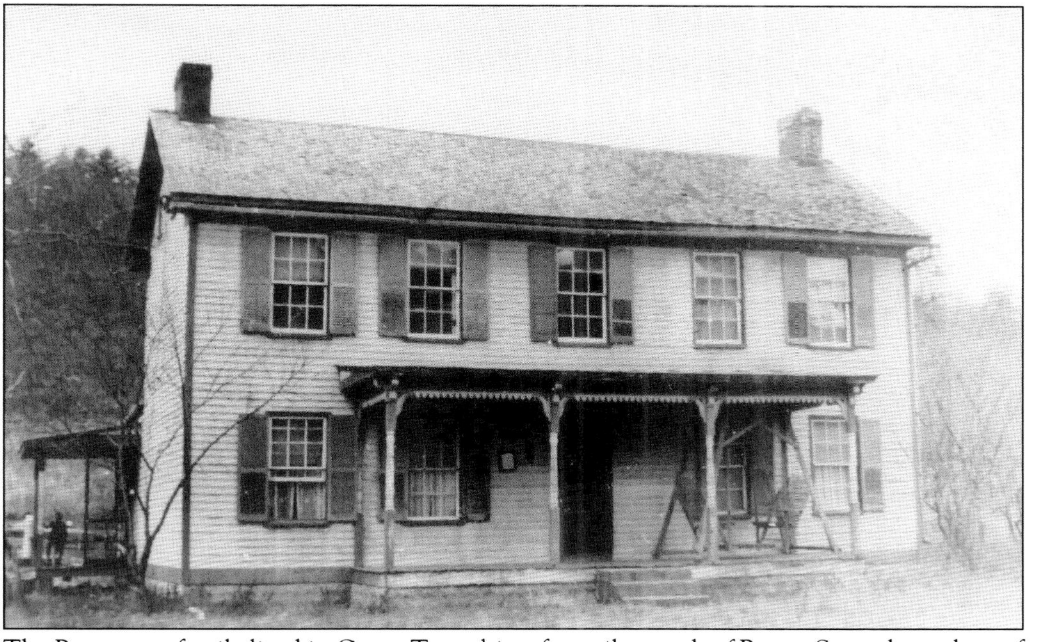

The Puntenney family lived in Green Township a few miles north of Rome. Several members of the family were heavily involved in assisting runaway slaves on their journey north to freedom. This is a *c.* 1945 photograph of "Tanner" John Puntenney's home. Built in the 1850s, it was part of the Underground Railroad. (Author's collection.)

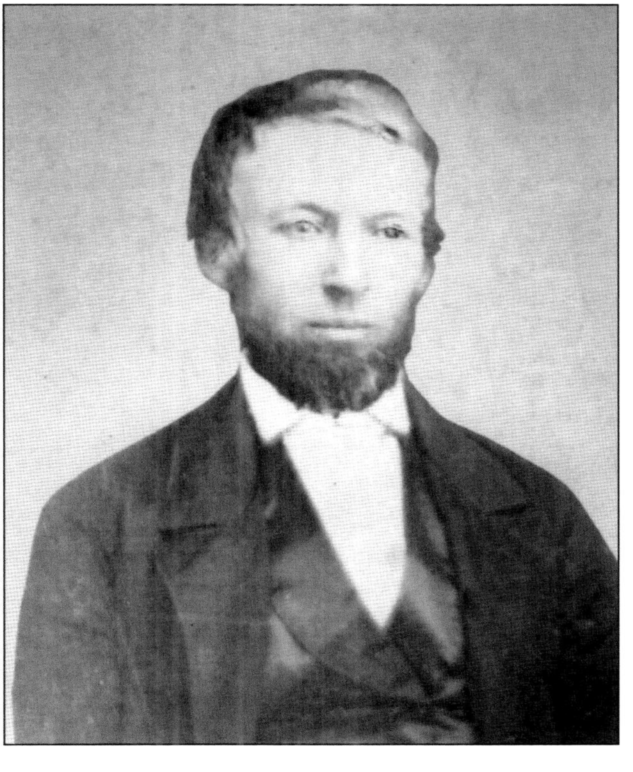

The Reverend James Caskey (1807–1854) grew to manhood on a farm between North Liberty (Cherry Fork) and Youngsville in an abolitionist home and neighborhood. He was ordained to preach in the Associate Reformed Presbyterian church. During his career, he served churches in West Union and in the Brown County villages of Russellville and Ripley. All of these congregations were antislavery and had many members involved in the Underground Railroad. (Author's collection.)

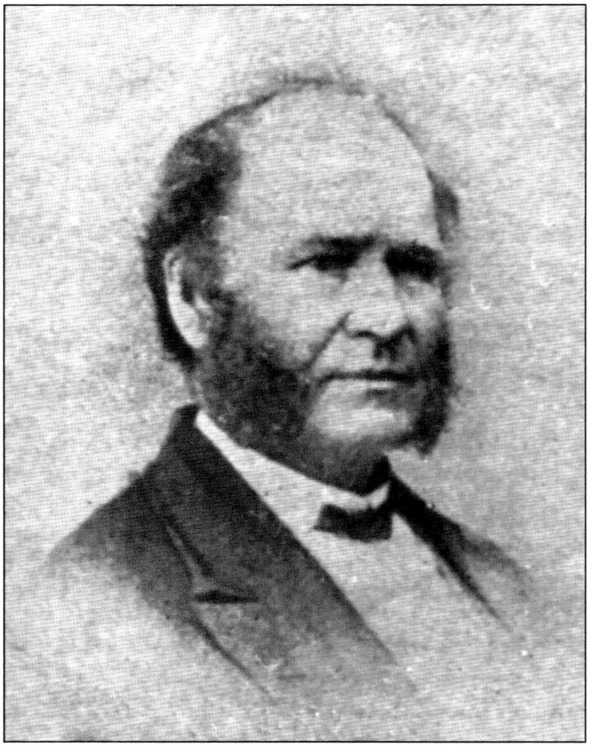

John T. Wilson was a merchant, soldier, banker, statesman, and philanthropist. He helped organize the 70th Ohio Regiment during the Civil War and enlisted in Company E of that military unit at age 50. In 1884, he personally financed the construction of the county's children's home that is still in use today. He was an abolitionist and is believed to have used his Tranquillity home on the Underground Railroad. (Courtesy Adams County Genealogical Society.)

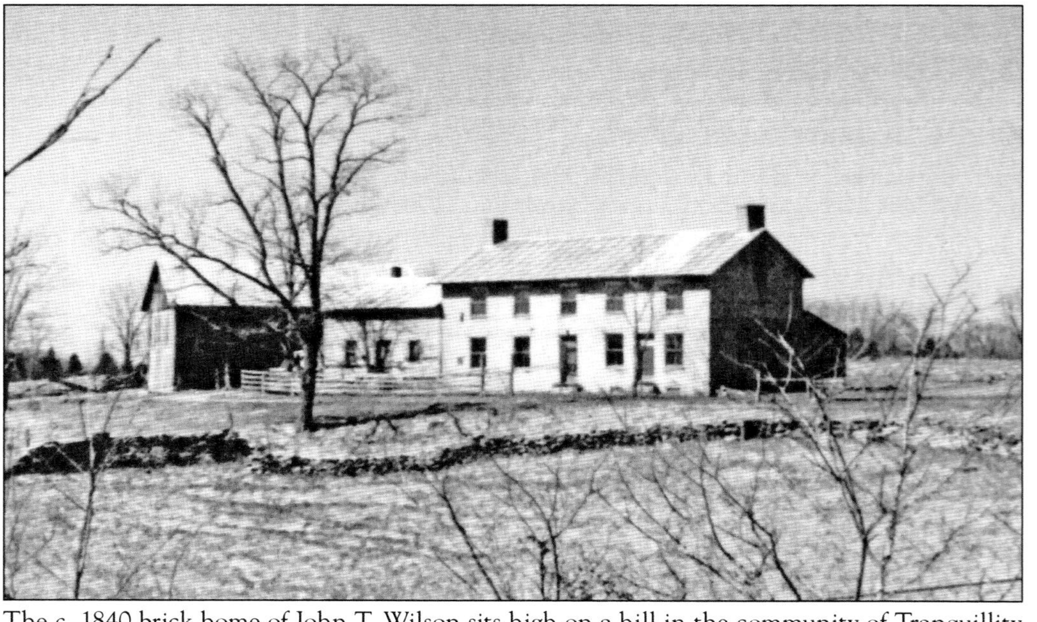

The c. 1840 brick home of John T. Wilson sits high on a hill in the community of Tranquillity overlooking George's Creek valley. By the time this view was taken in 1976, the house had been abandoned for 14 years and was starting to deteriorate. The historic home has been placed on the National Register of Historical Places and is now undergoing major restoration efforts. (Courtesy Ralph and Patricia Alexander.)

Six

MILITARY

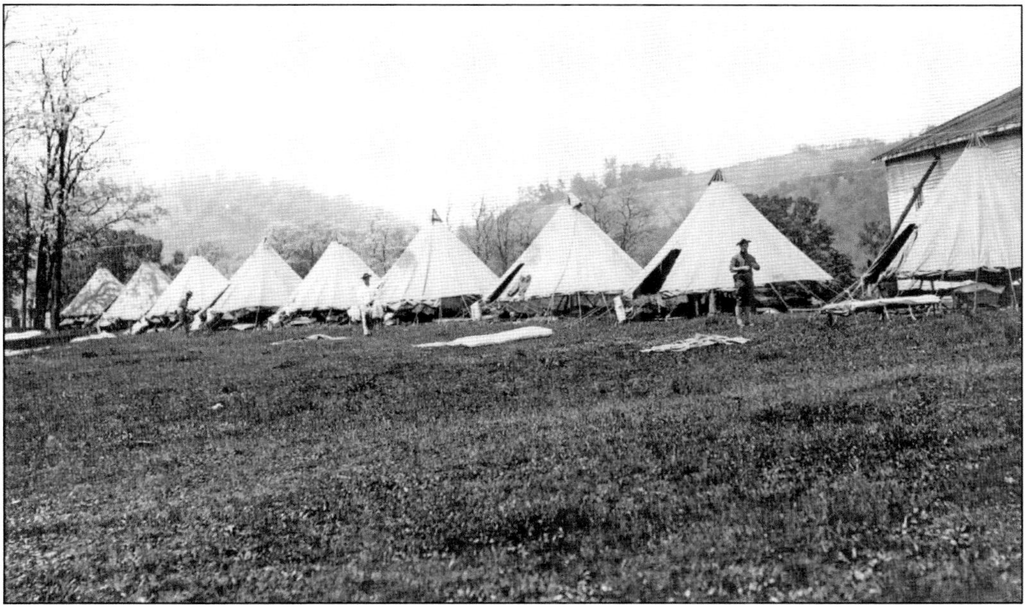

In 1883, a company of the Ohio militia was organized in Manchester. Known as Ellison's Light Guards, its first commander was Capt. Daniel R. Shriver, a Civil War veteran. Disbanded and reorganized several times throughout the ensuing century, this unit eventually became known as Company B of the 216th Engineer Battalion of the Ohio National Guard. The unit is currently disbanded. It is shown here bivouacked in Manchester in 1906. (Author's collection.)

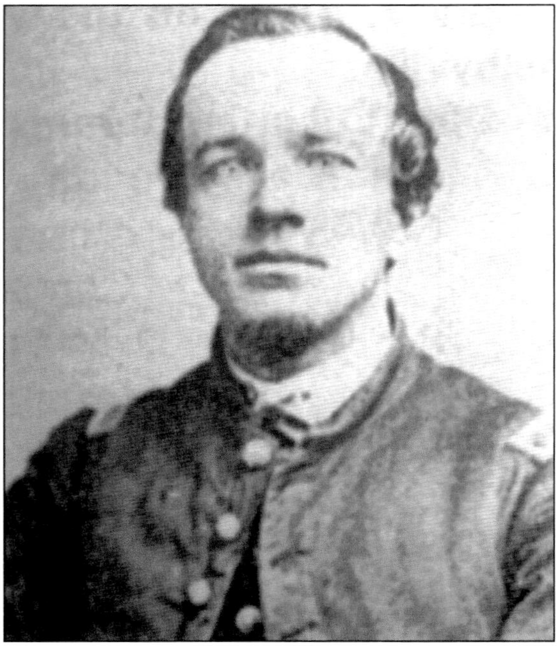

William H. H. Reddick (1840–1903) was from Locust Grove. As a member of Company B of the 33rd Ohio Regiment, he volunteered to become a member of Andrews' Raiders. The Raiders captured a locomotive at Big Shanty, Georgia, in an attempt to destroy railroad bridges and tear up tracks. For his services, he was awarded the Congressional Medal of Honor from President Lincoln. (Courtesy Adams County Historical Society.)

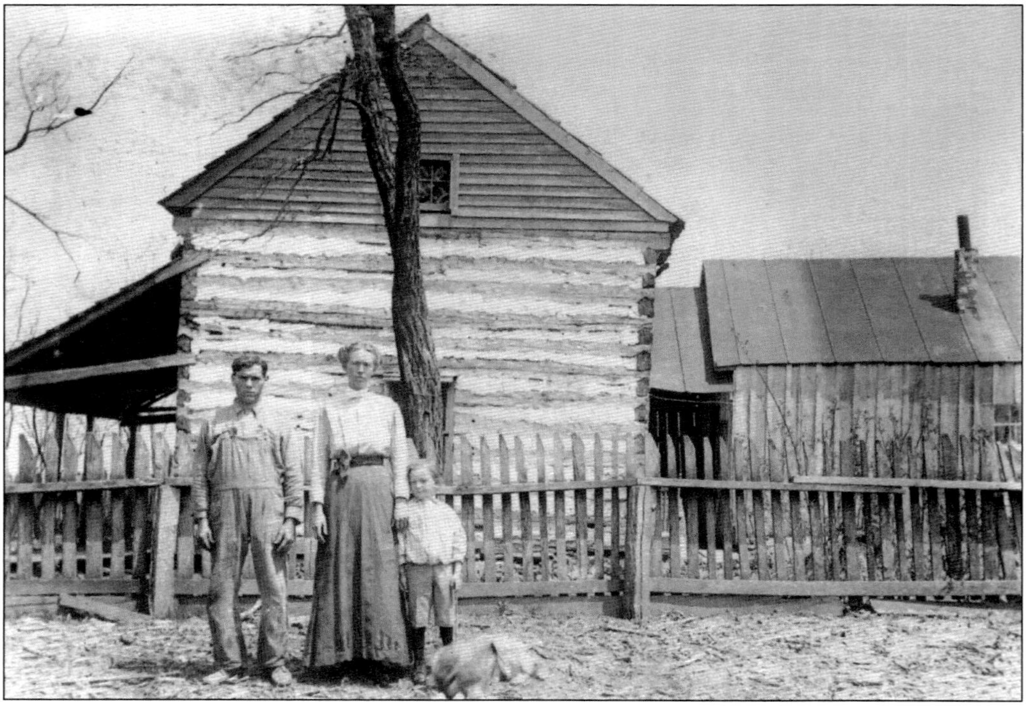

This log house, located north of Locust Grove, was built by Revolutionary War soldier William Pemberton in 1796. The George W. Reddick family was living here during the early years of the Civil War. Their son, William Henry Harrison Reddick, left this home to enlist in the 33rd Ohio Regiment. As a volunteer member of Andrews Raiders, he became the sixth soldier to receive the Congressional Medal of Honor. (Courtesy Lester and Jean Wallis.)

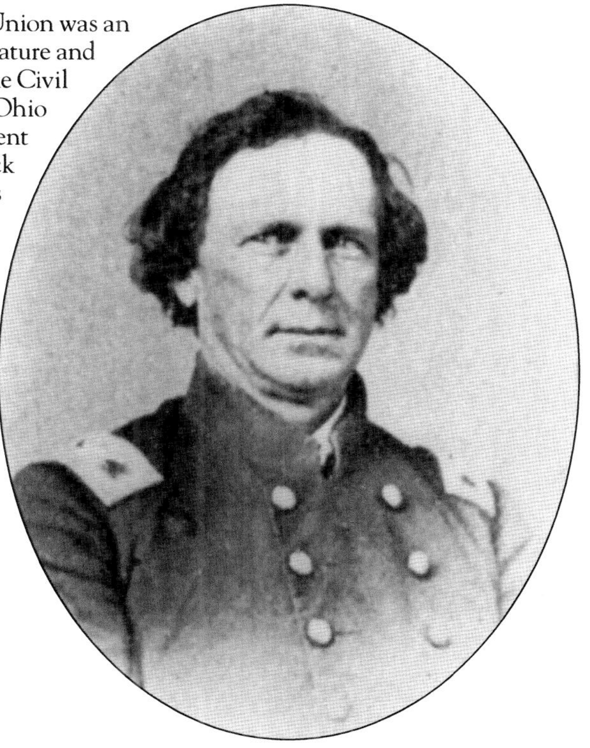

Joseph R. Cockerill (1818–1875) of West Union was an attorney and had served in the Ohio Legislature and the U.S. House of Representatives. After the Civil War began, he was commissioned by the Ohio governor to organize the 70th Ohio Regiment and to serve as its colonel. Despite his lack of formal military training, Cockerill was commended for his battlefield conduct. He was later brevetted a brigadier general. (Courtesy Adams County Historical Society.)

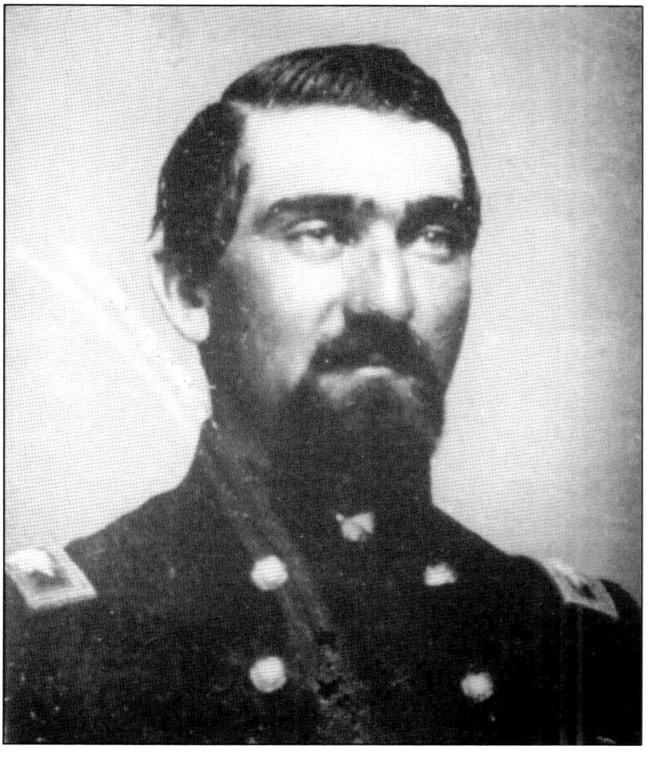

Armstead T. M. Cockerill (1841–1870) was a son of Col. Joseph R. Cockerill. At the outbreak of the Civil War, he enlisted in the 24th Ohio Regiment. He was immediately commissioned a first lieutenant and only months later promoted to captain. In December 1862, at the age of 21, he received the rank of lieutenant colonel, commanding the 24th Regiment. He received the promotion to colonel in October of 1863. (Courtesy Adams County Historical Society.)

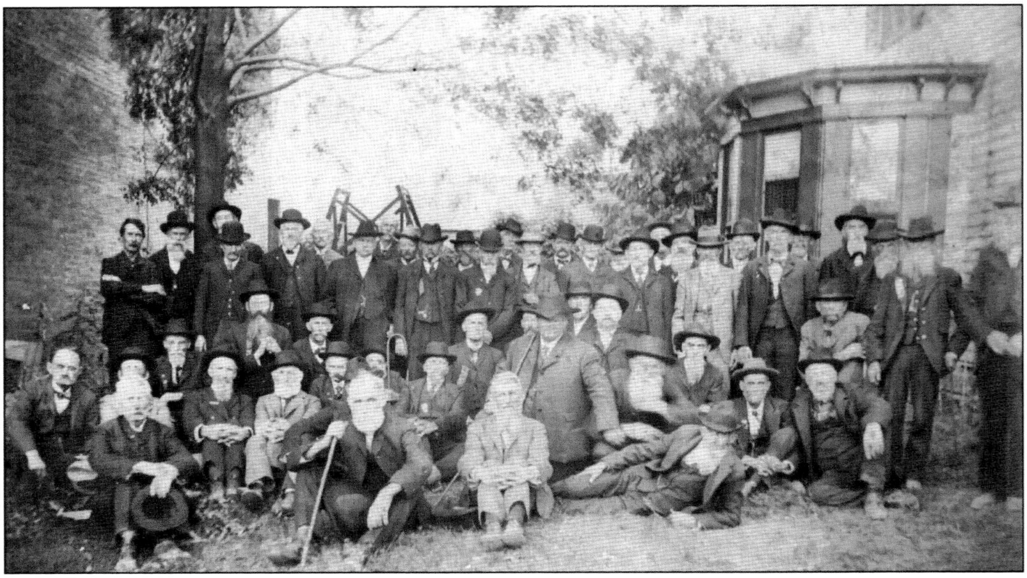

Following the Civil War, many veterans groups were organized. On November 27, 1885, in Cincinnati, the 70th Ohio Regimental Association was formed and officers elected. The association began holding reunions throughout Adams and Brown Counties for several years. This group photograph was taken October 21, 1904, at the reunion in Winchester. The members are posing between the Fenton home and the Winchester Bank building. (Author's collection.)

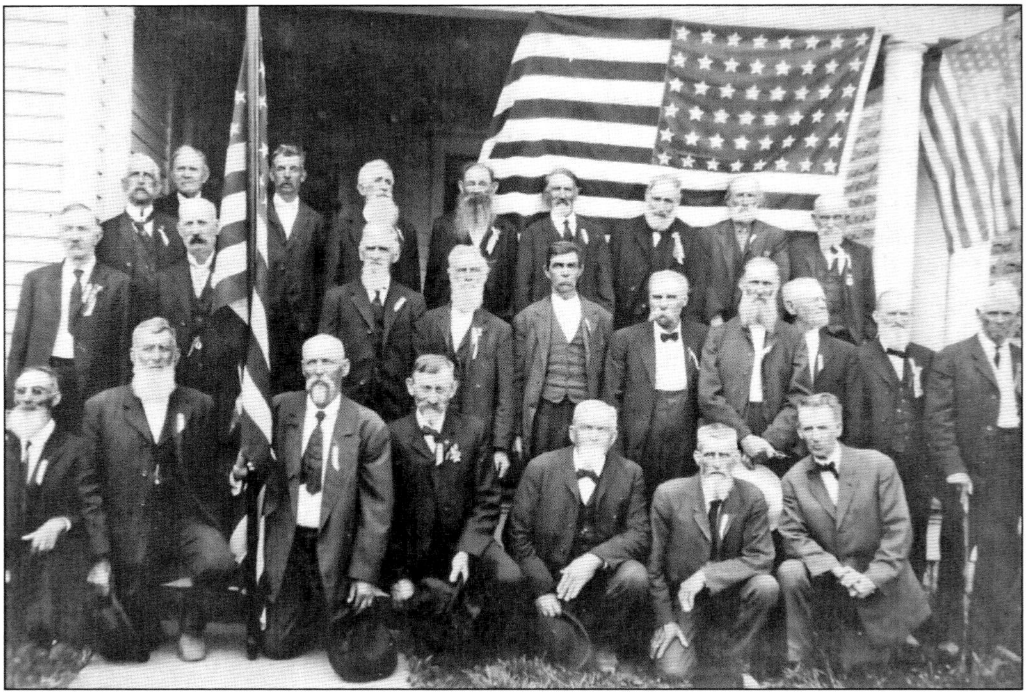

A few years after the reunion in Winchester, the 70th Ohio Regimental Association met in the village of Seaman. The former soldiers were entertained in the Rector Hotel on First Street, where they were photographed on the front porch. (Courtesy Adams County Genealogical Society.)

Benjamin F. Coates (1827–1899) was a physician and moved to West Union in 1853. He was elected to the Ohio Senate and was serving in that position when he was appointed lieutenant colonel of the 91st Ohio Regiment. He was promoted to colonel of the regiment in 1864 and brevetted brigadier general in March 1865. In later years, he owned and operated the Mineral Springs resort near Peebles. (Courtesy Larry Strayer.)

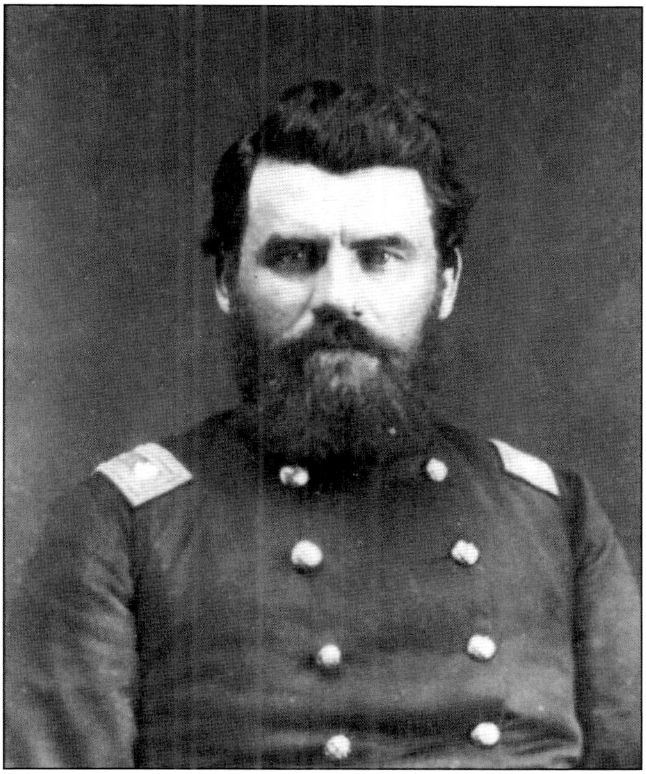

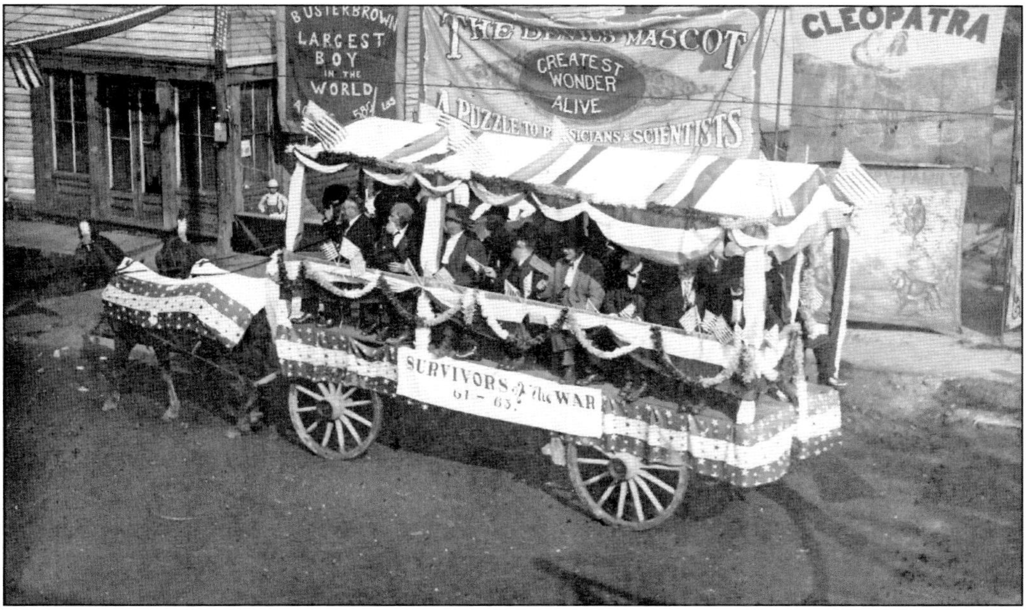

The residents of Winchester threw a grand celebration in 1915 in observance of their village's centennial. In the huge parade, this wagon was one of the primary attractions, carrying more than a dozen aged Civil War veterans. The war had ended 50 years earlier. Sideshow posters are seen in the background. (Author's collection.)

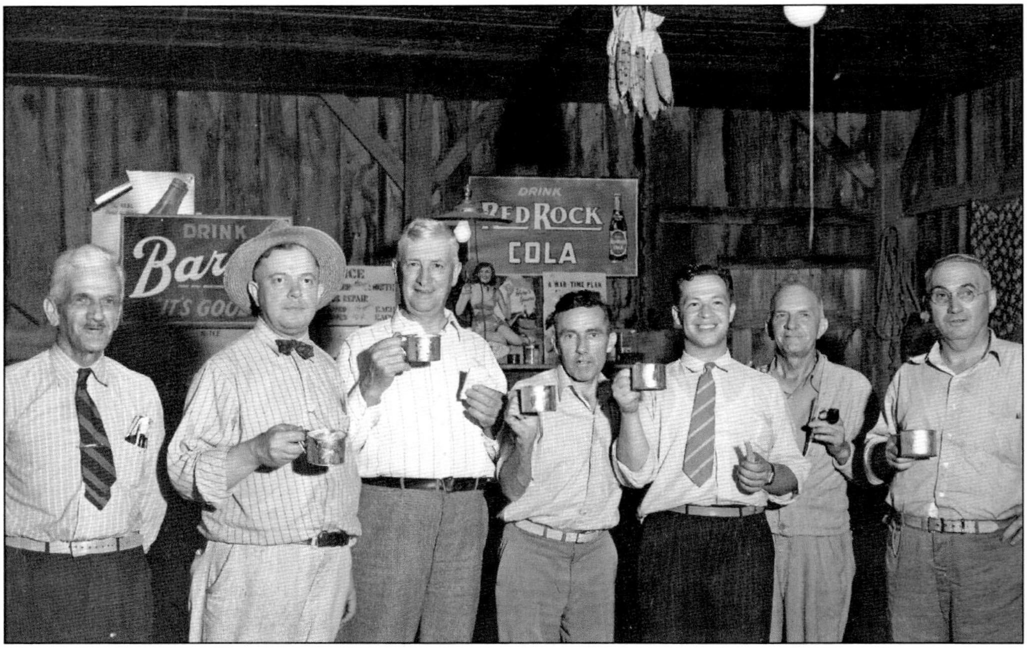

World War II was raging in 1943, and Eustice Stultz decided to do his part and enlist. His friends and coworkers from the West Union Post Office decided to send him off with a party at the clubhouse of the Adams County Country Club. Here toasting Stultz are, from left to right, J. D. Williams, Loran Grooms, George Watson, Ted Brodt, Eustice Stultz, Ira Shell, and Ernie Dunkin. (Courtesy Adams County Historical Society.)

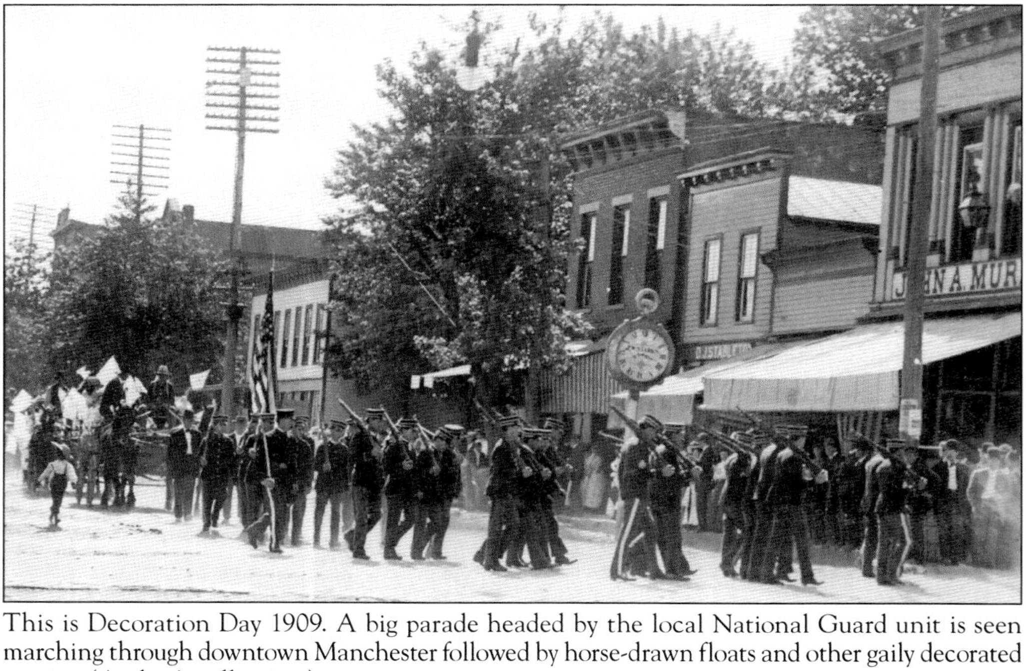

This is Decoration Day 1909. A big parade headed by the local National Guard unit is seen marching through downtown Manchester followed by horse-drawn floats and other gaily decorated entries. (Author's collection.)

Seven

Transportation

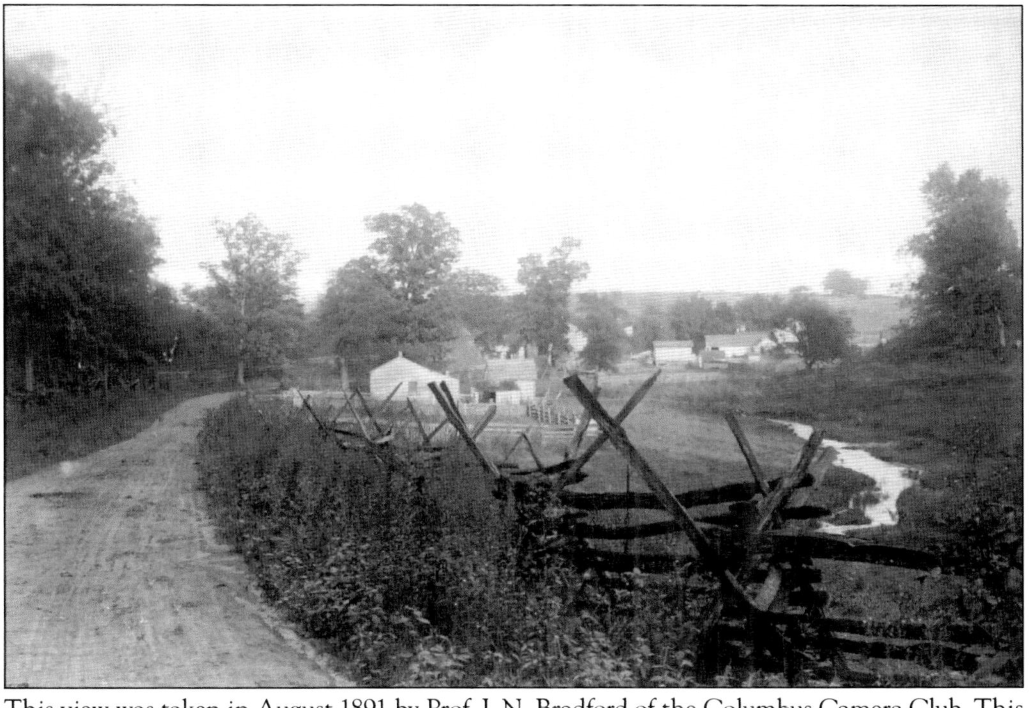

This view was taken in August 1891 by Prof. J. N. Bradford of the Columbus Camera Club. This is approaching Locust Grove from the west on present-day Ohio Route 73. It is believed this road followed an ancient animal migratory trail that was also used by Native Americans. Many of the earliest roads used by the first explorers and settlers were these existing paths that had been trod for centuries. (Courtesy Lester and Jean Wallis.)

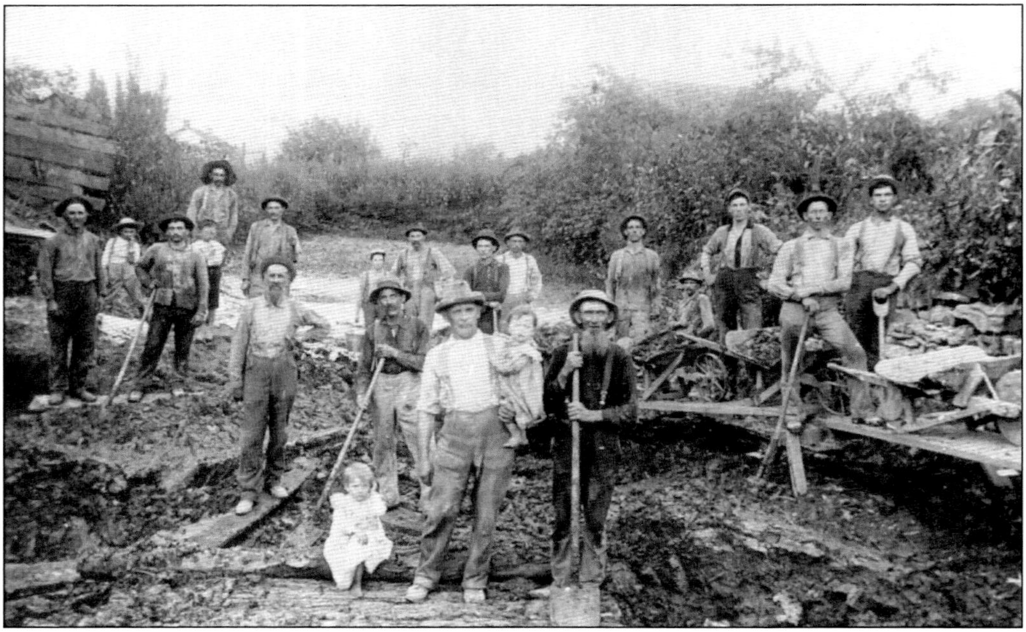

Photographer Lizzie Treber took this photograph of a work crew improving old Zane's Trace near the historic Treber Inn around 1895. The trace at that time was known as the Maysville and Zanesville Pike. It appears the workers are preparing to build a small bridge or install a culvert. (Courtesy William and Bessie J. Sininger.)

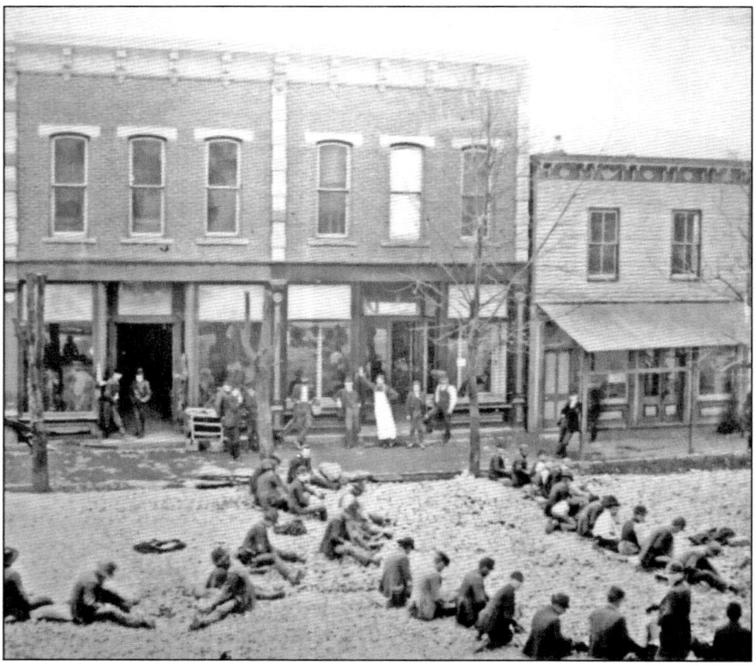

This is a rare view of workers busily knapping rock on Second Street in Manchester about 1905. They were literally making gravel by hand using small knapping hammers designed for that purpose. Notice how most of the laborers are seated, with a few on their knees. This method of gravelling the village streets and county roads was an effective means for landowners to work off their property tax. (Courtesy Lois Kidd.)

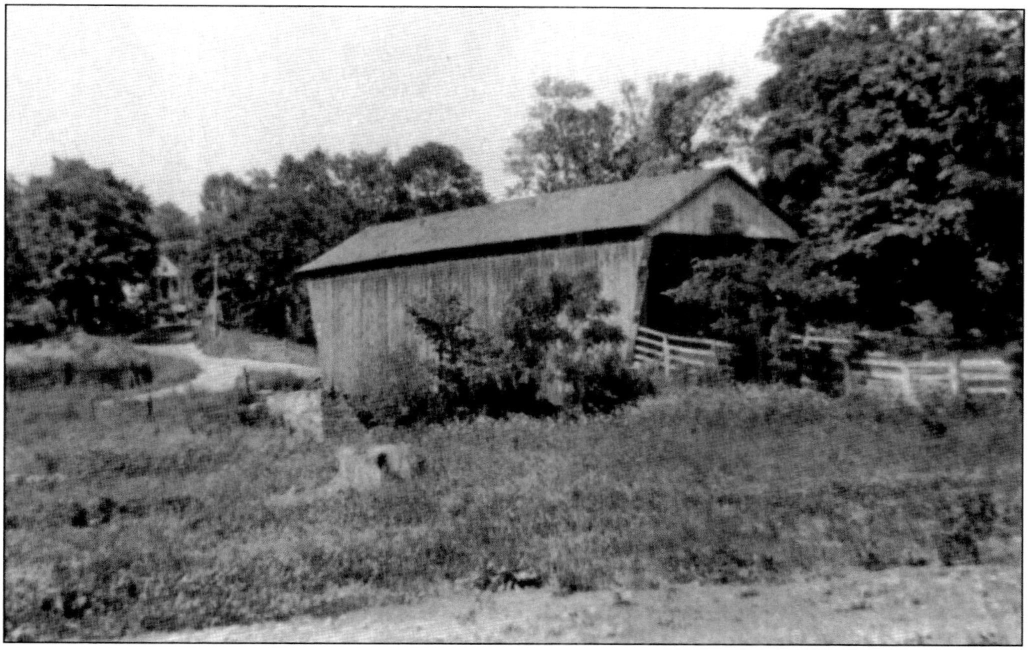

There were never many covered bridges built in Adams County. Only 18 have been documented. One of the most scenic was this small structure built over George's Creek in the community of Tranquillity. Constructed in 1864 during the Civil War, it was of multiple king post architecture with arches. It served the public until 1942, when it was replaced by the state. This photograph was taken about 1915. (Courtesy Richard and Paula Gaston.)

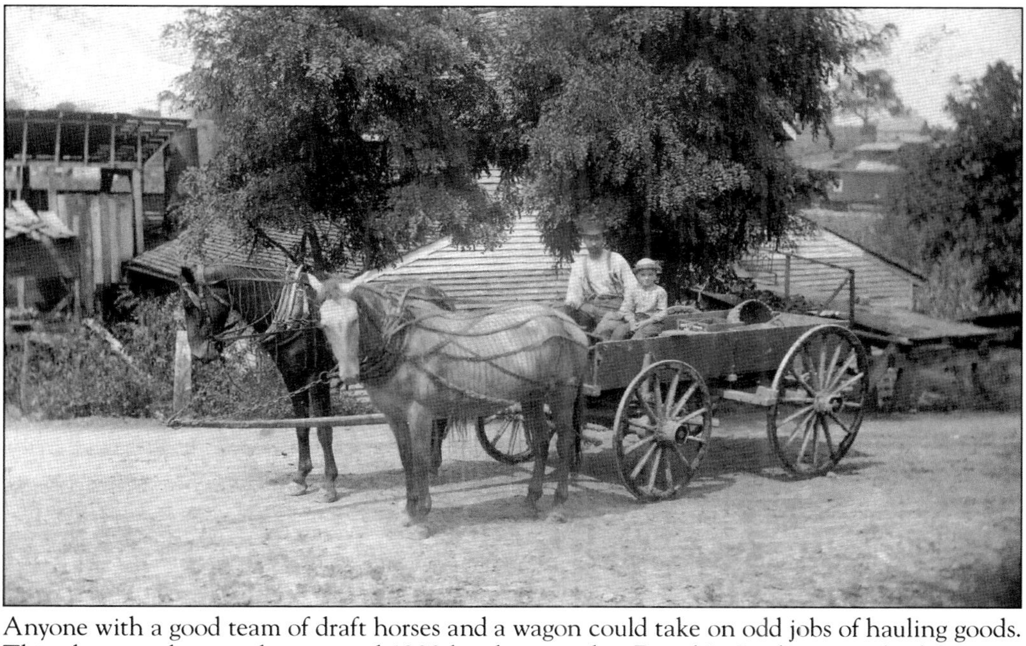

Anyone with a good team of draft horses and a wagon could take on odd jobs of hauling goods. This photograph was taken around 1900 by photographer David I. Gardner on a backstreet in Peebles. The man and boy are not identified. (Courtesy John and Carol Wickerham.)

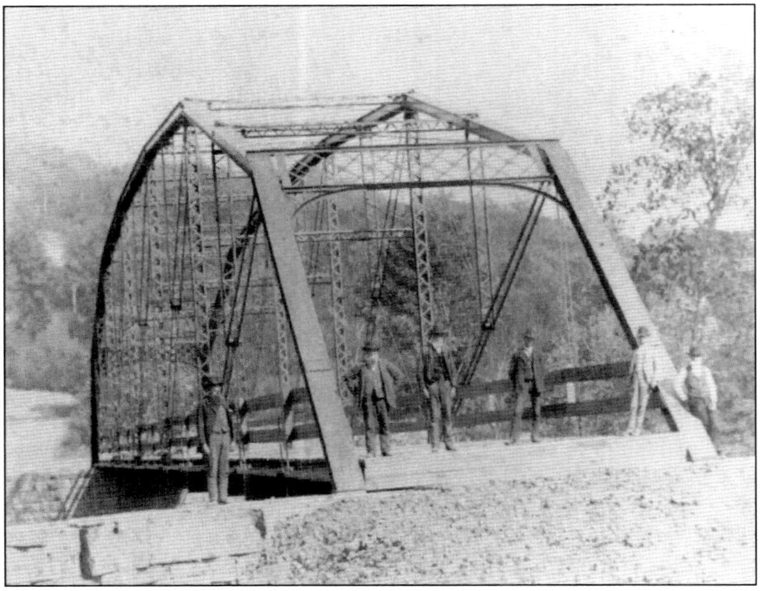

The big, camel-backed, through-truss Beasley Fork Bridge was erected in 1888. It spans Ohio Brush Creek, connecting Monroe and Brush Creek Townships. The structure continues to carry traffic today on Beasley Fork Road and is the second-oldest bridge in use in Adams County. This photograph was taken by David I. Gardner as the bridge was being completed. (Author's collection.)

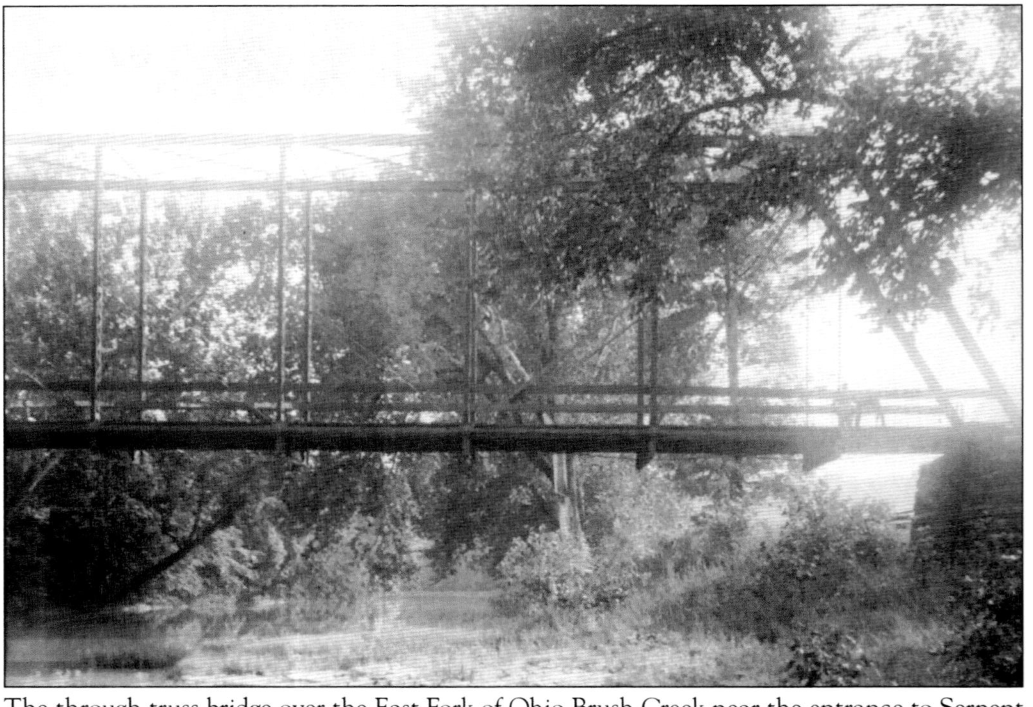

The through-truss bridge over the East Fork of Ohio Brush Creek near the entrance to Serpent Mound Park is photographed here in August 1891. This creek-side view was taken by Frank H. Howe, a member of the Columbus Camera Club. Howe was the son of Henry Howe, who authored one of the earliest histories of Ohio. This bridge was probably constructed in the 1880s. It was removed in the 1980s. (Courtesy Lester and Jean Wallis.)

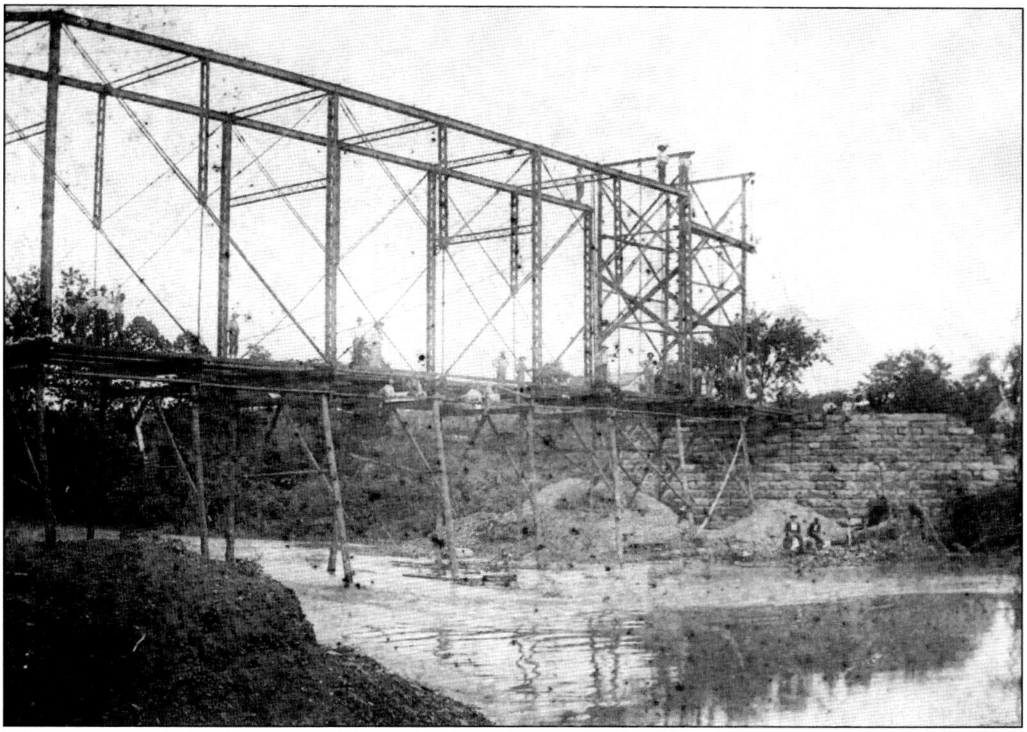

The photographs on this page illustrate how some of the through-truss bridges were built in the late 19th century. In the photograph above, a camel-backed bridge is being constructed over the East Fork of Ohio Brush Creek at Lawshe in 1896 by the Champion Bridge Company. Notice the temporary wooden supports holding the new structure over the creek. Pictured below is the newly completed bridge sitting high and dry on its new stone abutments. The construction of the roadbed up to the top of the abutments on each end was obviously the final phase of construction yet to be done. This bridge stood the test of time until its removal by the county about 1983. David I. Gardner took both of these photographs. (Both author's collection.)

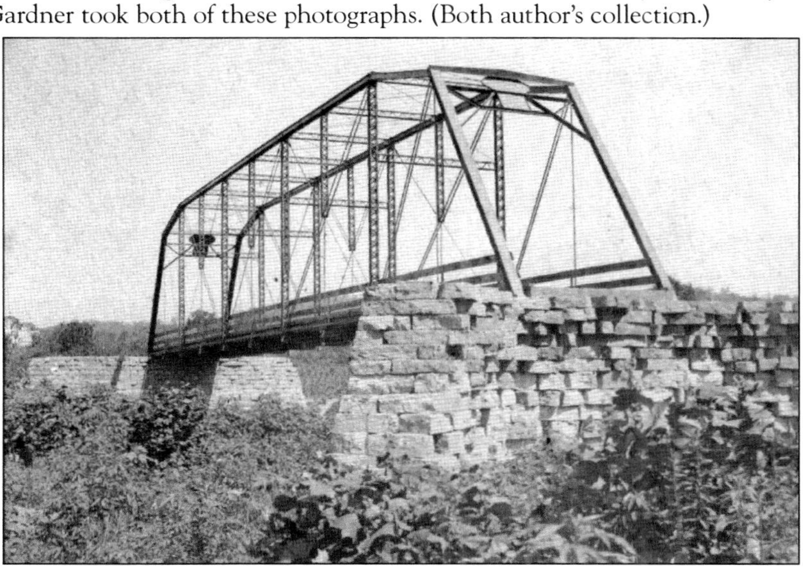

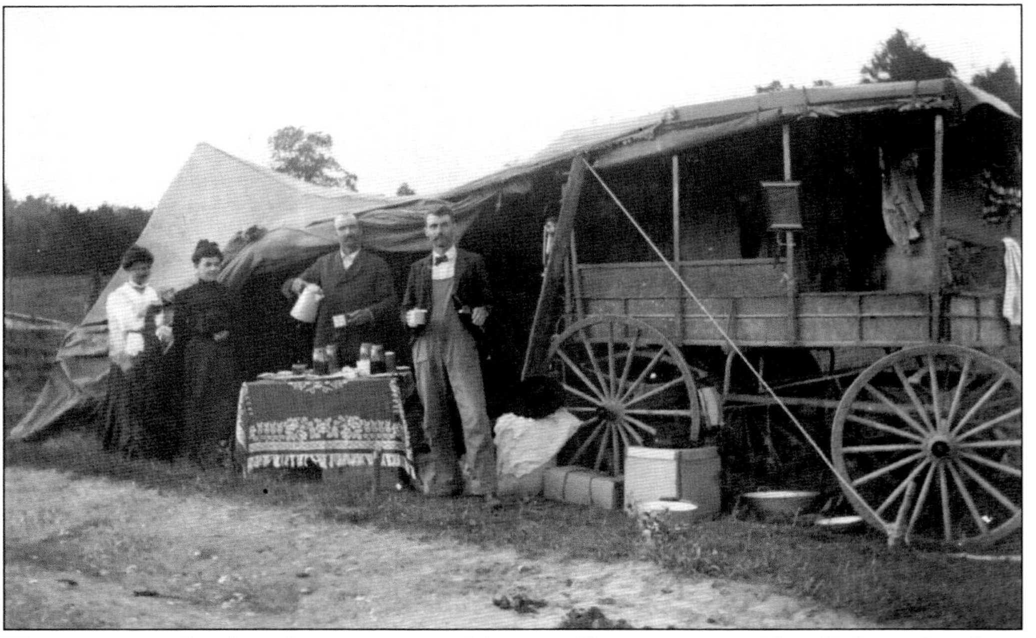

The urge to travel and see the country is nothing new. Here are some unidentified travelers about 1905 in their early version of a recreational vehicle. This photograph was taken by Winifred Johnson Holmes in the Peach Mountain–Mineral Springs area. (Courtesy Adams County Historical Society.)

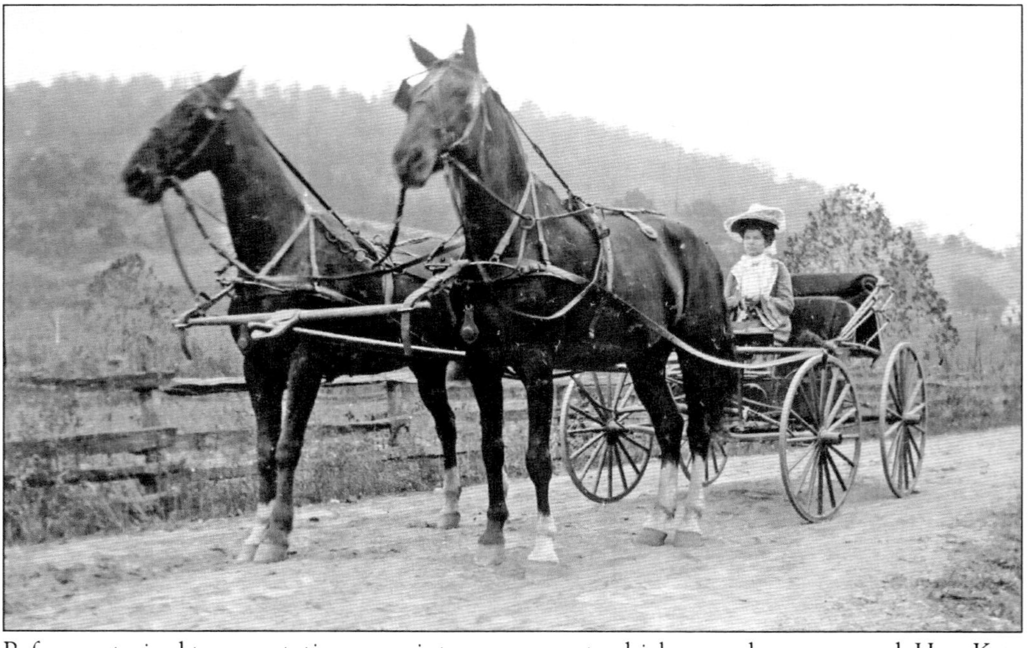

Before motorized transportation came into vogue, most vehicles were horse powered. Here Kate Smith of the Peach Mountain–Mineral Springs area shows off her matched pair of horses and new buggy. Winifred Johnson Holmes took this photograph around 1905. (Courtesy Adams County Historical Society.)

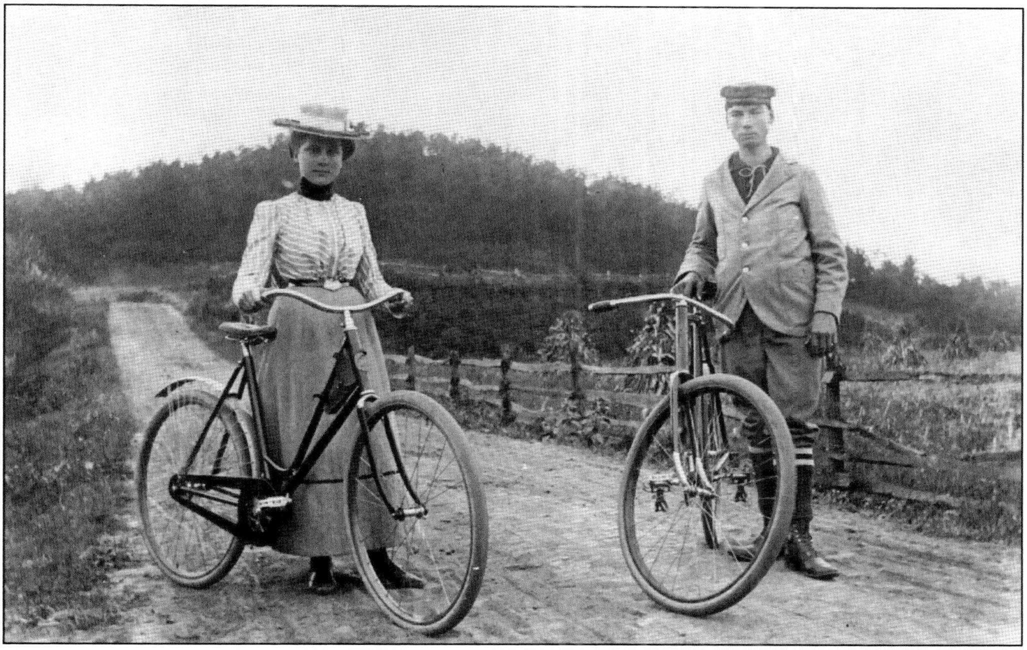

Winifred Johnson Holmes and her father, George Johnson, lived in the Mineral Springs community within sight of the big resort hotel. Here a young "Winnie" and her father are wheeling on nearby Turkey Creek about 1902. (Courtesy Adams County Historical Society.)

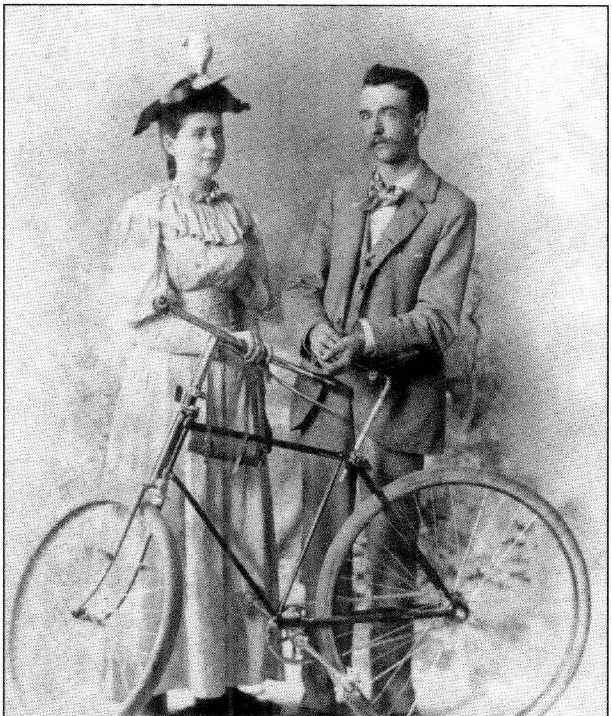

Sherman Edgington, son of Civil War captain L. L. Edgington of West Union, is shown with an unidentified girlfriend about 1890. Bicycles became the rage in the United States in the 1880s and Gay Nineties. Many people used them for basic transportation needs as opposed for pleasure. Sherman Edgington was probably thinking of pleasure in this case. (Courtesy Adams County Historical Society.)

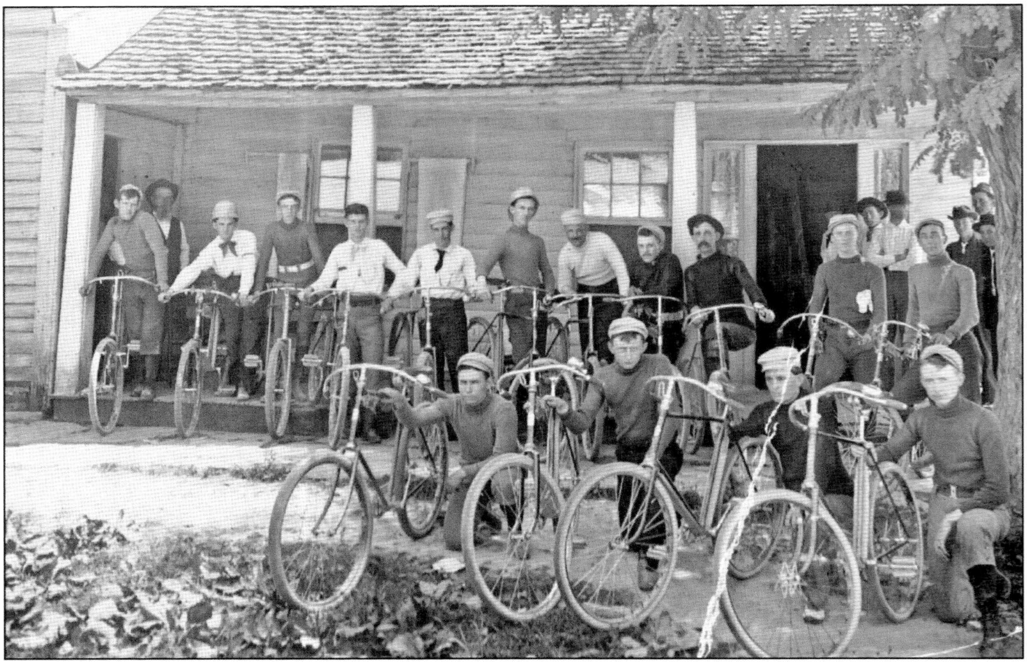

In the summer of 1887, members of the Peerless Bicycle Club of Portsmouth, Ohio, travelled from their hometown to Peebles on the Cincinnati, Portsmouth, and Virginia Railroad. From there they headed on their bicycles for the Serpent Mound Park, stopping in Locust Grove at David Eylar's Grove House hotel. After having lunch, they posed for David I. Gardner to take this picture and headed on towards "the Mound" on their wheels. (Author's collection.)

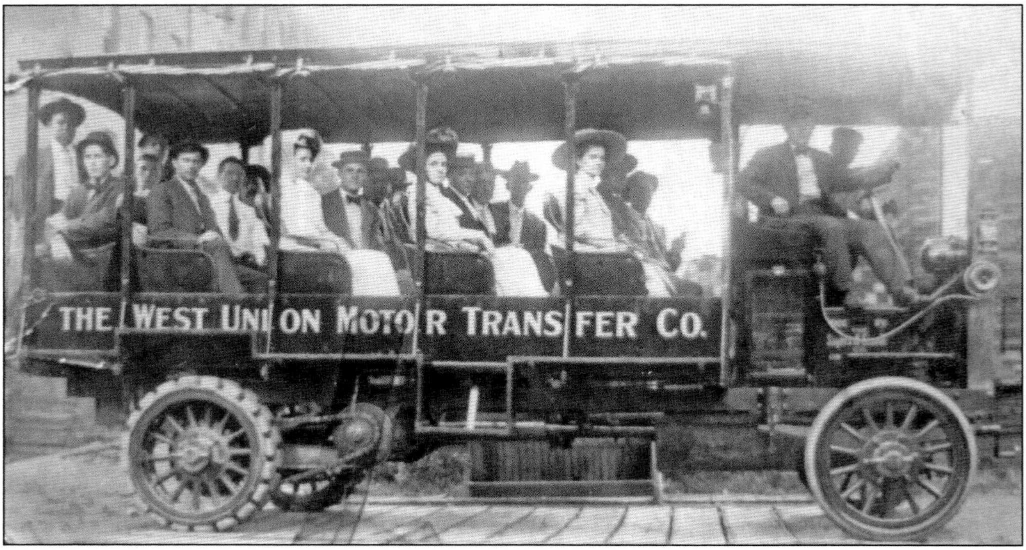

In 1909, the West Union Motor Transfer Company was organized. The company ordered a large bus—then referred to as an "automobile"—to begin running two trips each day from the county seat to the depot in Winchester. The vehicle had solid rubber tires, was chain driven, and could carry up to 30 passengers. After the novelty wore off, the business faltered, and it was sold not long after. (Courtesy John Brodt.)

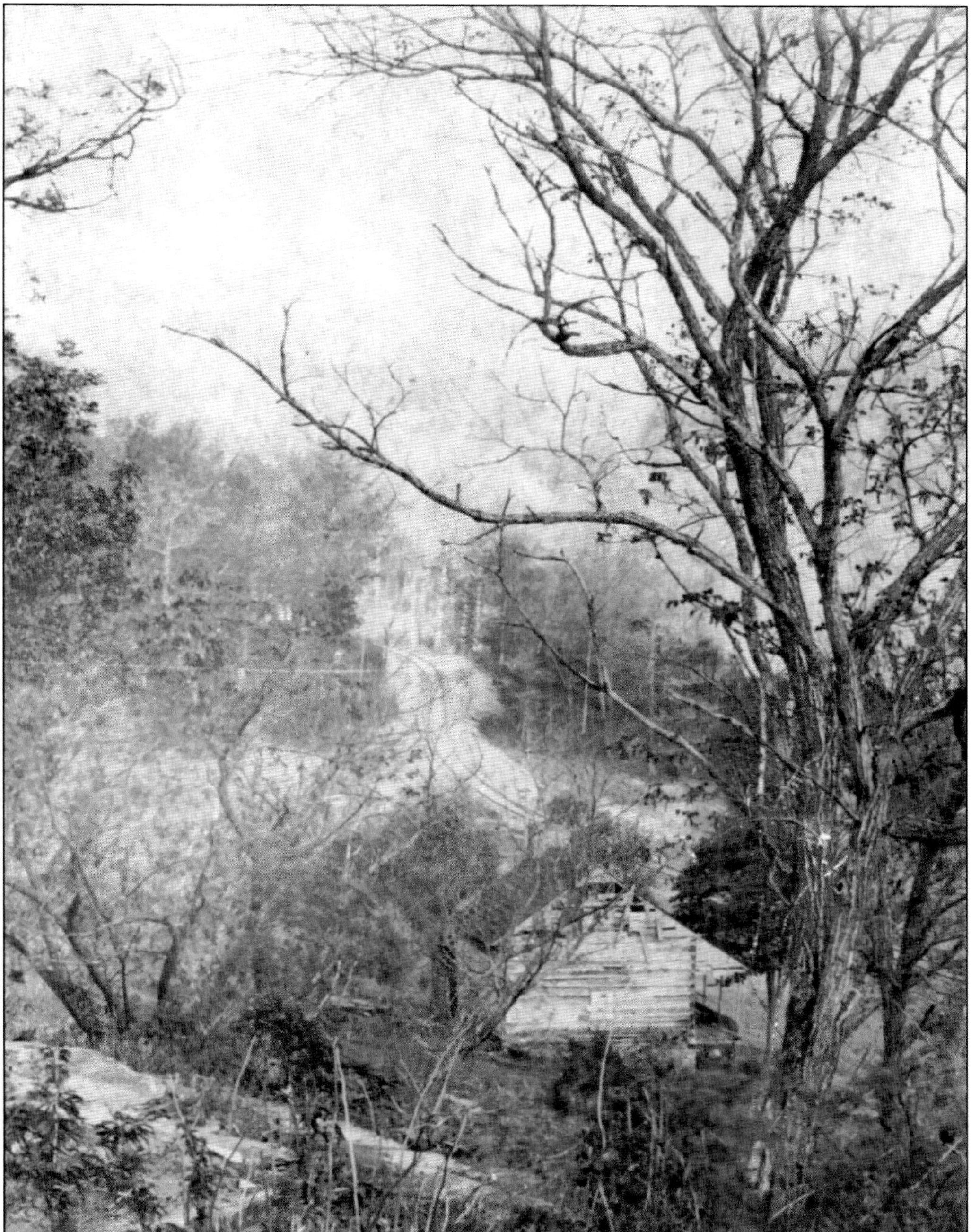

Shortly after the construction of the Cincinnati and Eastern Railway (later known as the Cincinnati Portsmouth and Virginia Railroad) in 1882, photographer David I. Gardner shot this long-distance view showing how the new railroad snaked its way through the woods just west of Peebles. The structure seen in the foreground was a log house built in 1817 by David Gardner, the namesake grandfather of the photographer. The house stood until 1902, when it was razed by the railroad. (Author's collection.)

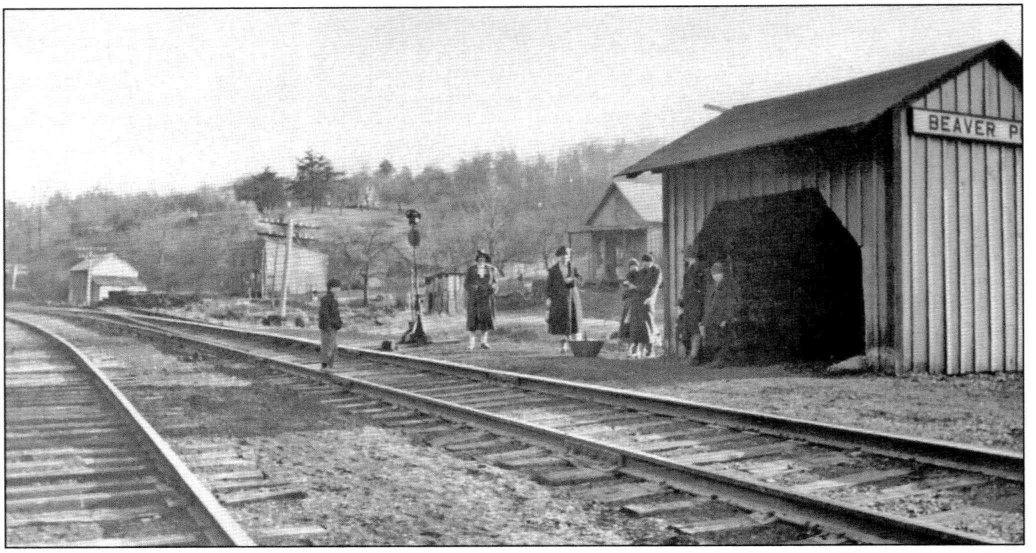

The new railroad cut through a small community in Franklin Township named Beaver Pond. A small station was built there in 1882 to serve customers of the nearby Mineral Springs resort. In later years, as shown here, the station was removed and replaced with a simple flag-stop shelter. This photograph was taken around 1910. (Courtesy John and Carol Wickerham.)

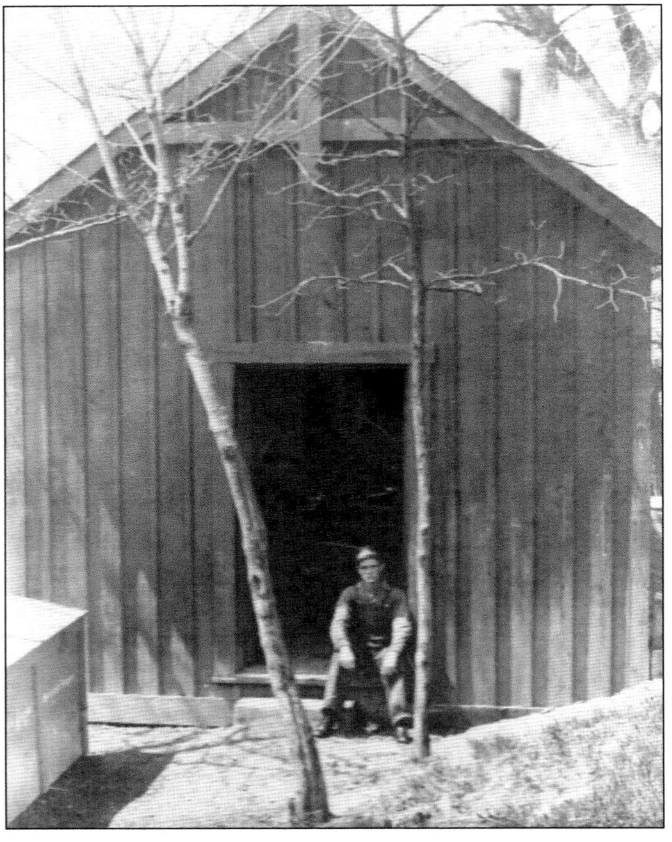

Lawshe was greatly enhanced in size and economic activity when the Cincinnati and Eastern Railway was built through the community in 1881–1882. The railroad built a station, large water tank with a nearby pump house, multiple sidings, and tool sheds. Shown is a c. 1905 view of the railroad's pump house, located on the northwest end of the West Fork Bridge. Pump operator Charles A. Montgomery is seated in the doorway. (Author's collection.)

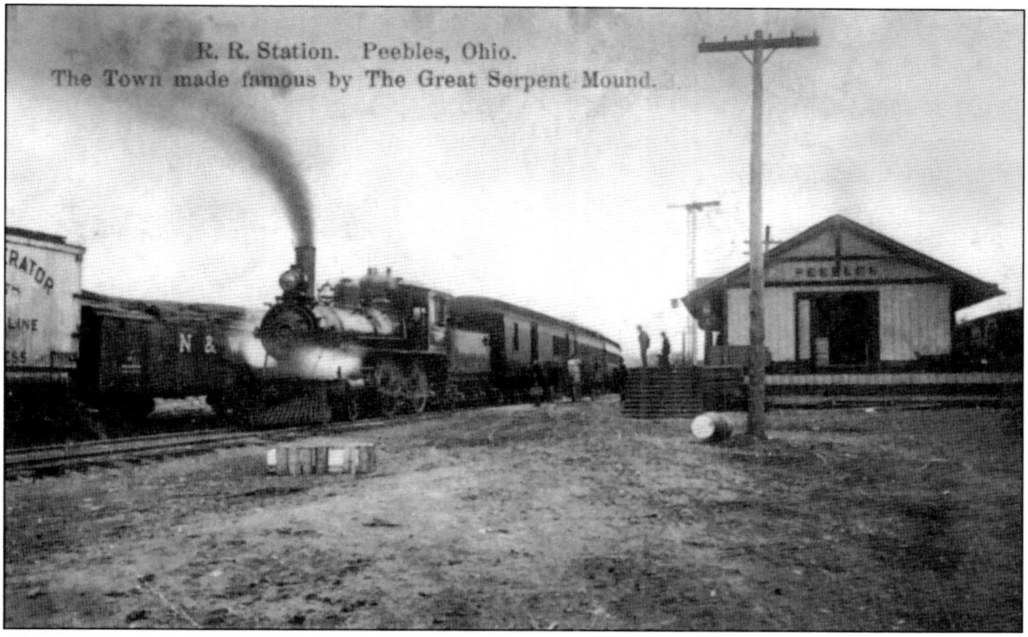

This is a *c.* 1909 picture-postcard view of the Peebles railroad station. The first station was built in 1881–1882 but burned a few years later. This structure replaced it and stood until the 1970s, when arsonists torched it. (Author's collection.)

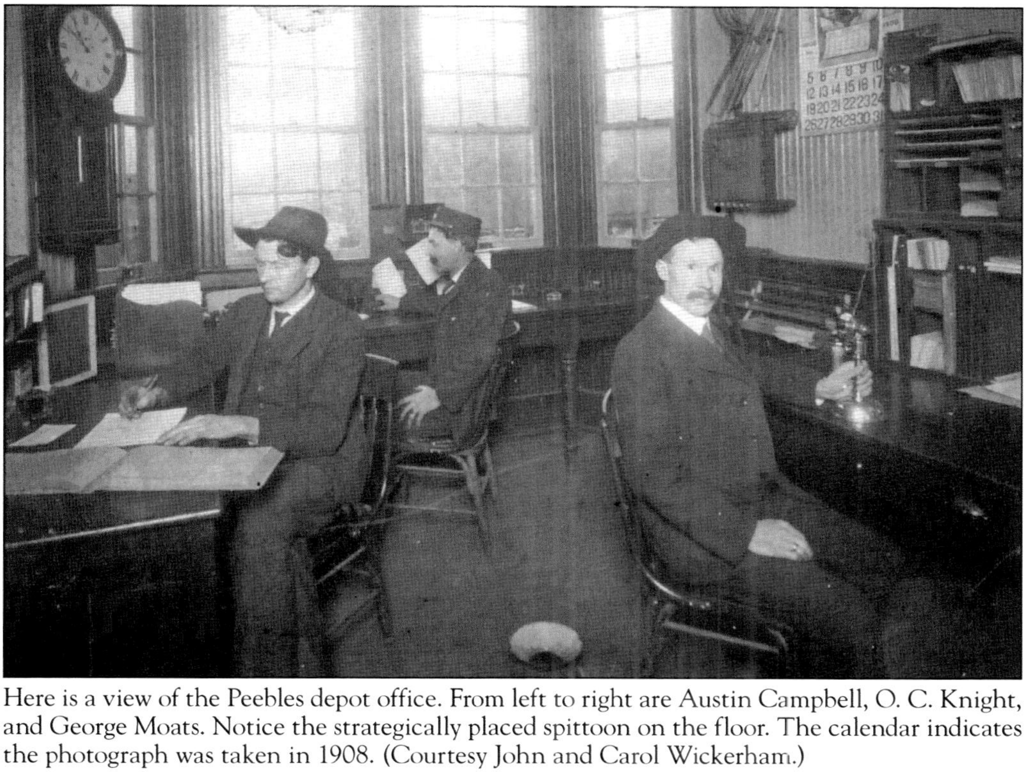

Here is a view of the Peebles depot office. From left to right are Austin Campbell, O. C. Knight, and George Moats. Notice the strategically placed spittoon on the floor. The calendar indicates the photograph was taken in 1908. (Courtesy John and Carol Wickerham.)

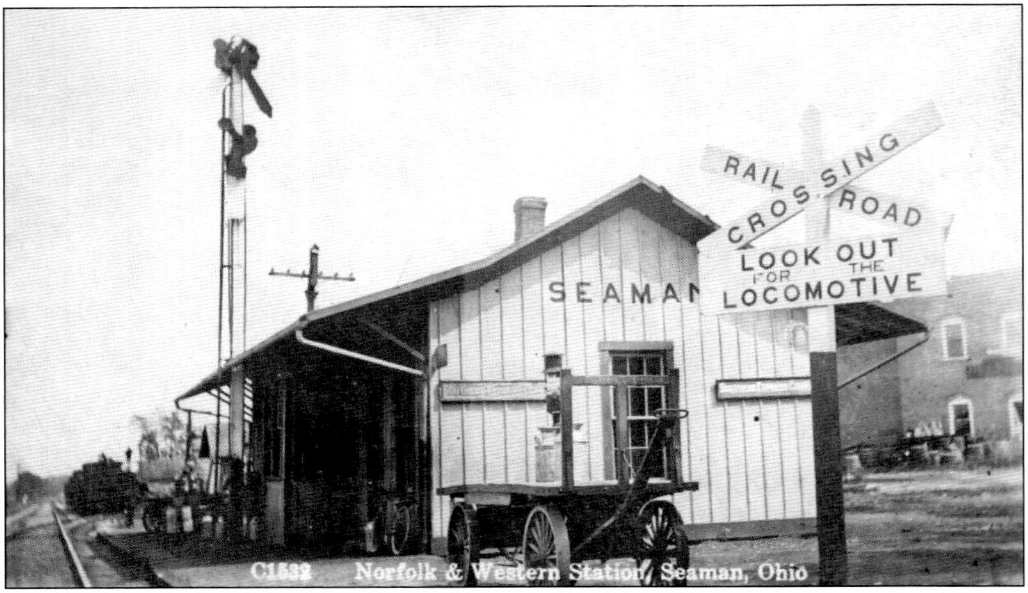

The village of Seaman counts this small railroad depot as its genesis. Constructed in 1882 on the newly constructed Cincinnati and Eastern Railway, it was named Seaman's Station in honor of Franklin Seaman, who donated the land upon which the structure was built. The little train station sat in vacant farmland until 1887, when a home and store were built across the road, spurring the growth of a new town. (Author's collection.)

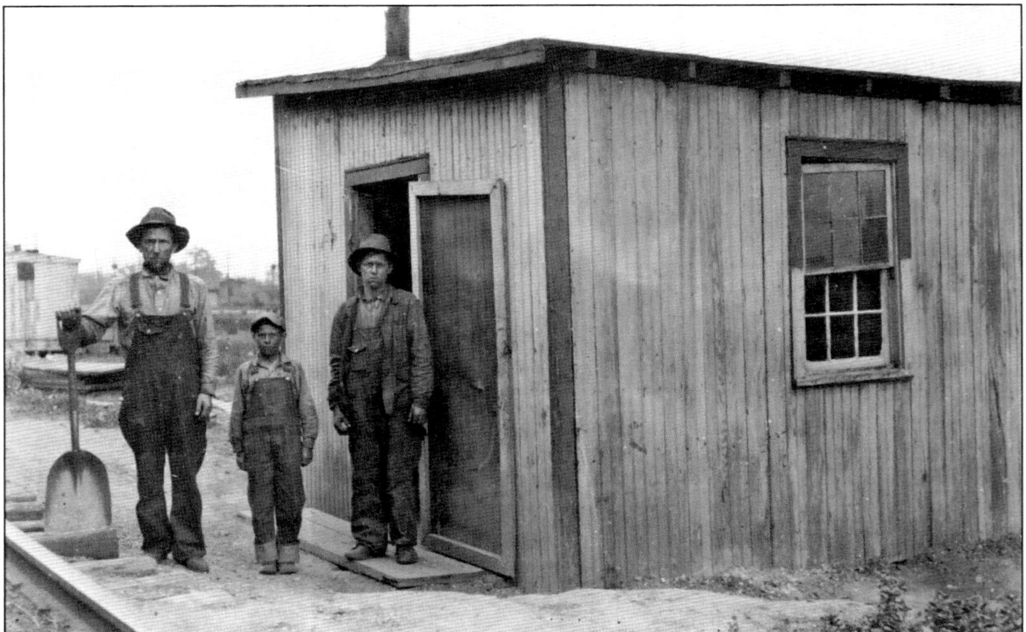

The area in which Seaman's Station was constructed was all farmland. It was not until late 1887 that a small village started growing around the depot and eventually assumed the name of Seaman. This is a c. 1935 photograph of railroad work hands at the tool shed just a few yards east of the depot. From left to right, they are Fred, Ira, and Porter Wickerham. (Author's collection.)

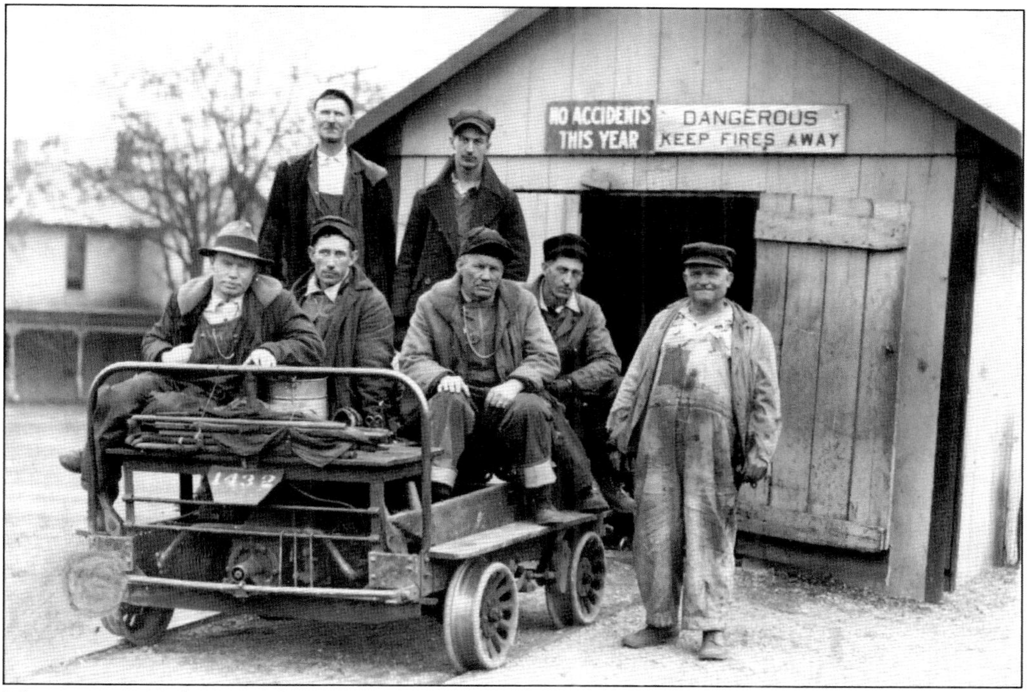

This is a c. 1935 photograph of a Lawshe railroad section gang posing on a motorcar—the successor of the former handcar. From left to right, members of this crew include (first row) Bill Wingo, Elvis Storer, S. M. Wingo (foreman), Bob Blackburn, and Pete Plummer; (second row) Billy Rhoades and Carl Blackburn. (Author's collection.)

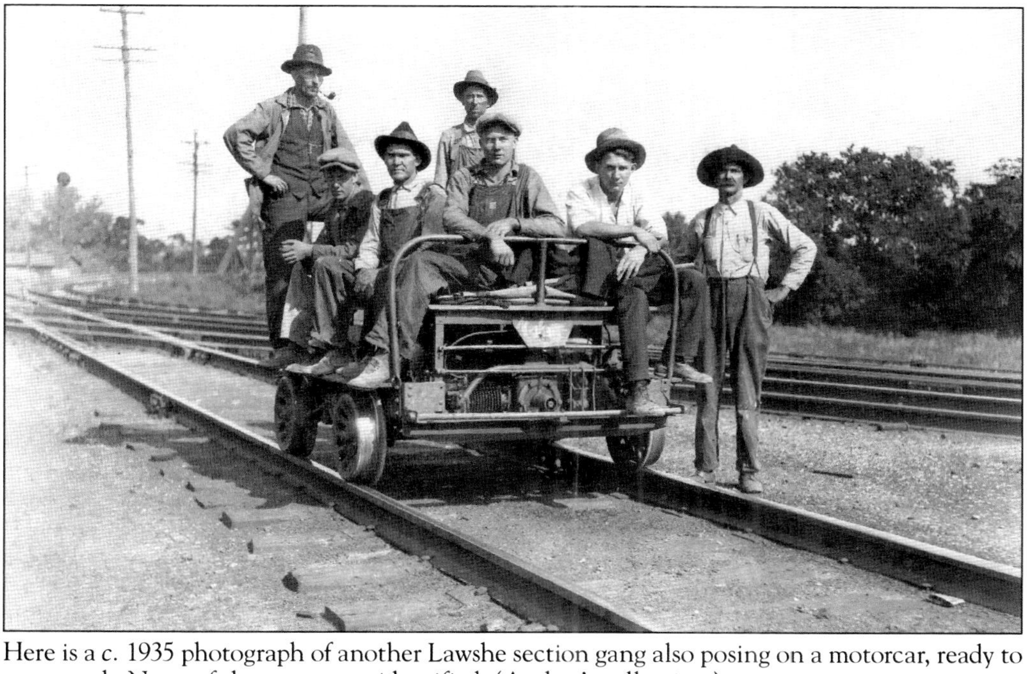

Here is a c. 1935 photograph of another Lawshe section gang also posing on a motorcar, ready to go to work. None of these men are identified. (Author's collection.)

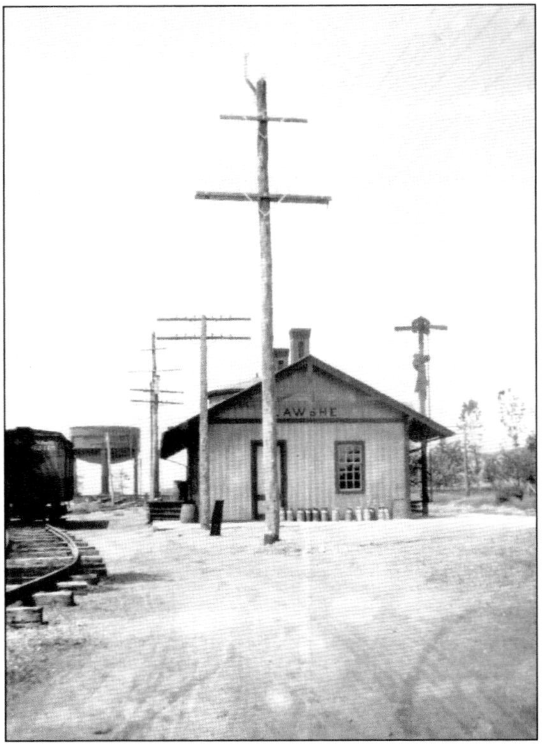

The railroad station at Newport, later renamed Lawshe, was built in 1882. In this *c.* 1925 photograph, the large metal water tank that replaced the original wooden tank can be seen in the background. This view was taken with the photographer aiming at the east end of the depot. This station was closed in 1948, eventually torn down, and replaced with a small flag-stop shelter. (Courtesy Adams County Historical Society.)

The largest trestle built for the Cincinnati and Eastern Railway was over Shimer Run, a short distance west of Peebles. The trestle stretched almost 500 feet in length and stood 90 feet above the little stream. Peebles photographer Jennie McAdow Broomhall took this view of it about 1895. A close look reveals the end of a train on the far side of the trestle. (Courtesy Lester and Jean Wallis.)

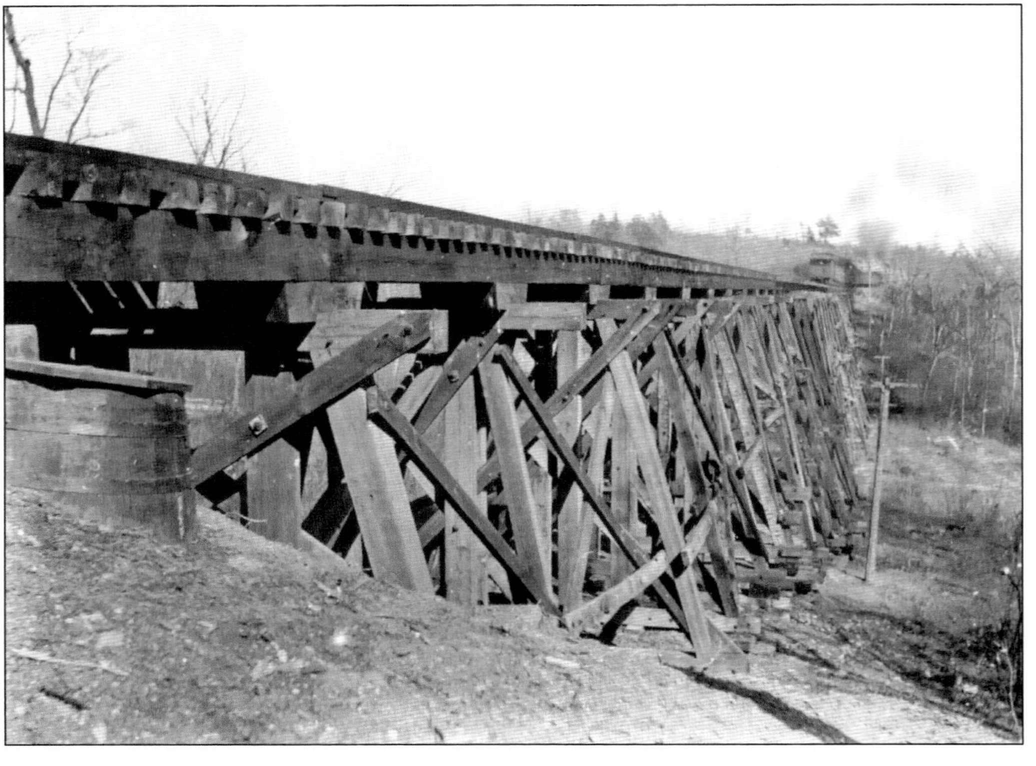

This photograph of the Shimer Trestle was taken the same day as the preceding view. This shows how small Shimer Run was at that time. Although difficult to detect, there are three women and a young child posing in the foreground on the base of the trestle to give perspective to the size of the structure. (Courtesy Lester and Jean Wallis.)

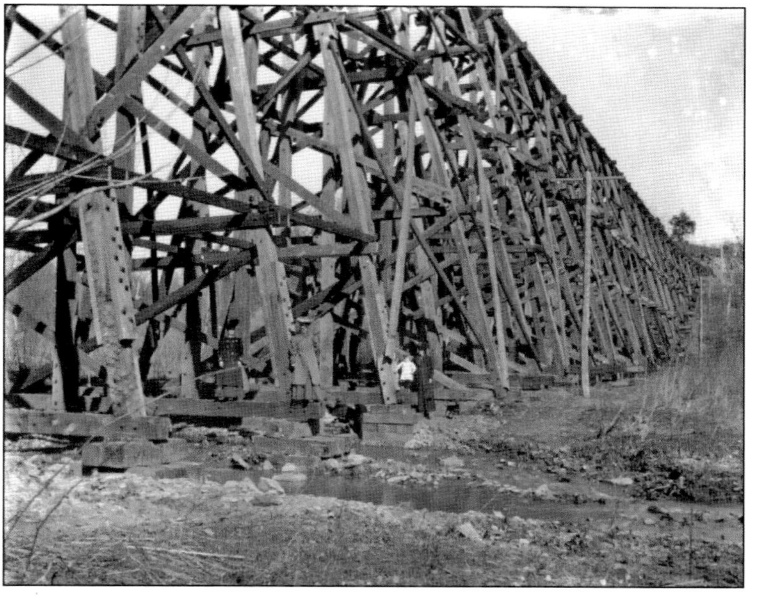

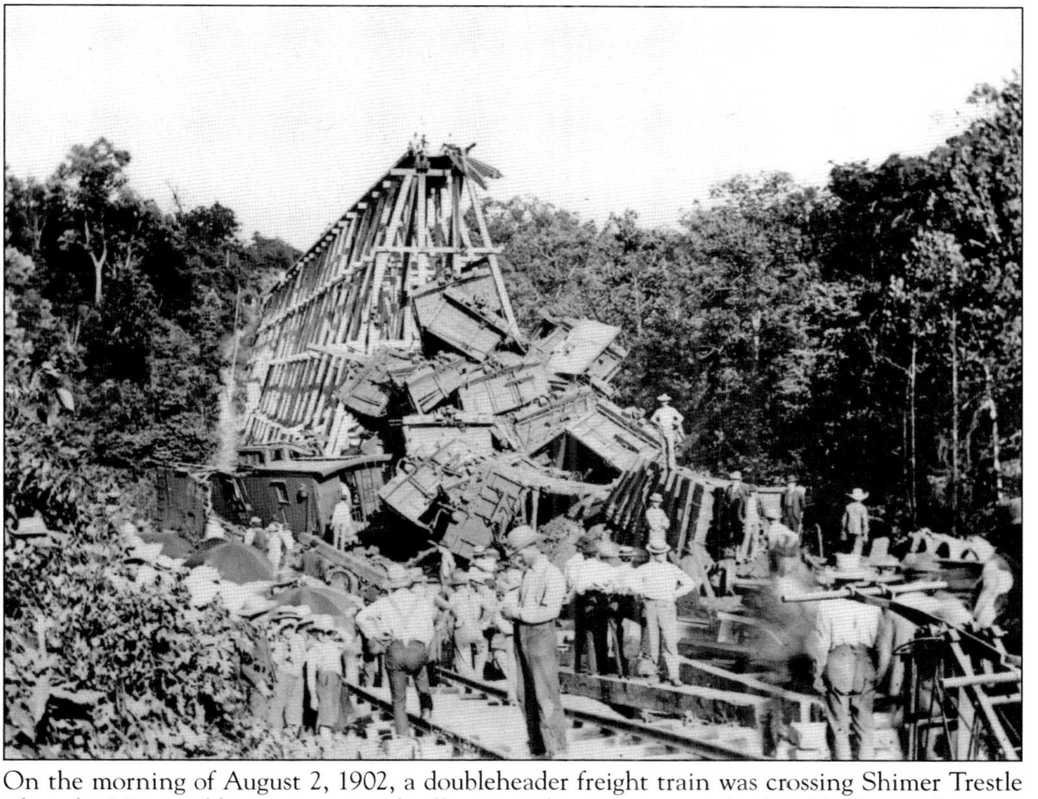

On the morning of August 2, 1902, a doubleheader freight train was crossing Shimer Trestle when the 20-year-old structure started collapsing. Close inspection of railroad bridges and trestles was not yet a priority and, in this case, one railroad worker lost his life as a result. Photographer David I. Gardner took this scene of the wreckage just hours after the tragedy. (Courtesy Adams County Historical Society.)

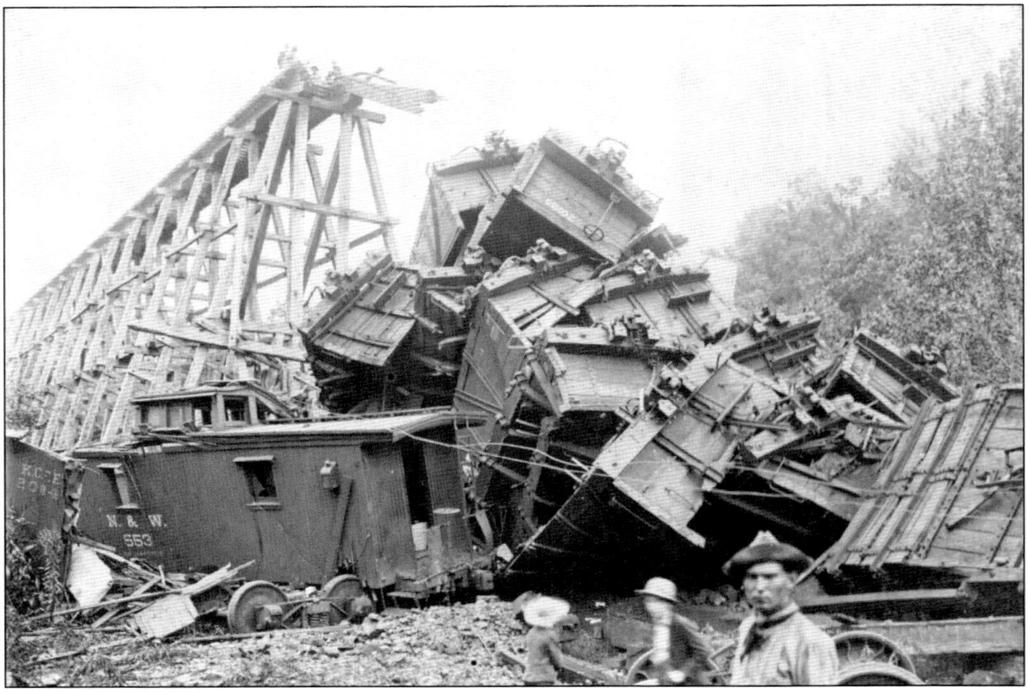

Since there were two photographers at the Shimer wreck—Broomhall and Gardner—it is unclear who took the two photographs on this page. Both shots are unmarked. This is an excellent view of the caboose and some of the demolished coal hoppers. (Author's collection.)

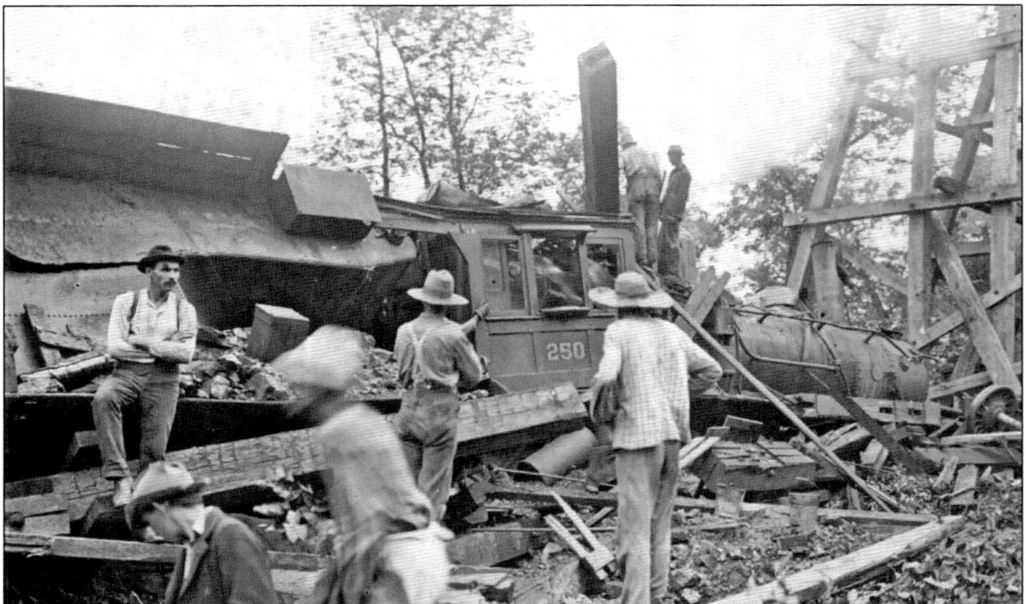

Here is another view of the wreckage of the Shimer Trestle collapse. Of the two locomotives pulling the train, the one in the lead made it safely across. The second one, shown here, was not so fortunate. (Author's collection.)

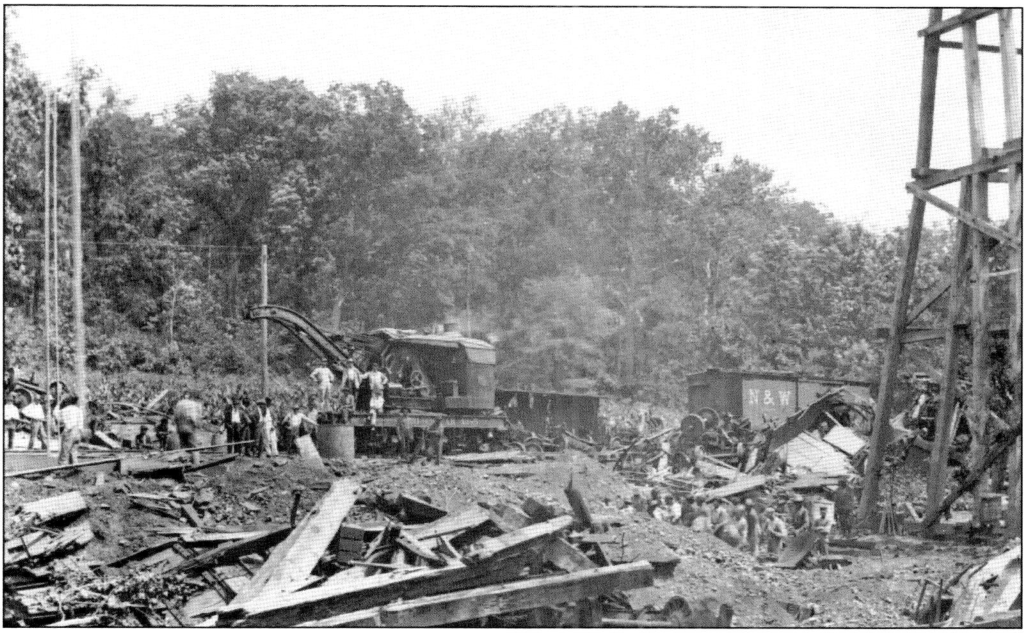

This is a David I. Gardner photograph of the cleanup of the Shimer Trestle collapse. The railroad's steam-powered crane was put to good use. In the wreck, four crewmen were seriously injured but all recovered. Brakeman Robert Foley of Portsmouth, Ohio, was the only fatality. Literally hundreds of curious onlookers visited the wreck site daily until the trestle was repaired. (Author's collection.)

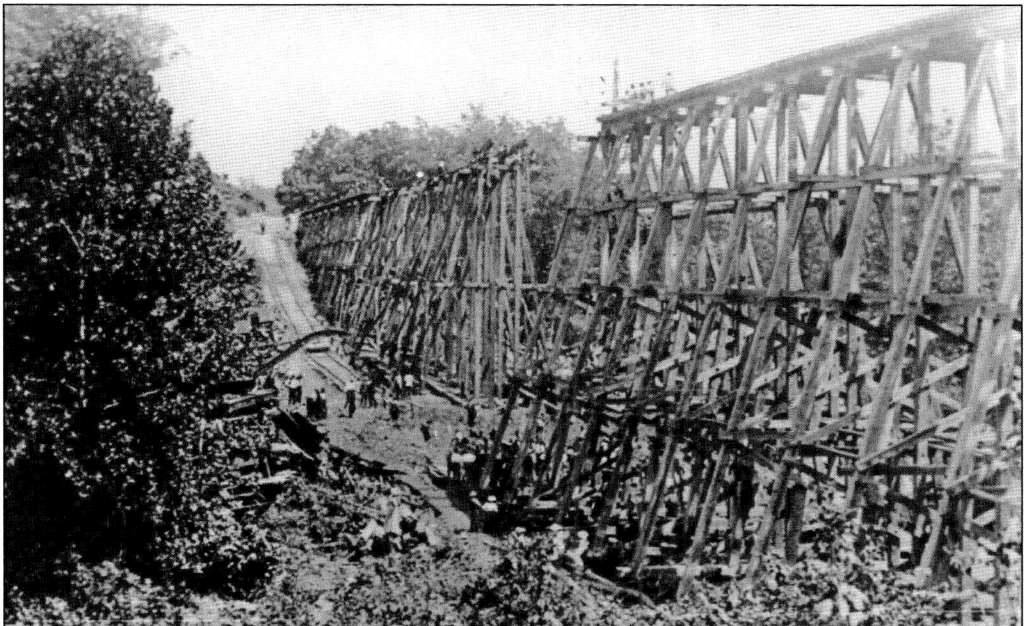

This view of the Shimer Trestle being repaired was taken by David I. Gardner only a few days after the collapse. Within a week, the trestle was reopened. (Courtesy Adams County Historical Society.)

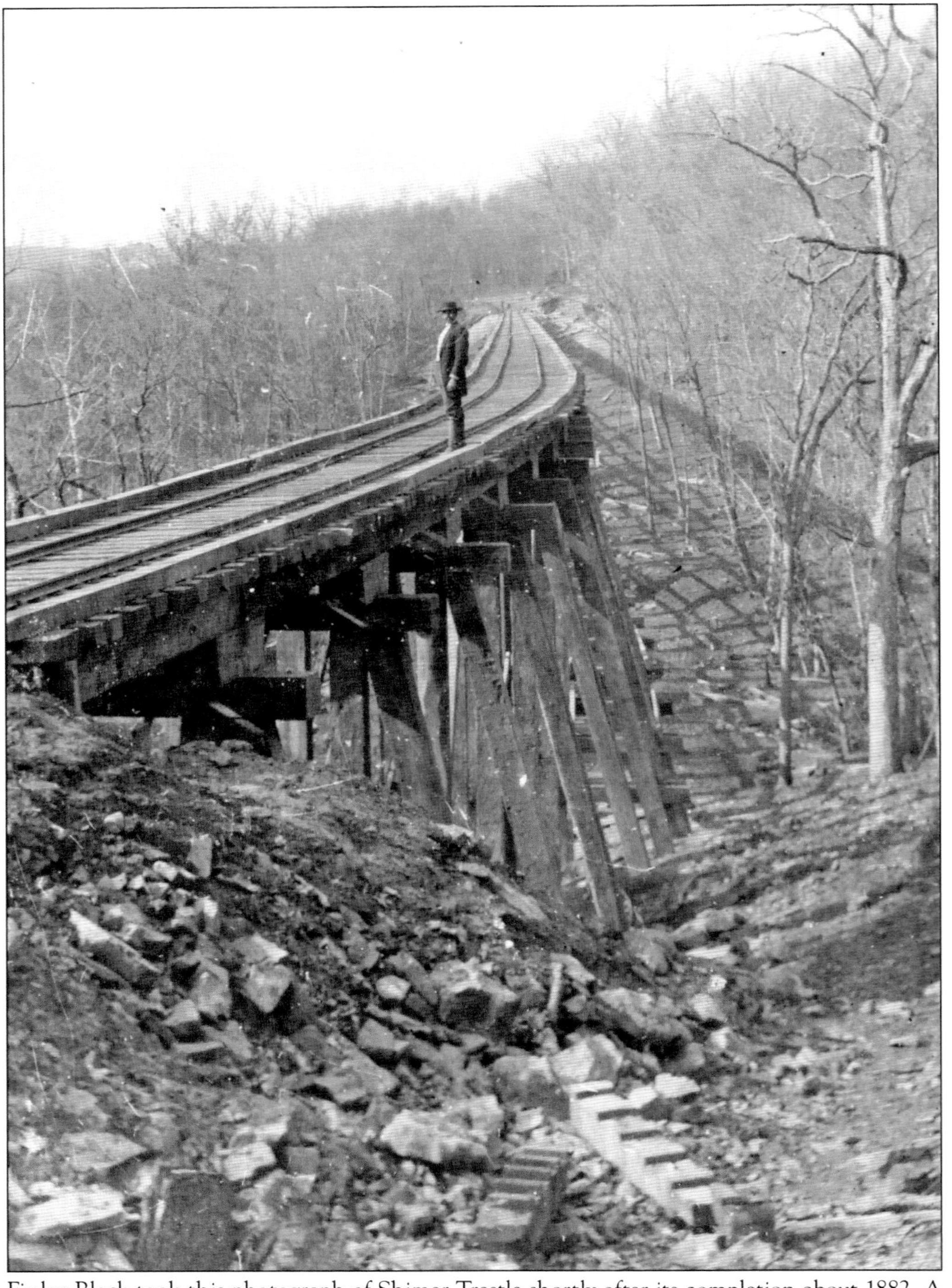

Finley Black took this photograph of Shimer Trestle shortly after its completion about 1882. A wintertime view, the late afternoon sun is casting a long shadow of the trestle on the nearby trees. At this time, the tracks were laid for narrow-gauge trains. Notice how the trestle was built in a curve. (Courtesy Lester and Jean Wallis.)

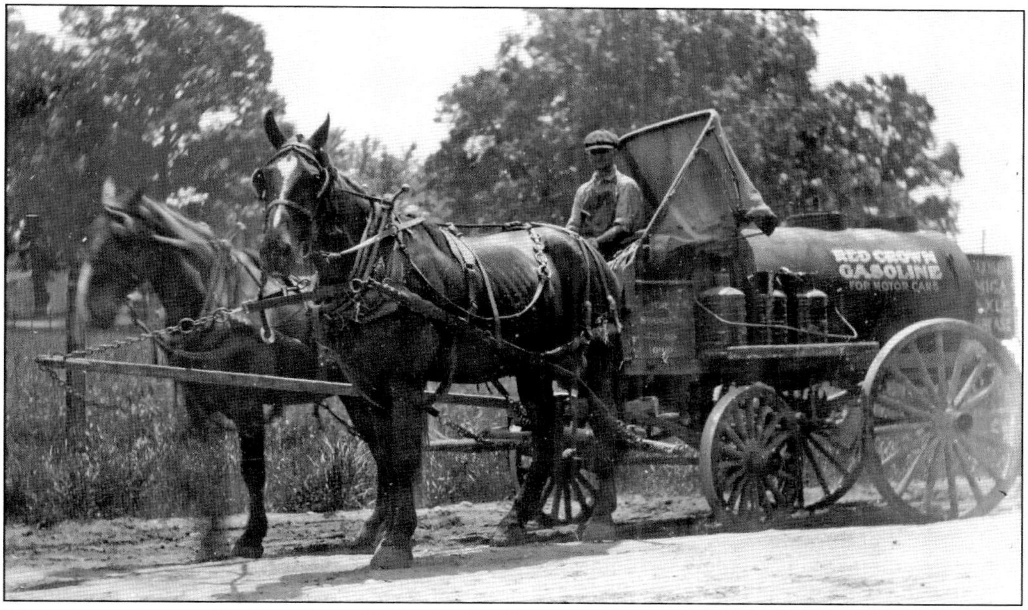

This view, taken in Peebles about 1910, clearly illustrates the transformation of American society from horses to motorized vehicles. Here the photographer, Jennie McAdow Broomhall, shows a teamster hauling "Red Crown Gasoline for motor cars" with a team of draft horses. The side of the wagon reads, "The Standard Oil Co. (Ohio)." On the rear of the vehicle, a sign urges potential customers to "Use Mica Axle Grease." (Courtesy Lester and Jean Wallis.)

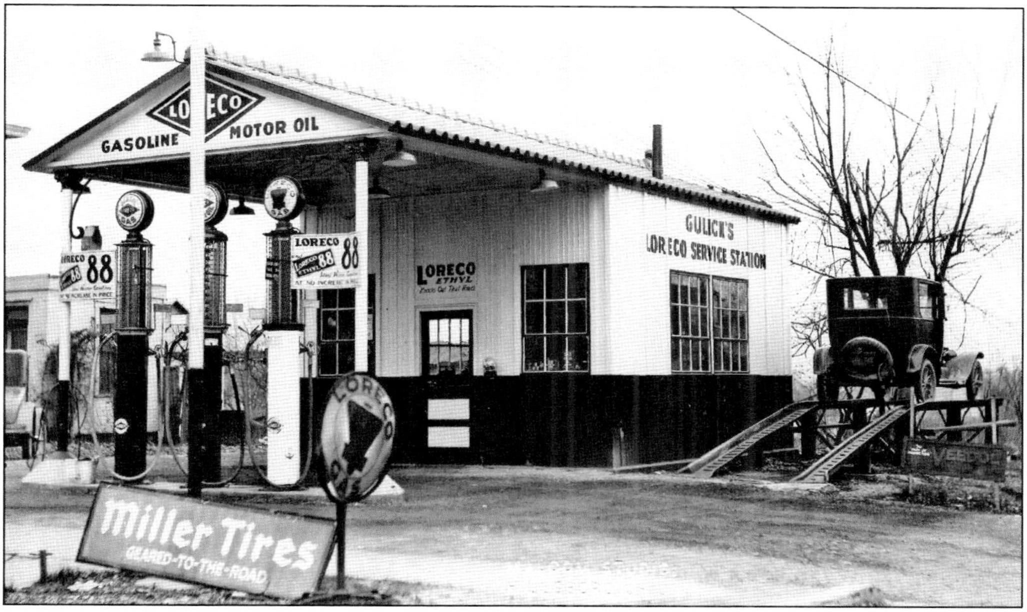

As motorized traffic increased in the early 20th century, related businesses began cropping up. These new commercial ventures became known as service stations. Here motorists could purchase fuel and lubricants, get a flat tire fixed, or receive badly needed mechanical services. This is a c. 1927 view of Max Gulick's service station behind the courthouse in West Union. Built in 1925, it stood until 1967. (Courtesy Tom Hughes.)

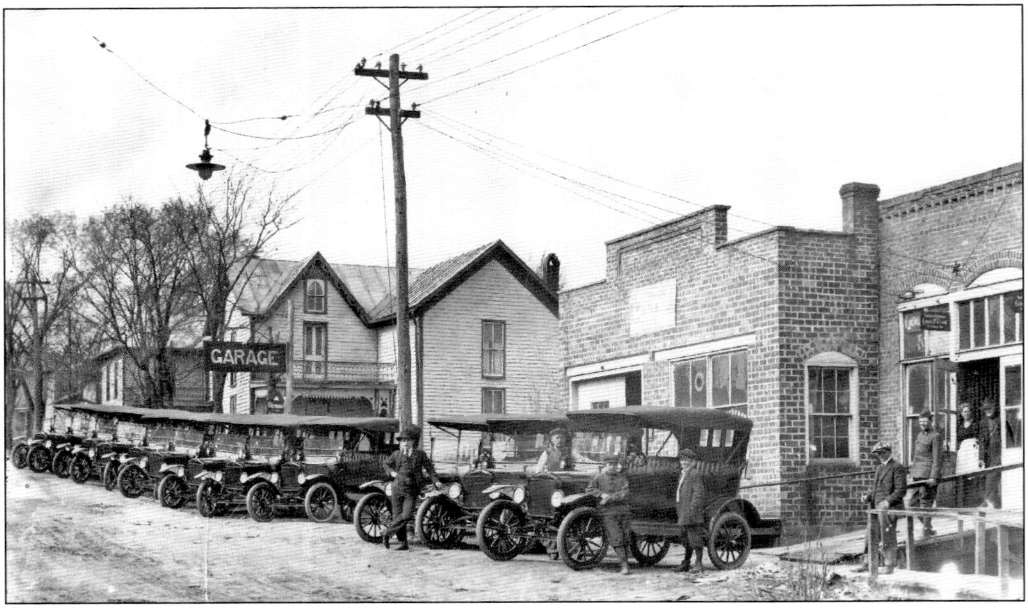

Taken in 1918 or 1919 on south Main Street in Peebles, this view shows the Suffron Ford dealership. The Suffron family had at one time operated a stove factory on this site. This photograph was taken by David I. Gardner. (Author's collection.)

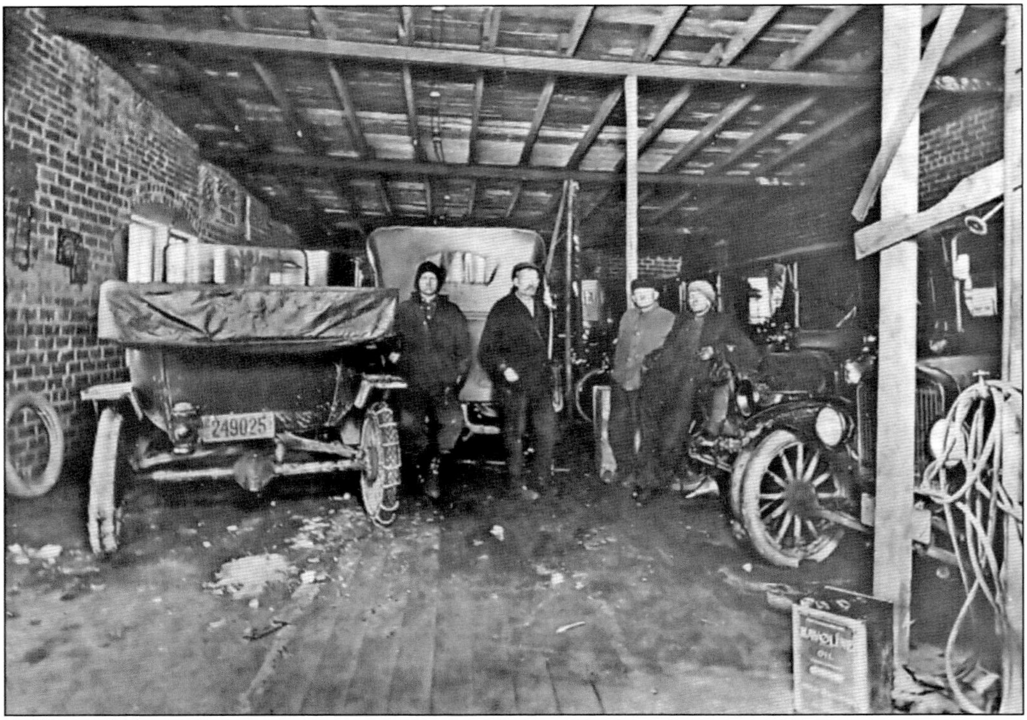

This is a c. 1920 interior view of the garage at the Suffron Ford dealership in Peebles. The photograph was taken in the winter, as attested by the men's heavy overcoats and the tire chains on the rear wheels of the truck seen on the left. (Courtesy Holly Johnson.)

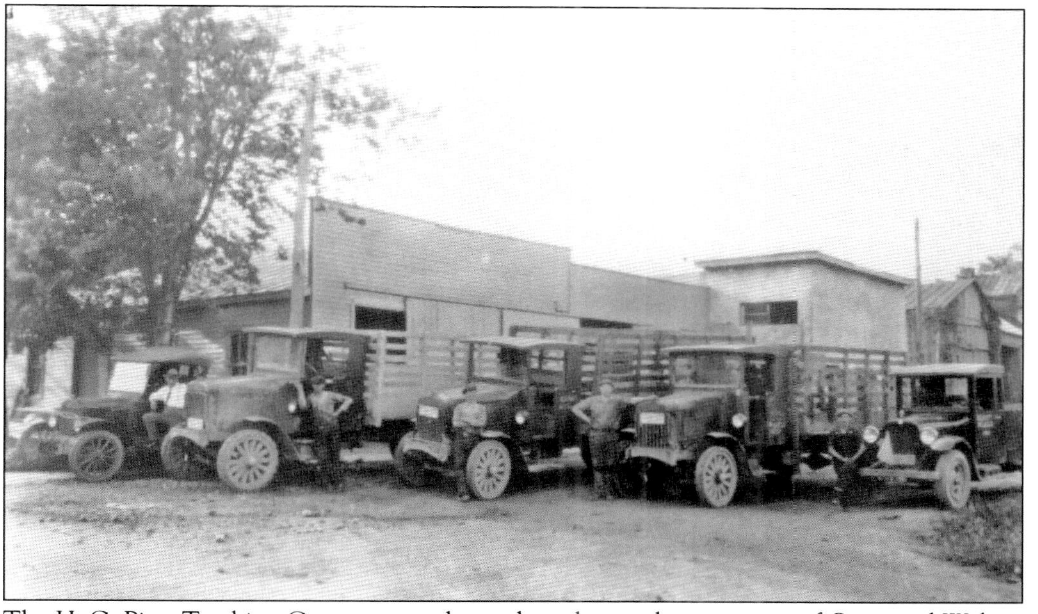

The H. G. Piatt Trucking Company was located on the northwest corner of Cross and Walnut Streets in West Union. This picture was taken in 1925. The drivers, from left to right, are H. G. Piatt, Oscar Young, Oral Harris, Claude Washburn, and Fred Stone. (Courtesy Phil Hawkins.)

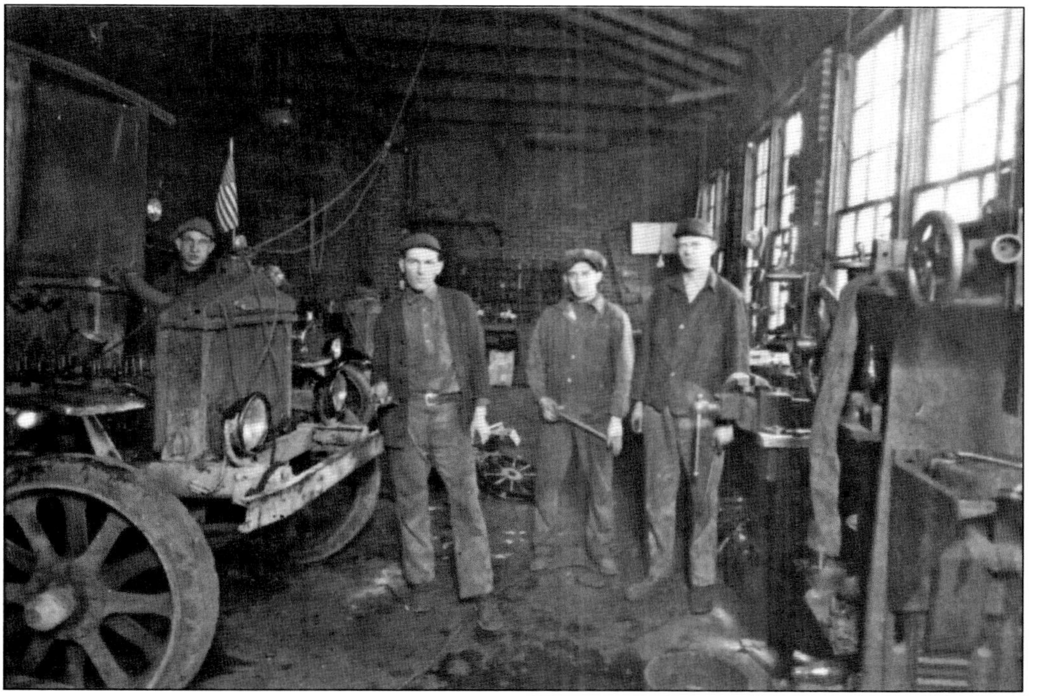

The W. C. Neu garage was a fixture in downtown Winchester for several decades. This view was taken around 1925. Notice the solid rubber tires on the truck undergoing repairs. (Author's collection.)

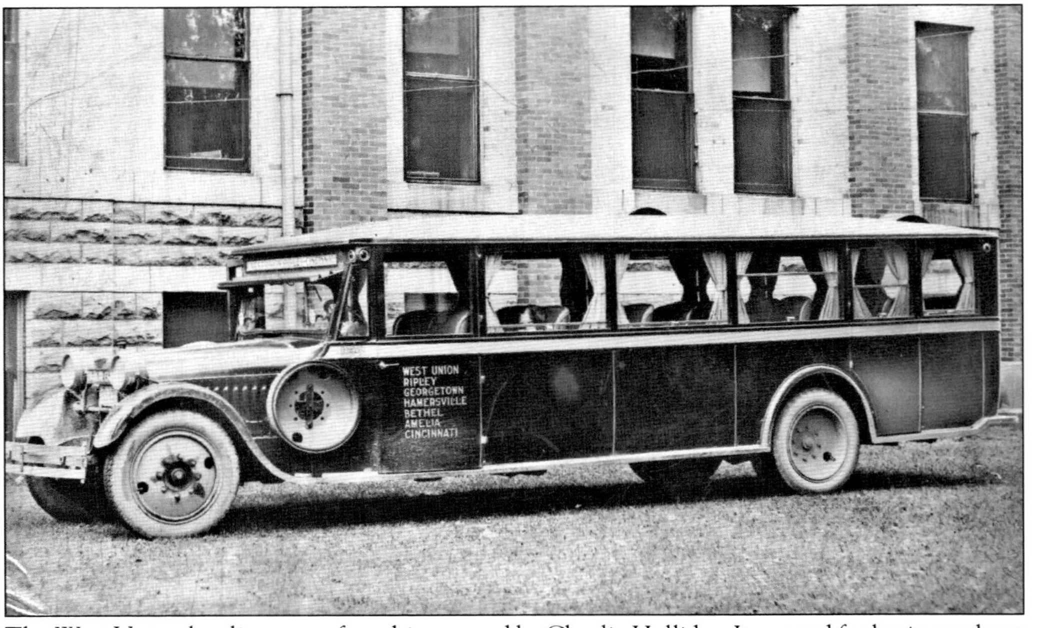

The West Union bus line was a franchise owned by Charlie Holliday. It opened for business about 1930, and the drivers included Ray and Fred Holliday, Marion "Stinger" Knechtly, and George Plummer. It ran regular routes from West Union through Ripley, Georgetown, Hamersville, Bethel, Amelia, and ended at the Dennison Hotel at Fifth and Main Streets in Cincinnati. It was eventually bought by the Blue and Gray Bus Line. (Author's collection.)

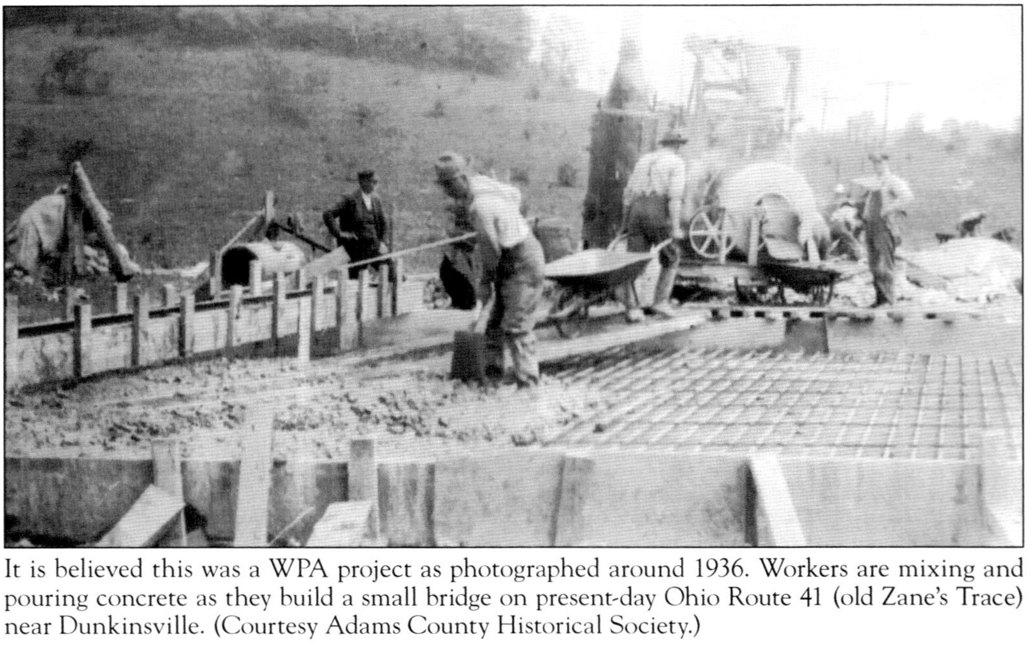

It is believed this was a WPA project as photographed around 1936. Workers are mixing and pouring concrete as they build a small bridge on present-day Ohio Route 41 (old Zane's Trace) near Dunkinsville. (Courtesy Adams County Historical Society.)

Eight

Village and Country Life

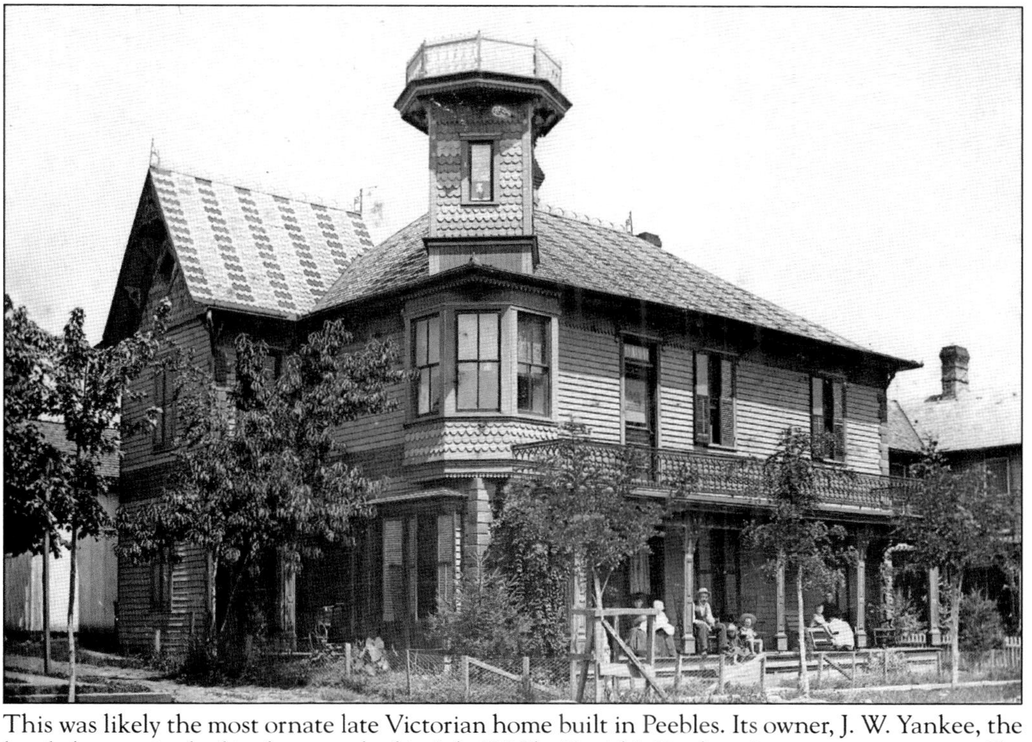

This was likely the most ornate late Victorian home built in Peebles. Its owner, J. W. Yankee, the local pharmacist, had it photographed in July 1896 by David I. Gardner. Its corner tower topped by a widow's walk, the decorative tile roof, intricate wrought-iron railing for the second-floor porch, and shingle-style siding helped make the home a work of art. It no longer stands. (Courtesy John and Carol Wickerham.)

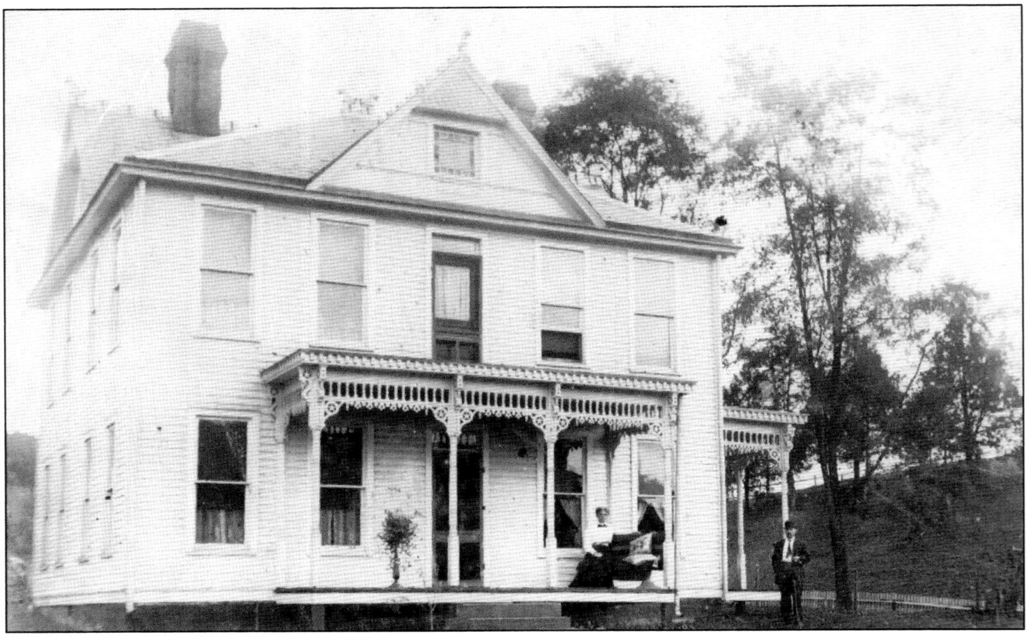

Robert Caraway Jones lived in this stately home in Blue Creek. He named his property Cedar Heights Farm. The home possessed a number of architectural embellishments, including corbelled chimneys, decorative roof crests, a slate roof, and a stained-glass window in the front gable. Jones bought the house from Nelson Jones. It no longer stands. (Courtesy Adams County Historical Society.)

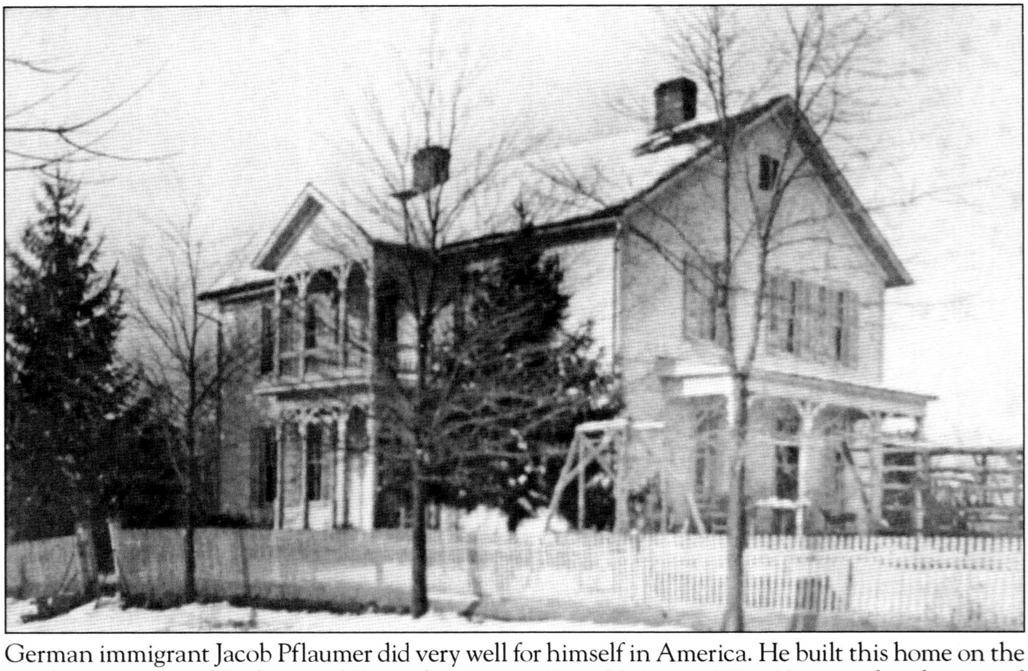

German immigrant Jacob Pflaumer did very well for himself in America. He built this home on the northwest corner of Walnut and Second Streets in West Union in 1882. He owned and operated the Hood Flouring Mill in the village for over 30 years. He also operated a lumberyard and planing mill in the county seat for several years. The home was razed in the 1990s. (Author's collection.)

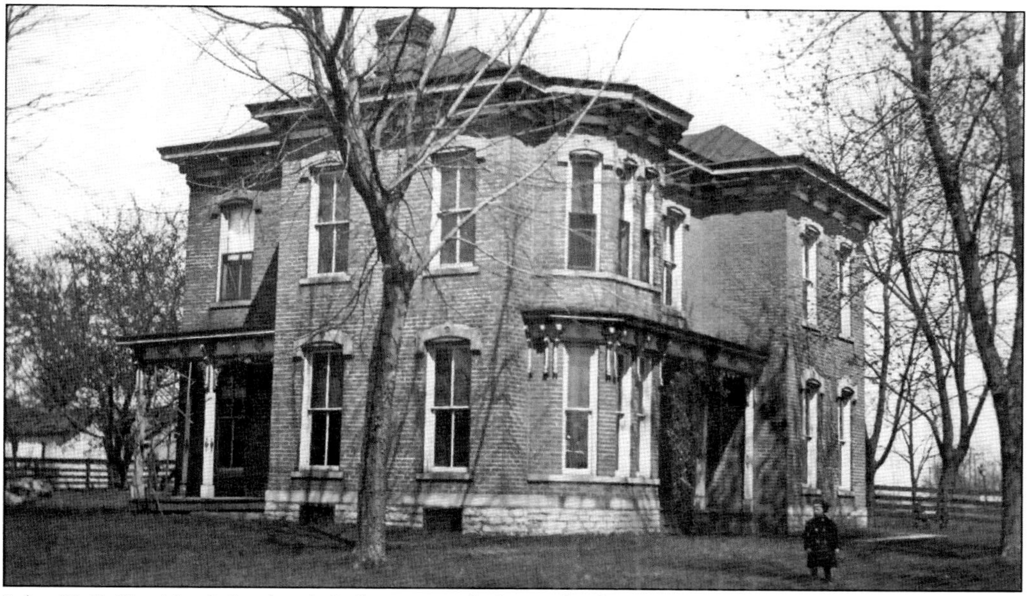

John K. Pollard had this brick Italianate-style home built on Mulberry Street in West Union in 1884. A former officer in the Civil War and county sheriff, Pollard had been elected to two terms in the Ohio Senate. Pres. William McKinley appointed him consul general of the United States to Mexico, where he was serving when he died in 1899. (Courtesy Valerie Young.)

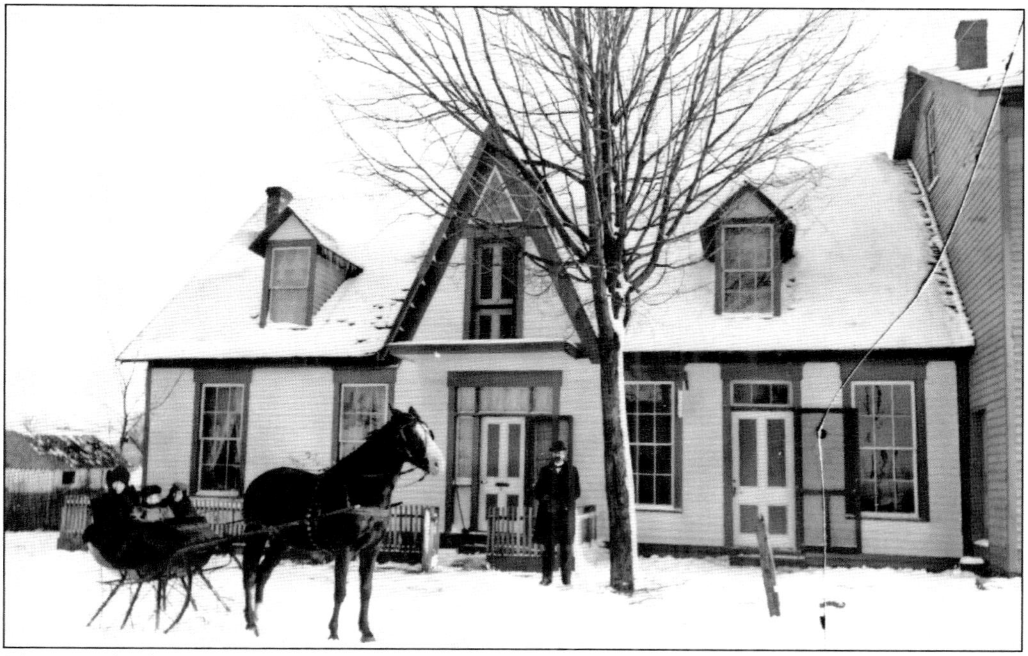

This was the home of Dr. Oliver T. Sproull, located in Bentonville. A native of Adams County, he moved into this house about 1888 and remained here until 1901, when he moved his growing family to West Union. His daughter, Dr. Hazel L. Sproull, was the first practicing female physician in Adams County. Dr. Oliver Sproull is seen standing in front of his Bentonville home about 1895. (Courtesy William and Bessie J. Sininger.)

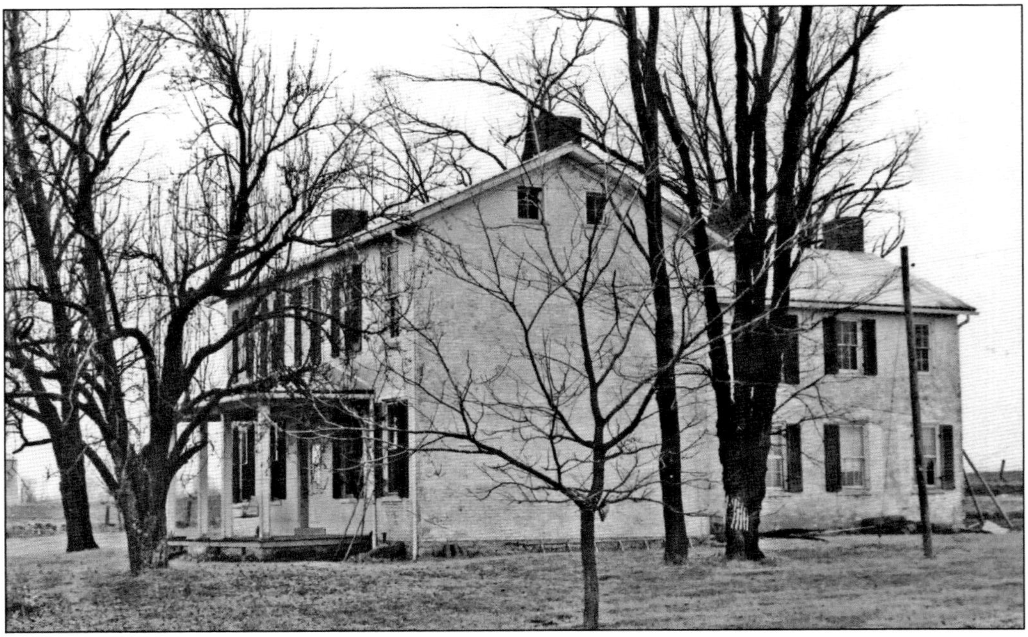

Paul and Martha Harsha moved to Adams County in 1846 and bought and operated a mill on Cherry Fork, where Harshaville is located today. Around 1848, they built this substantial brick home high on a hill overlooking their mill. They named their house Hillcrest. On July 15, 1863, Morgan's Raiders visited the farm, confiscating seven horses of the Harsha family. This photograph was taken of Hillcrest in 1984. (Author's collection.)

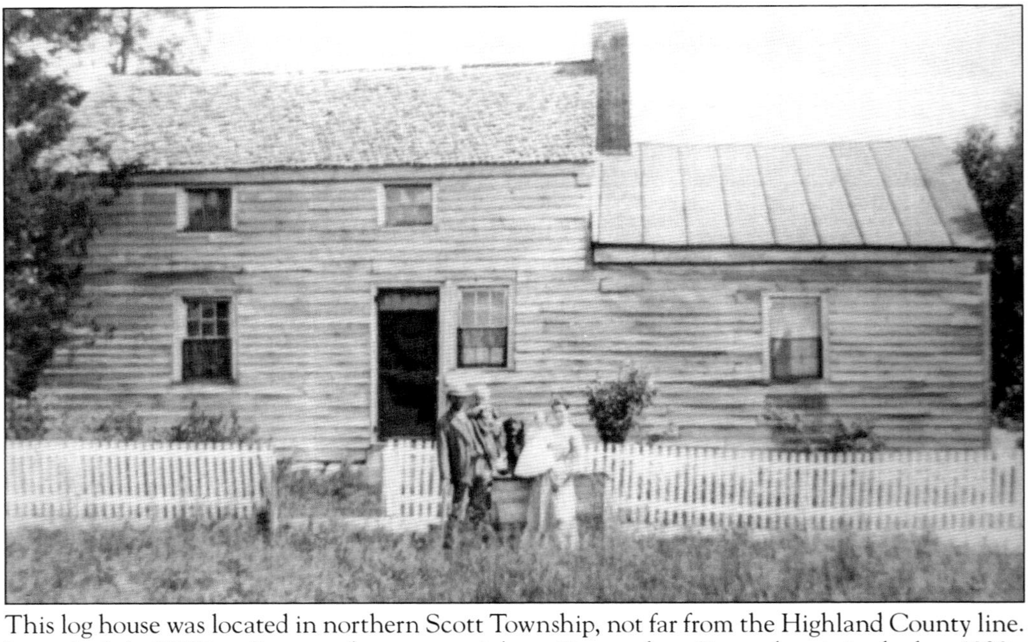

This log house was located in northern Scott Township, not far from the Highland County line. It was built by William Stroup, who came to Adams County from Pennsylvania in the late 1830s. Stroup was an abolitionist and used this home as a station on the Underground Railroad. This home no longer stands. The photograph was taken about 1905. (Author's collection.)

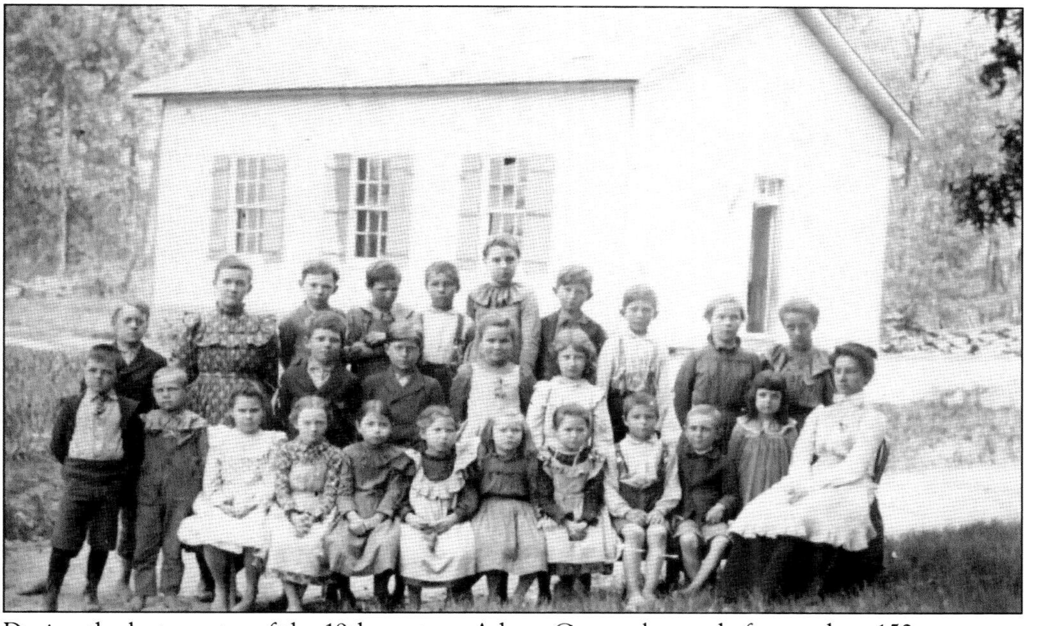

During the last quarter of the 19th century, Adams County boasted of more than 150 one-room rural schools. The schools were not graded, and all ages of students were mixed together in the single classroom. Most of these small institutions of learning were eventually consolidated and graded. This is a *c.* 1905 view of the Mt. Leigh School that stood northwest of Seaman in Scott Township. (Author's collection.)

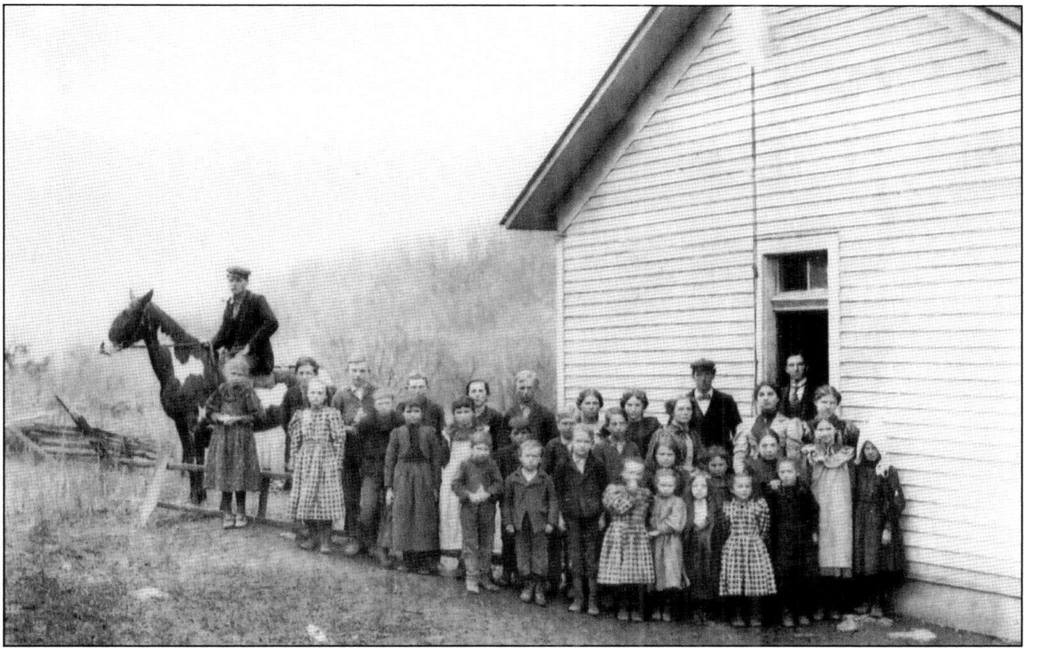

This is the Beasley Fork School in Monroe Township as photographed in 1908 or 1909. The teacher was Marsh Foster. Ed Cumings is mounted on the horse; the students are not identified. (Courtesy Mary Fulton.)

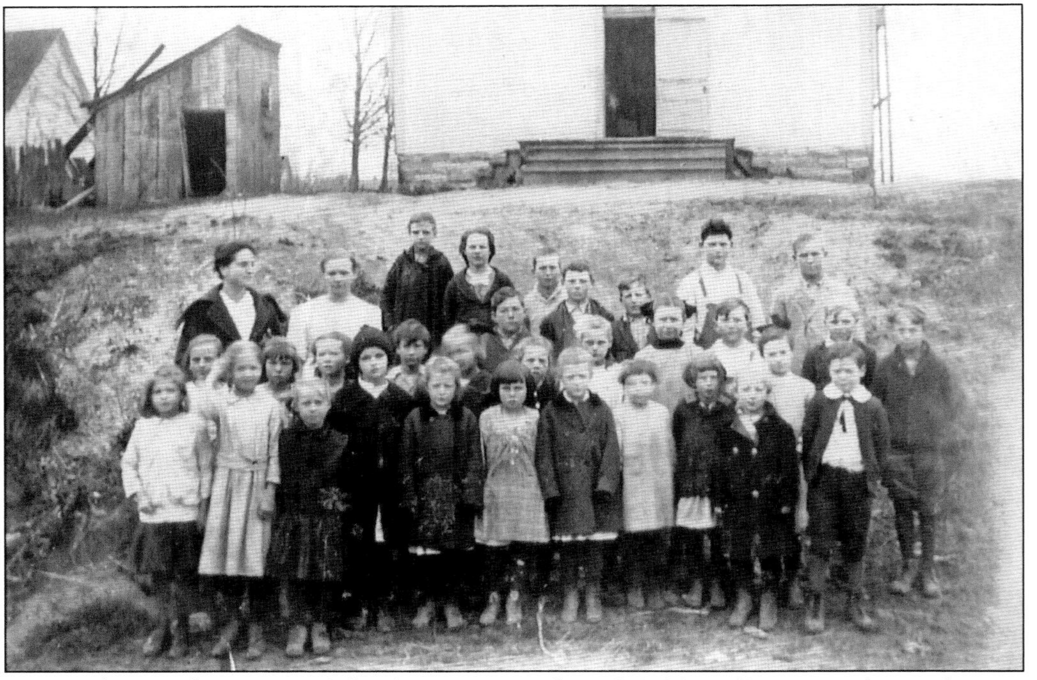

Here is the Lawshe Primary School as it appeared in 1919. Marie Davis was the teacher; no students are identified. This building was erected in 1902 and torn down in 1939. (Courtesy Mary Fulton.)

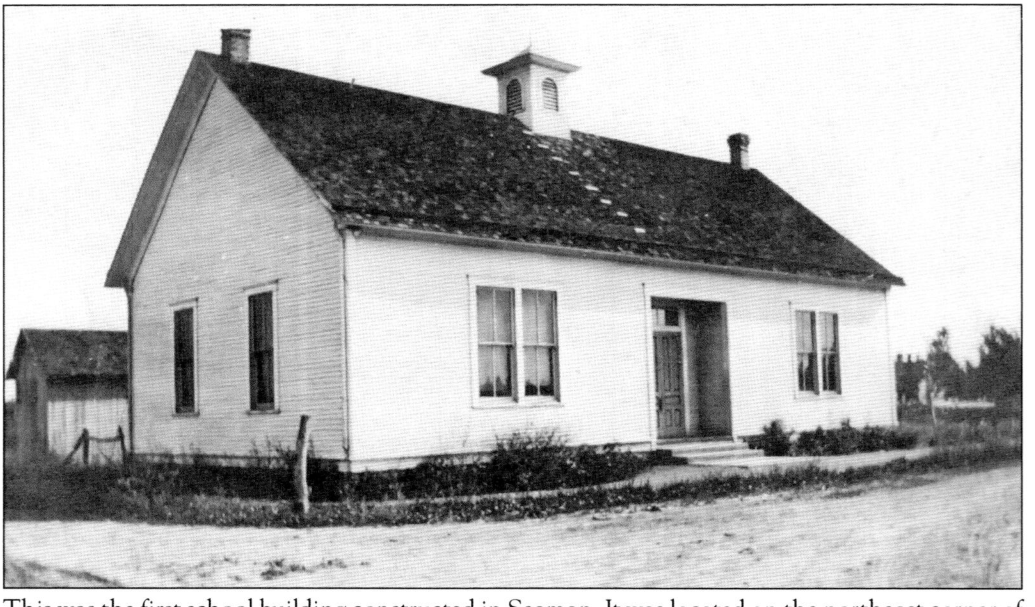

This was the first school building constructed in Seaman. It was located on the northeast corner of Columbia Avenue and Second Street. Erected in 1902, it was used through the 1915–1916 school year. It was then utilized by the village as a municipal building until 1927 and later converted into apartments. It was razed in 1960. This photograph was taken in 1912 by photographer J. E. Shriver. (Author's collection.)

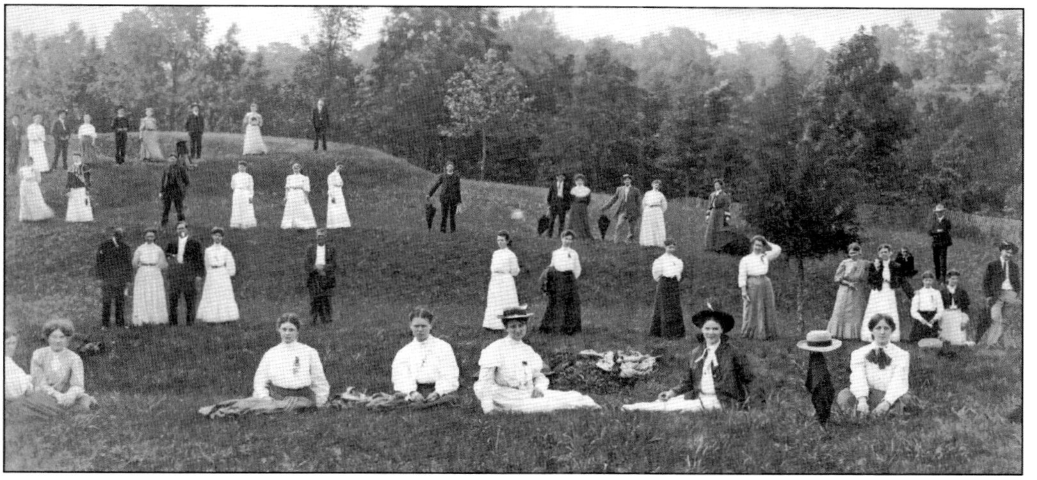

Normal schools were generally held during summer months and provided professional training for public school teachers. Many such schools were conducted in the county, and most of these summer sessions concluded with a field trip. Here is a picture postcard view of Adams County normal students posing on the folds of the Great Serpent Mound in 1906 on their final outing of the season. (Author's collection.)

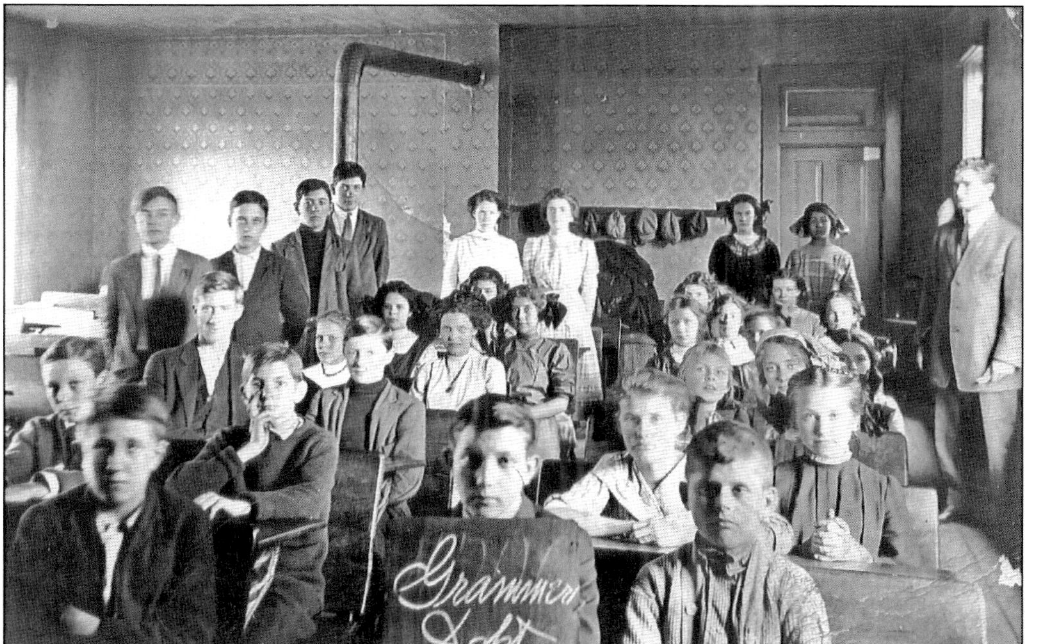

This view was taken in the Peebles Village School during the 1909–1910 school year. This was the grammar department in the seventh and eighth grades. Lon Morrison, the teacher, stands on the right. (Courtesy H. W. Johnson Jr.)

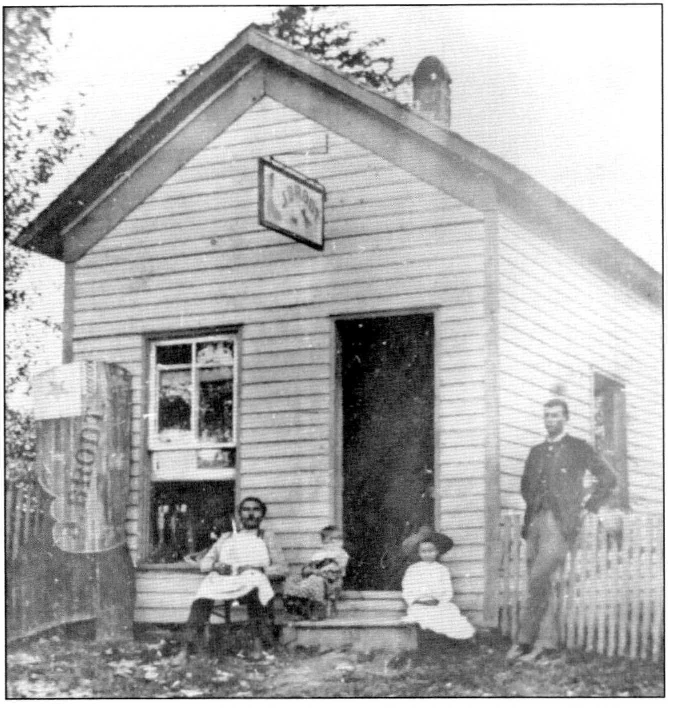

John J. Brodt was a boot and shoe manufacturer. Upon moving to West Union in 1884, he built this small shop to house his business. He made footwear here until 1905, when he changed professions, becoming a successful farm implement dealer. (Courtesy John Brodt.)

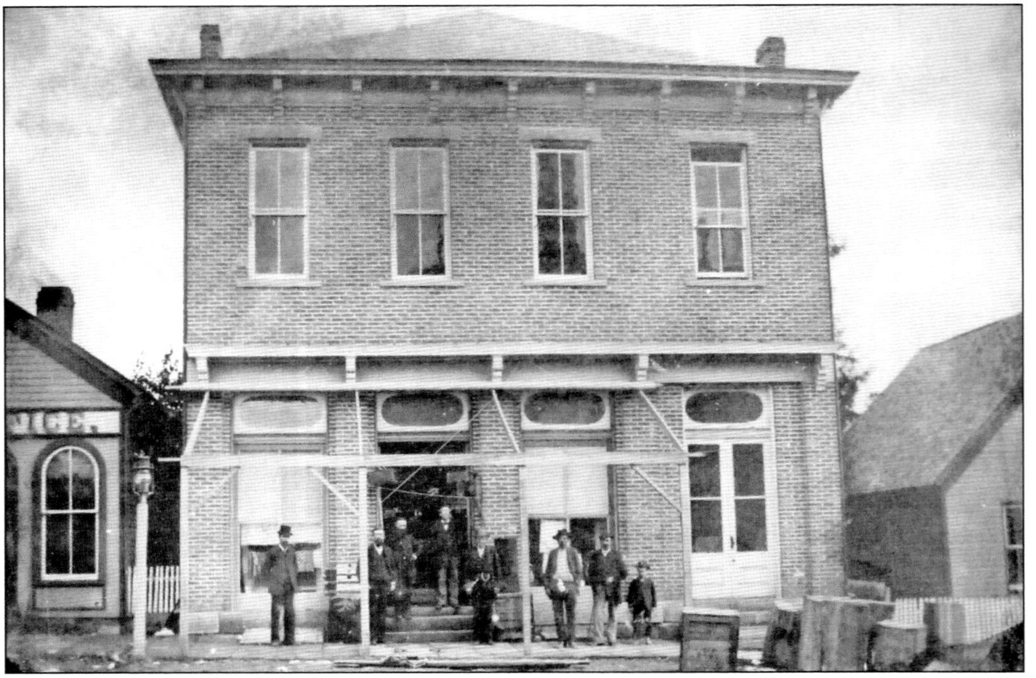

This structure was built in 1880 on Market Street facing the courthouse square. The local Masonic lodge built the second floor for its meeting hall, whereas the ground floor was rented to Connor, Boyles, and Pollard, "Dry Goods and Notion Merchant." This tintype was taken around 1882. The building was razed in the early 2000s. (Courtesy Valerie Young.)

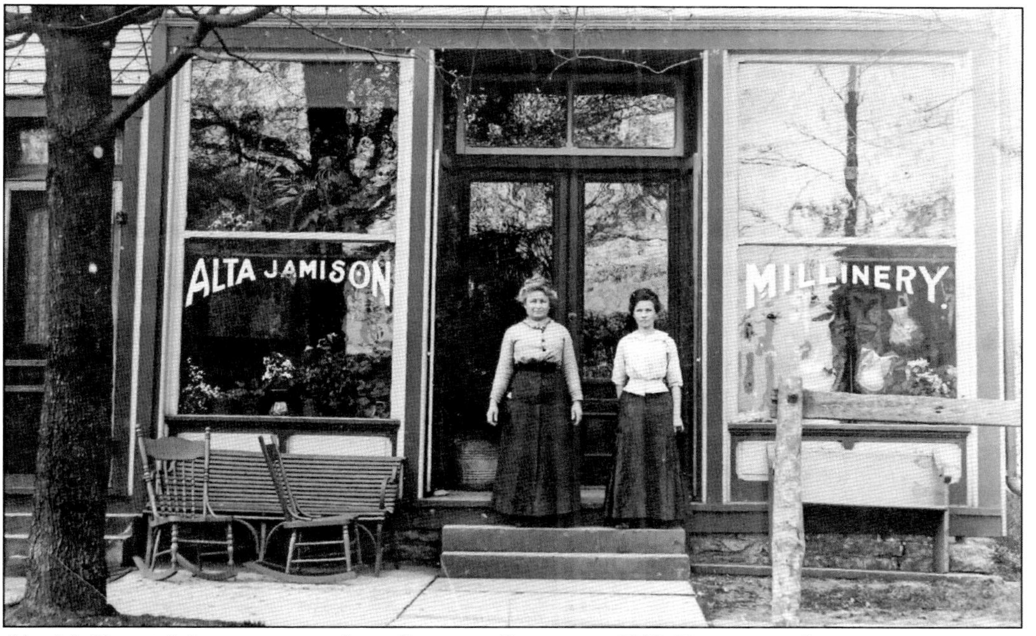

Alta McCormick Jamison opened a millinery in Seaman in 1898. Business in that young town must have been good, and her business lasted over 30 years. She is shown in this picture postcard on the left with her niece, Ella McCormick Cornelius, who assisted in the millinery. (Author's collection.)

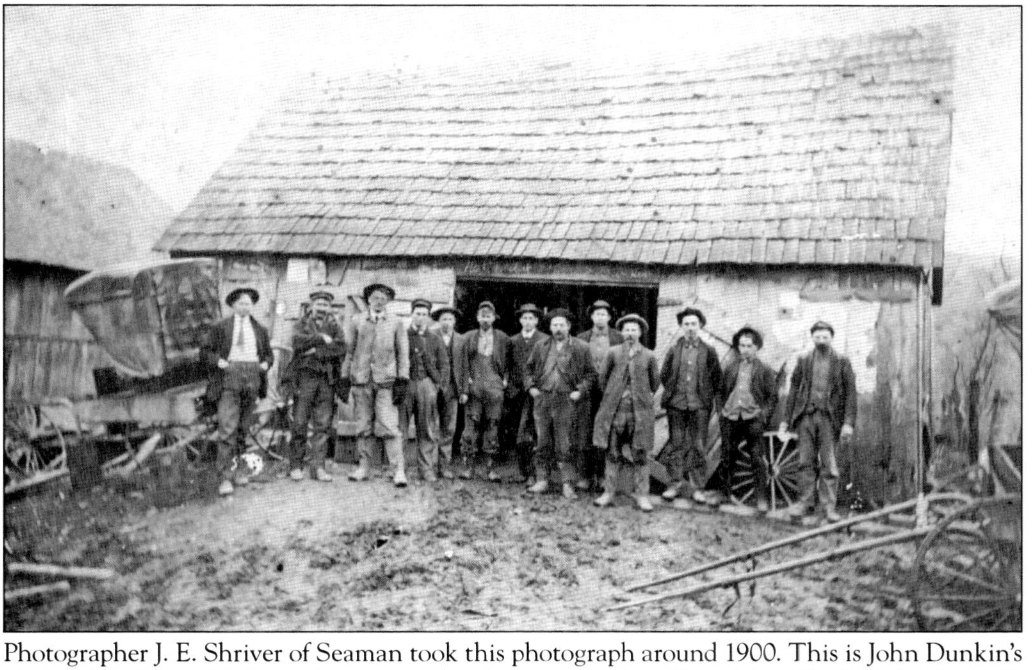

Photographer J. E. Shriver of Seaman took this photograph around 1900. This is John Dunkin's blacksmith shop, which was located in the tiny community of Dunkinsville, founded in 1841. Dunkin probably started smithing in the late 1890s and kept his shop in Dunkinsville until the mid-1920s. At that time, he and his wife, Cynthia Stratton Dunkin, moved to Seaman, where John continued blacksmithing for several years more. (Author's collection.)

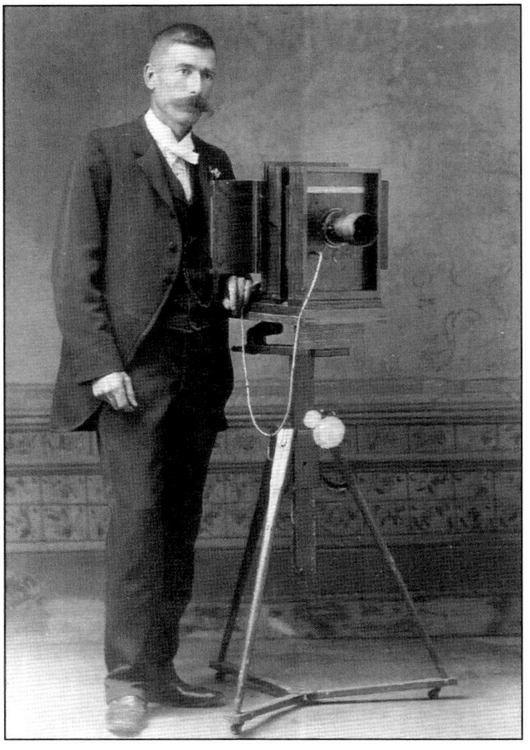

David I. Gardner helped preserve the history of the county with his photographic expertise. Born and reared in Adams County, he began his career in photography by 1888 and continued throughout most of his lifetime, not retiring until the 1930s. He died in 1942 at age 83. This photograph was taken of Gardner about 1895. (Courtesy H. W. Johnson Jr.)

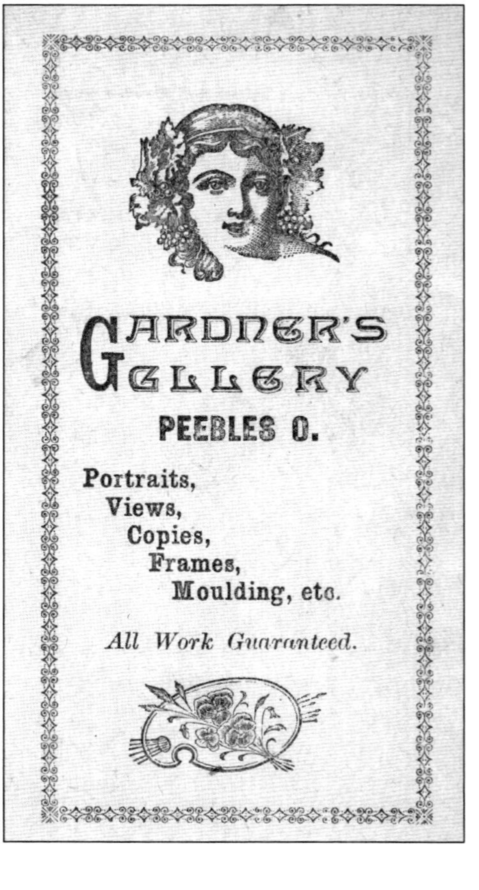

This is the front of a small advertising brochure produced by David I. Gardner. Printed around 1895, it reflects all the services he was offering his customers. (Courtesy H. W. Johnson Jr.)

In the mid-1890s, Peebles photographer David I. Gardner decided to expand his business. He opened this small shop in West Union, hoping to increase his patronage. How successful this second photography studio was is unknown. Notice Gardner's high-wheel bicycle parked beside his shop. (Courtesy Adams County Historical Society.)

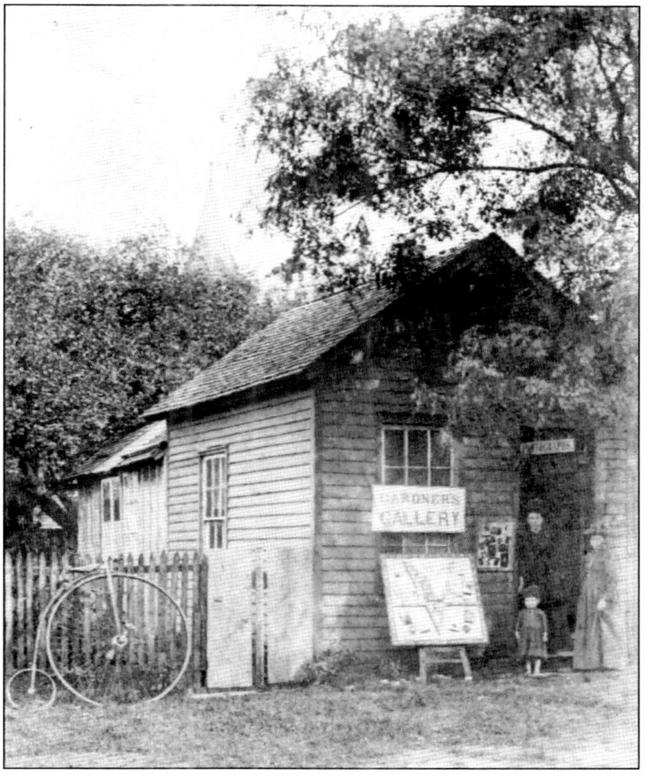

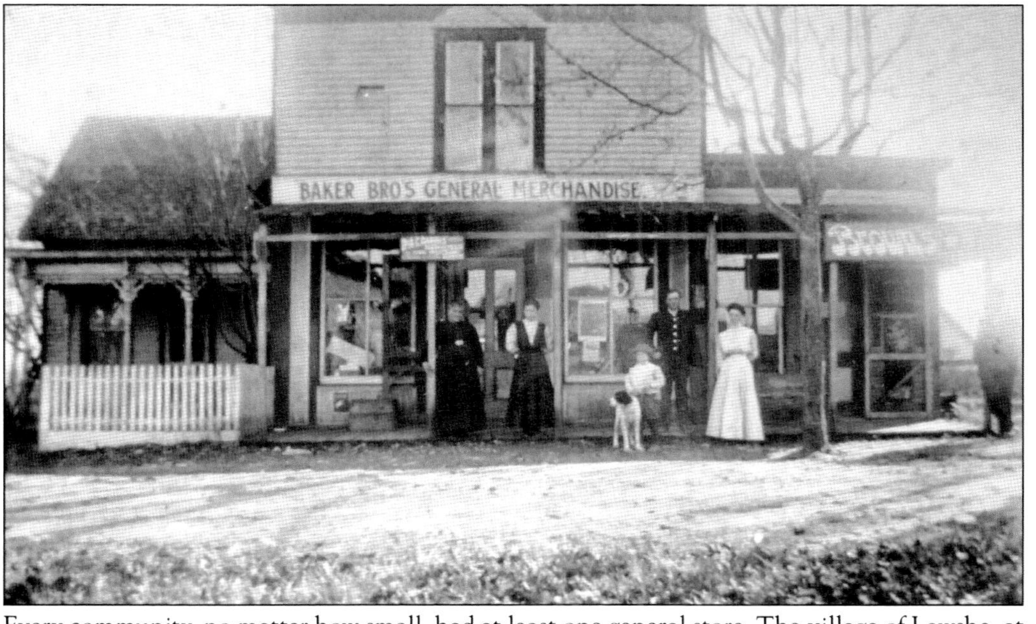

Every community, no matter how small, had at least one general store. The village of Lawshe, at the start of the 20th century, boasted of three such emporiums. The store that had the longest history in the town is pictured here about 1909. At that time, it was run by Hamer W. and George Baker—the Baker Brothers. The store closed in the mid-1970s. (Author's collection.)

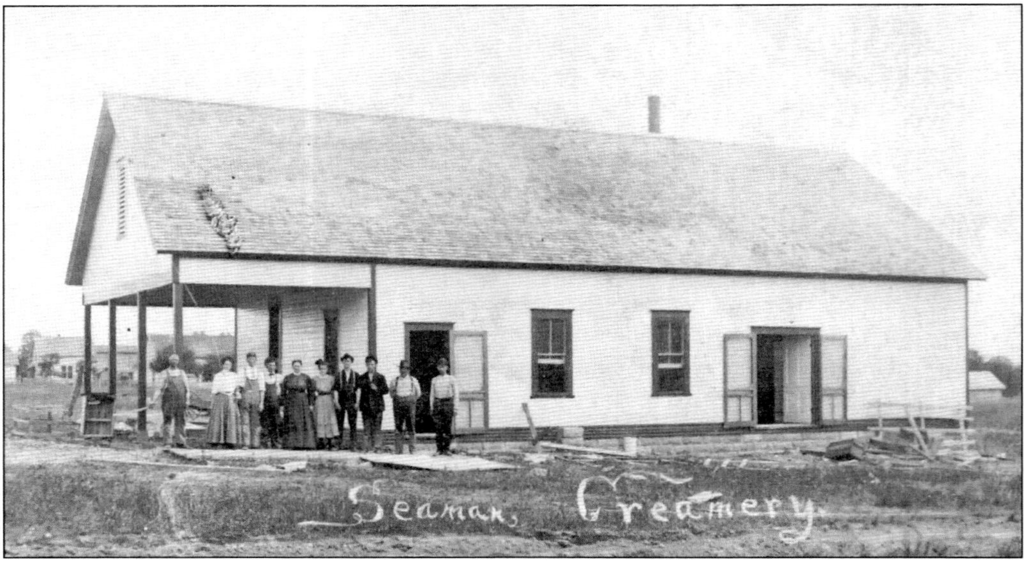

It is believed the two creameries shown on this page were built by the same company. The buildings appear to be identical in construction and size. The Seaman Creamery, pictured above, was erected in 1908 on the northeast corner of Broadway and Fourth Street by the Chicago Building and Manufacturing Company of Chicago, Illinois. A local group of shareholders owned and operated the creamery. The building was razed about 1960. The Manchester Creamery, shown below, was probably built around the same time as the Seaman Creamery. This building still stands on Eighth Street. A sign on the Manchester building as seen in this photograph indicates its builder was based in Chicago. It also states the material for the building came from Evansville, Indiana. Both the Manchester and Seaman Creameries bought fresh cream from local dairy farmers and converted it into creamery butter. (Both author's collection.)

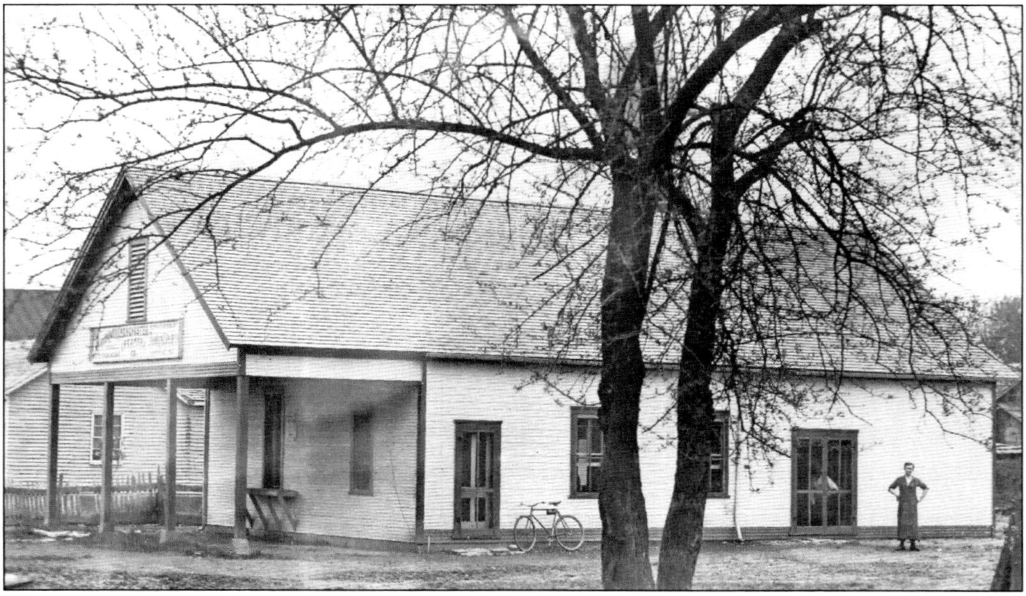

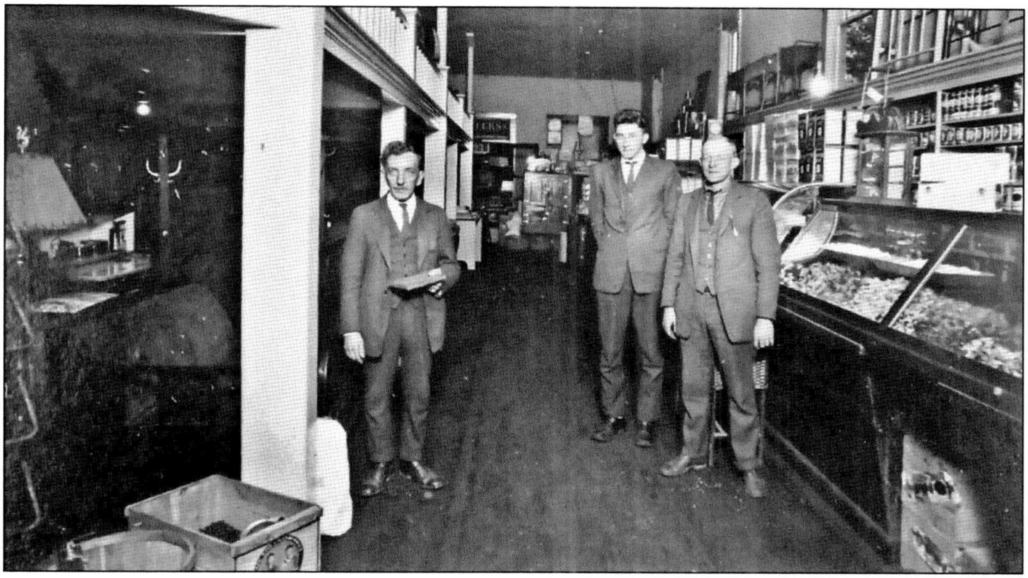

The Dot Food Store was located on Market Street in West Union across from the courthouse. Despite its name, the business sold other items, with an emphasis on furniture. Owner Charles E. Frame is standing on the left in this interior view of the store about 1915; the other two gentlemen are not identified. (Courtesy Mr. and Mrs. Robert C. Frame.)

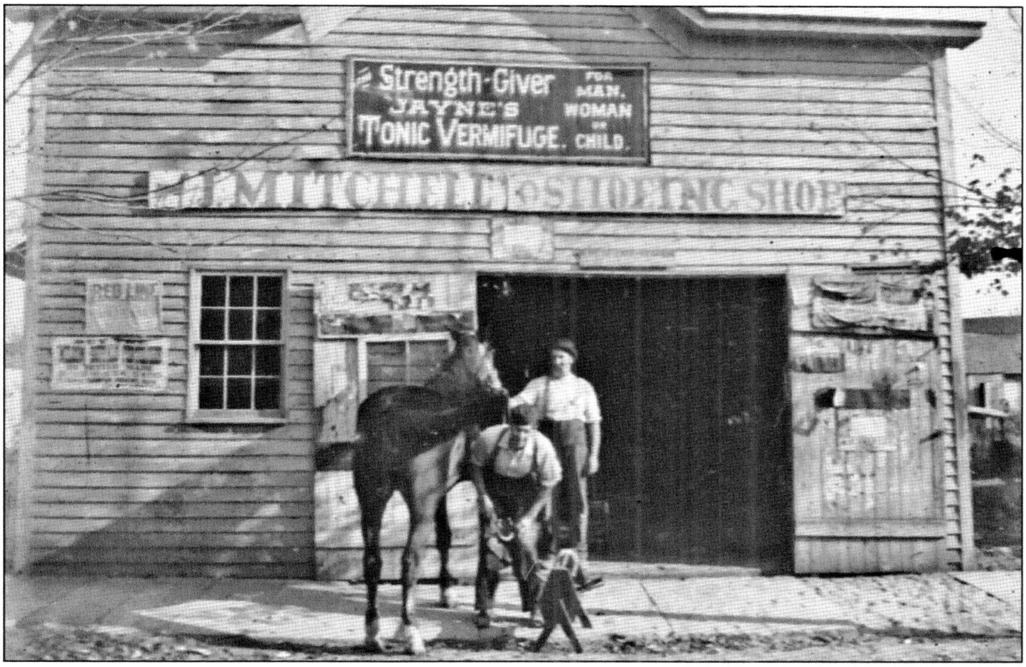

Peebles came into existence in 1883. That year saw an explosion of new structures being built, businesses opened, and homes erected. One of the first craftsmen to move into the new village that year was John B. Mitchell. A blacksmith by trade, Mitchell's specialty was horseshoeing. His was the first blacksmith shop in Peebles. He is shown here shoeing a horse in front of his Peebles shop around 1900. (Courtesy Lester and Jean Wallis.)

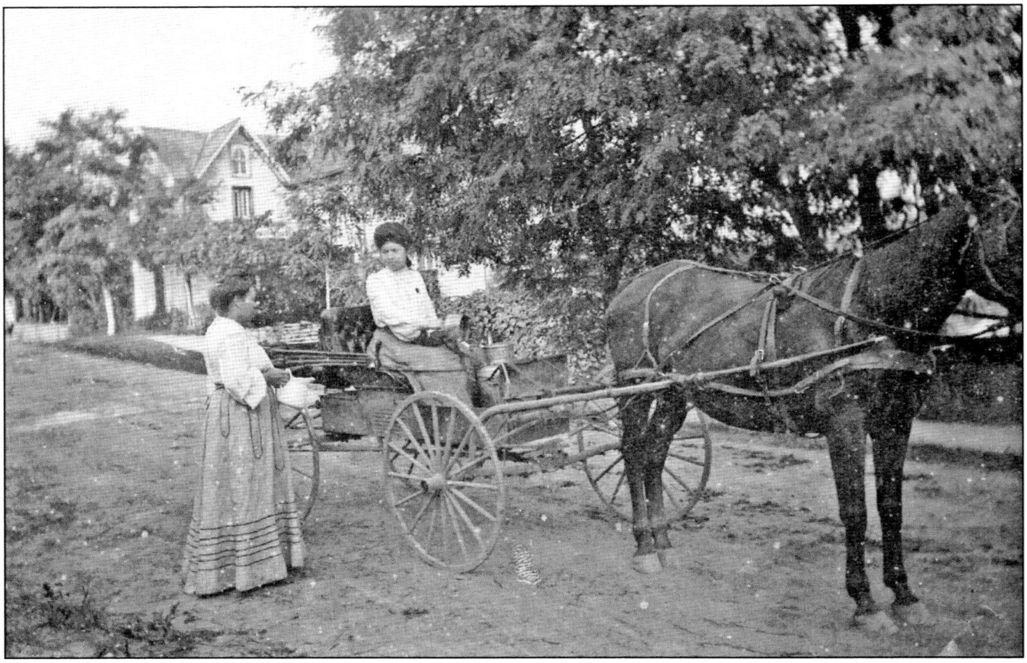

Here is a rare view of an early milk delivery route in Peebles taken about 1910. Clara Custer Bacon is selling a pitcher of milk to Jane Gardner. Bacon is holding the lid of her milk can, preparing to pour or dip milk into Gardner's pitcher. (Courtesy John and Carol Wickerham.)

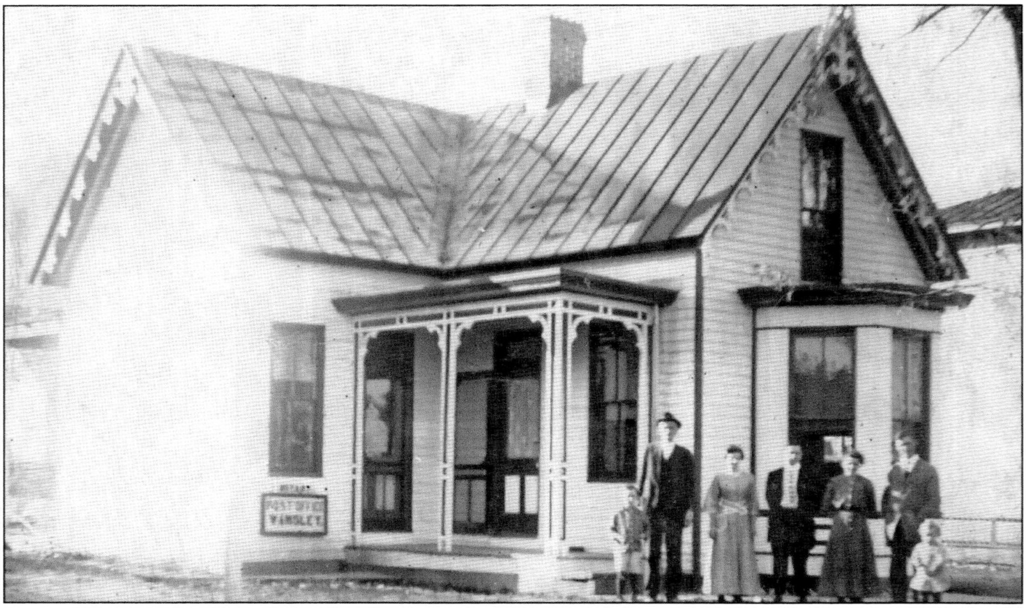

The little village of Wamsleyville was founded by William M. Wamsley in 1864. A post office was opened in the community in January 1869, with Wamsley appointed as the first postmaster. Shown here is a late Victorian cottage erected in Wamsleyville about 1885 by James and Sabrina Freeman. In 1909, when this photograph was taken, the village's post office occupied a side room in this home. (Author's collection.)

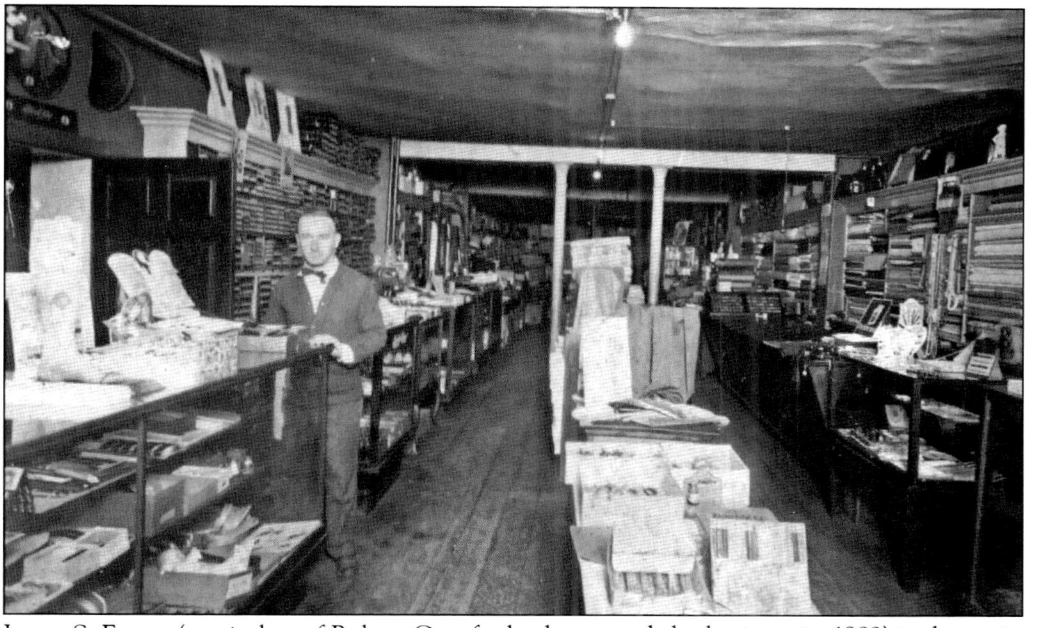

James S. Frame (son-in-law of Robert Crawford, who started the business in 1889) is shown in the Crawford and Frame Dry Goods Company in downtown West Union about 1925. Crawford and Frame Dry Goods provided sales and service to its customers for almost a century. Known as "Mr. Presbyterian," James Frame was a member of the West Union First Presbyterian Church and was the church's historian. (Author's collection.)

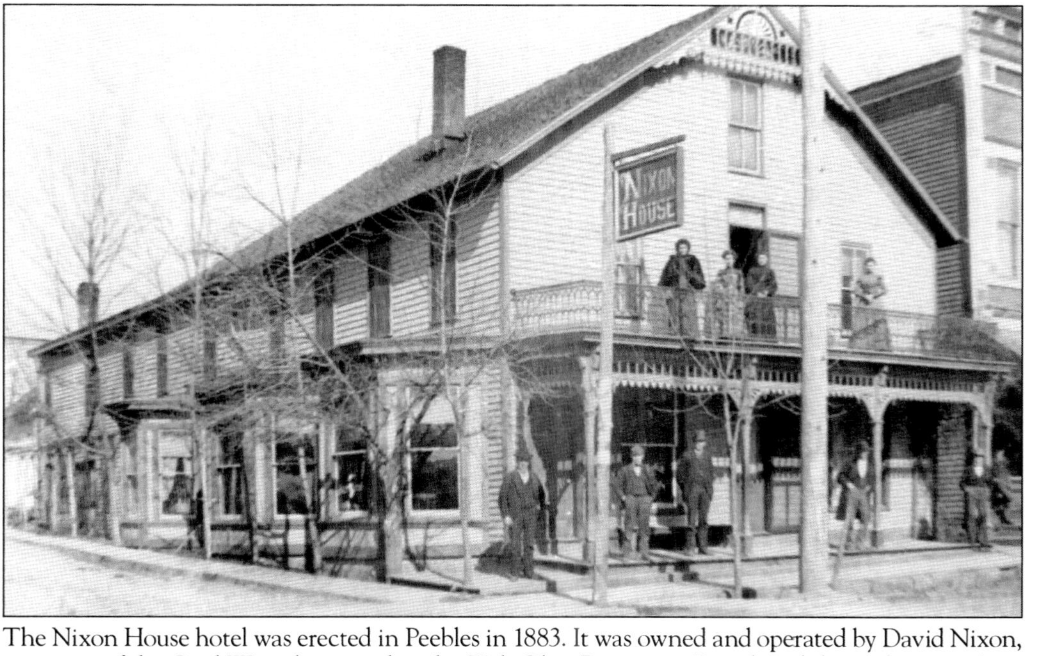

The Nixon House hotel was erected in Peebles in 1883. It was owned and operated by David Nixon, a veteran of the Civil War who served in the 70th Ohio Regiment. David, with his wife, Mary Ann Eakins, operated the hotel for 18 years before selling it to Francis and Alice Stultz. The hotel remained in business until 1917, when it was razed for commercial development. (Author's collection.)

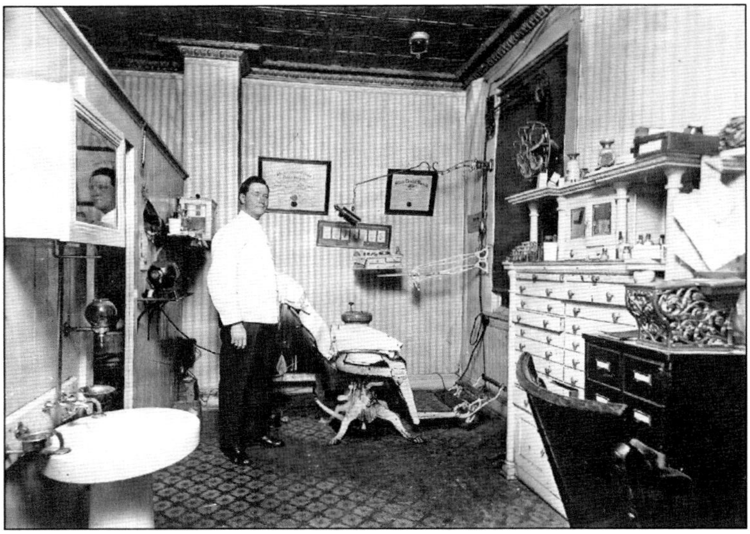

Dr. A. G. Hadley, a dentist, was among the early medical practitioners who opened an office in Peebles. Unfortunately the good doctor's future in the village was cut short when he died of pneumonia at age 30 in 1918. (Courtesy John and Carol Wickerham.)

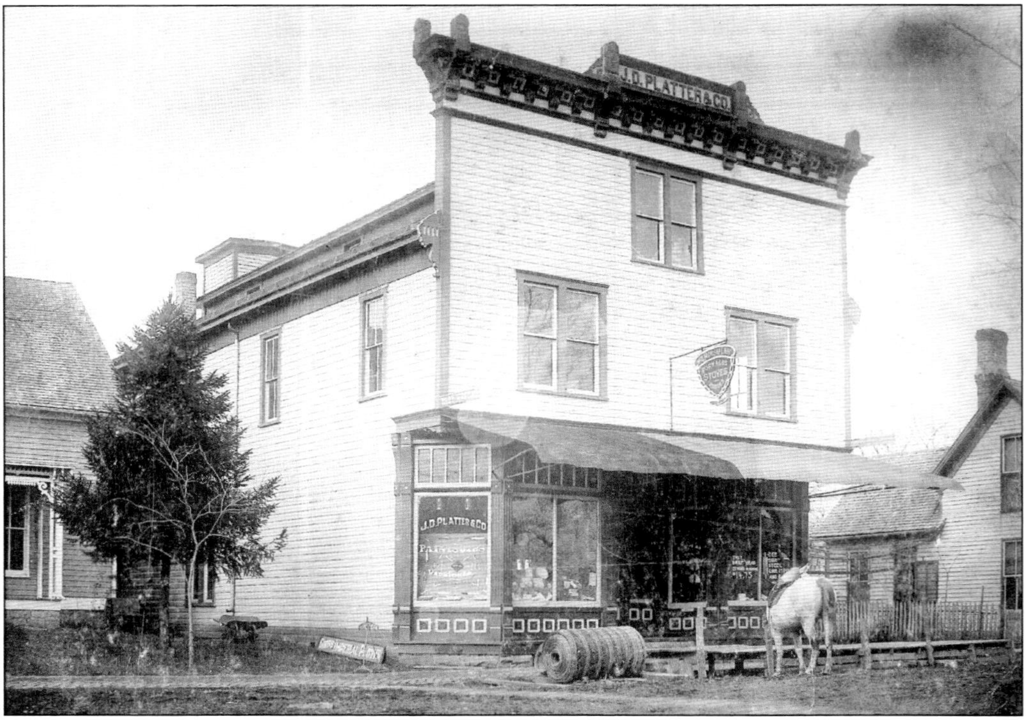

John D. Platter is credited with building the first business house in Peebles in 1883. He erected this large emporium about 1888 on the west side of north Main Street. Here, for several years, he sold hardware, farm implements, paints, Troy brand farm wagons, Peninsular brand stoves, Gibbs Imperial Plows, and just about whatever a person needed. James and Fred Morrison bought Platter's business in 1915. David I. Gardner took this photograph about 1905. (Courtesy John and Carol Wickerham.)

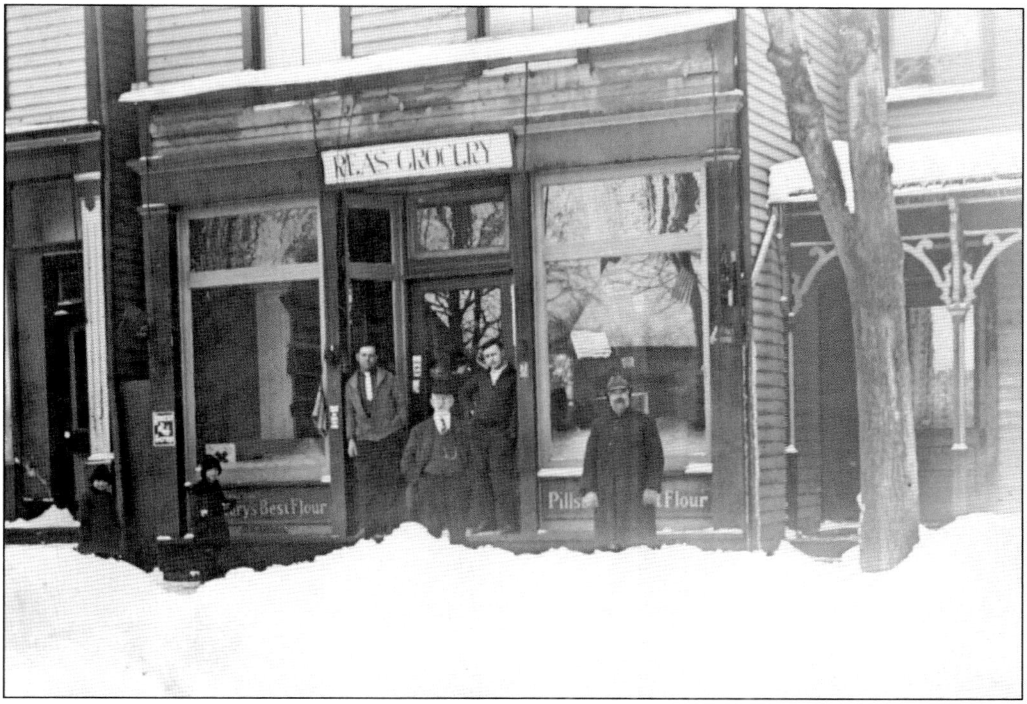

Every community needed a grocery. In the village of Winchester, James Rea decided to meet that need. Here is a *c.* 1905 view of Rea's Grocery on Main Street in the dead of winter. Rea ran this business for 40 years. (Author's collection.)

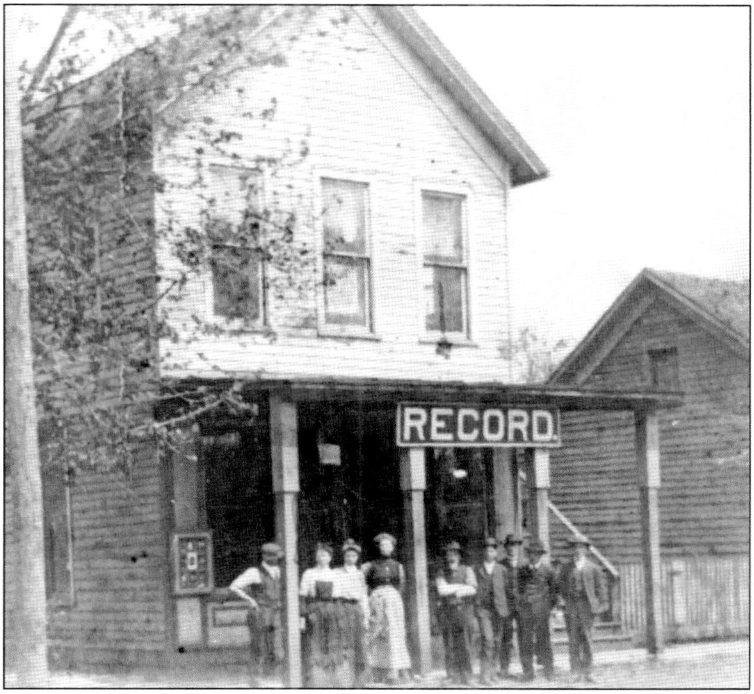

The *Adams County Record*, a Republican newspaper, was founded in 1902. It was published from 1904 to 1918 in this building that stood on the northeast corner of Mulberry and Market Streets in West Union. The *Record*'s first editor was Clarence J. Brown Sr., who was elected lieutenant governor of Ohio in 1918 while a resident of West Union. This photograph with the *Record*'s staff posing in front was taken around 1910. (Courtesy John Brodt.)

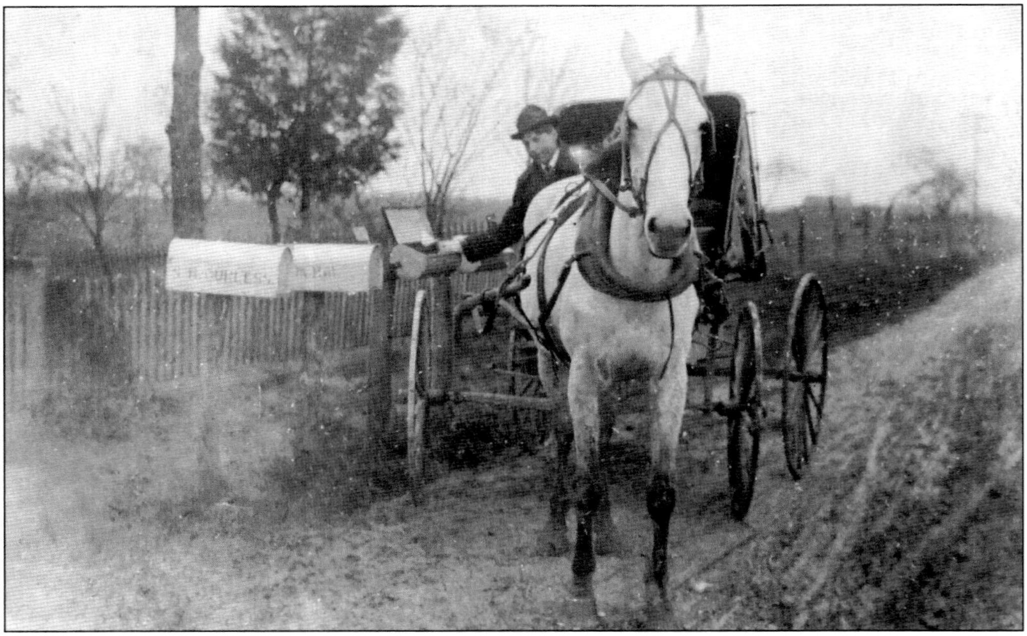

Mail carriers in horse-and-buggy days had to be tough characters. Dirt roads could be turned into mud following a storm, buggies provided little protection against the cold, sleet, and snow in the winter, and sometimes the horse's behavior could be very unpredictable. Here a carrier is seen delivering mail to S. B. Curless's mailbox in the vicinity of Youngsville around 1912. (Courtesy Adams County Historical Society.)

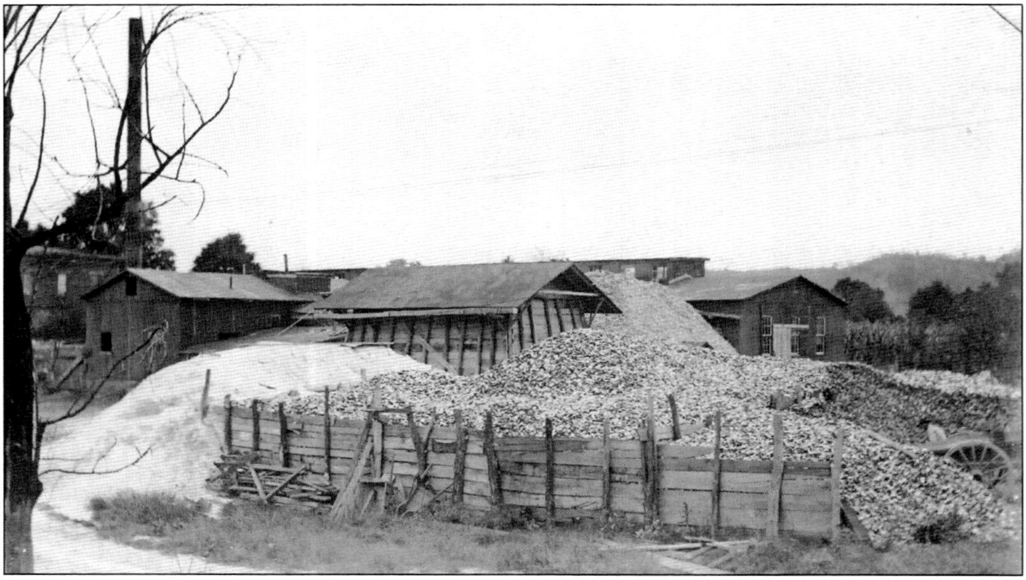

The Manchester Pearl Button Works was constructed in 1909 on Fourth Street. Mussel shells were harvested by the millions from the Ohio River, and button blanks were cut from them and shipped to New York City, where they were finished for the garment industry. Pictured is a c. 1912 view of the factory with mountains of used shells in the foreground. The factory closed in 1948. (Author's collection.)

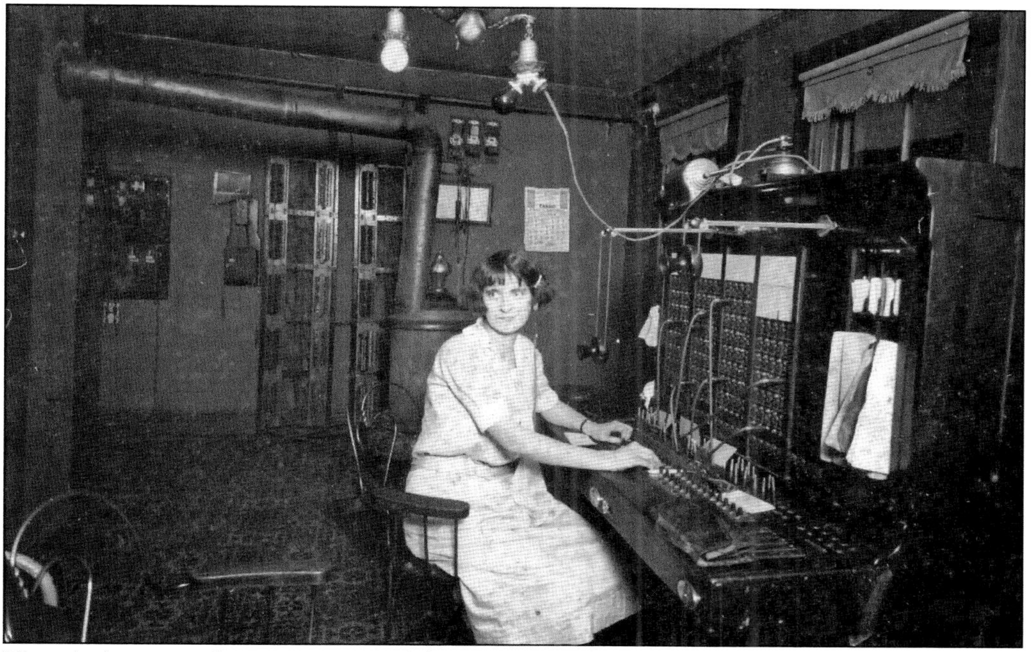

The telephone was slow in coming to Adams County. The first telephone line was strung in 1883, connecting Eureka Mills in Bentonville to Manchester and West Union. Acme Bell Telephone, established in 1899 in West Union, was the first local telephone company in the county. Pictured is Ida Florence Kennon Montgomery White, who served as a telephone operator in Peebles. This view was taken in November 1929. (Author's collection.)

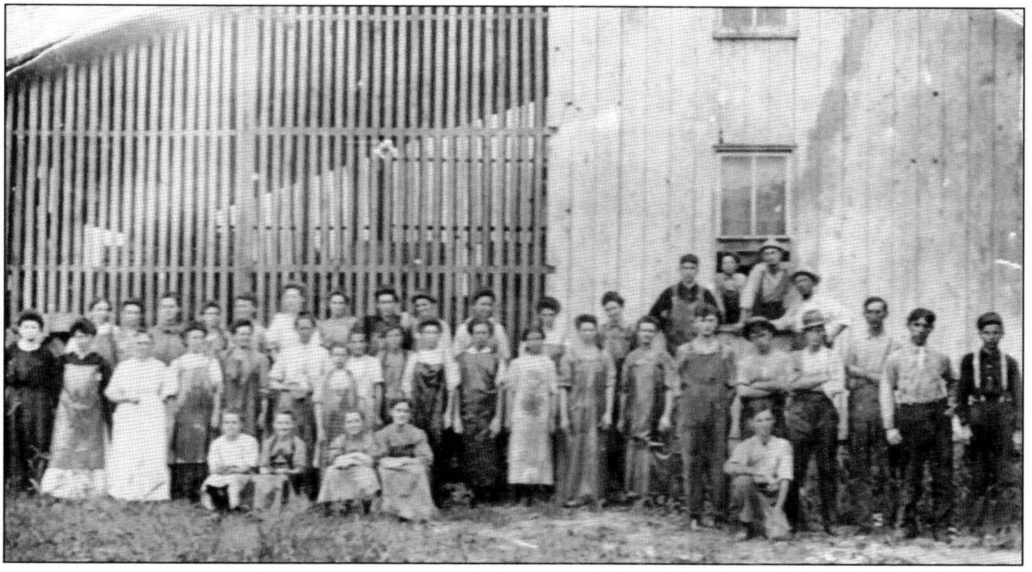

In 1900, H. T. Massie, with a small group of investors, built a canning factory in Winchester. The company contracted with local farmers to raise 75 acres of tomatoes to be processed by the new enterprise. Shown is a view of the factory with its workers around 1905. Several of the laborers were children, as child labor laws had not yet been enacted in Ohio. (Courtesy Adams County Historical Society.)

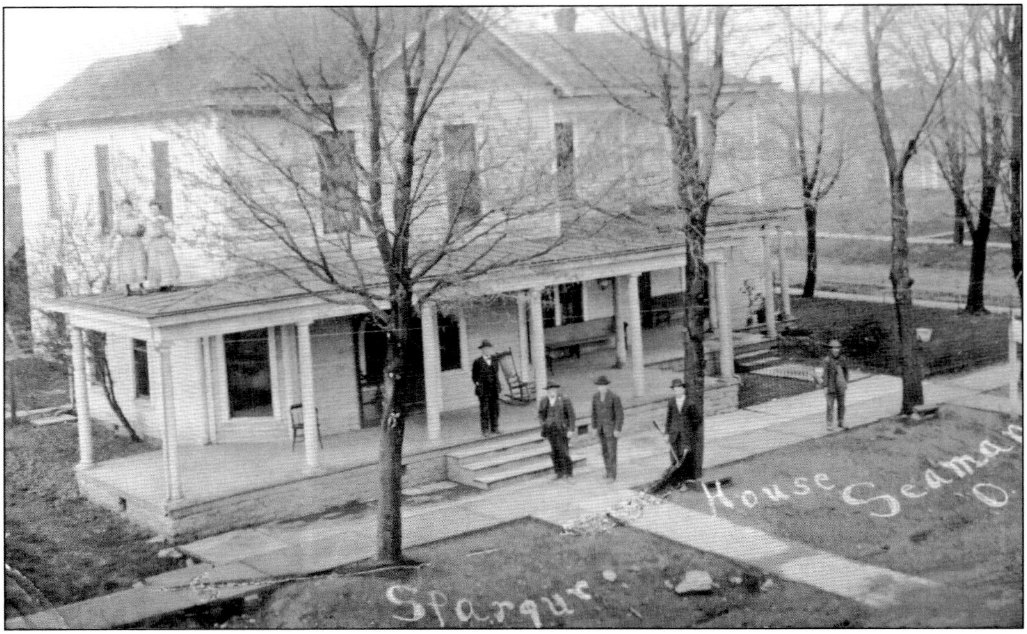

When John Q. Roads was building the first house and general store on the future site of the village of Seaman, he convinced a local farmer, James A. Young, to build a small hotel nearby. Young's new hotel was officially opened on July 4, 1888, and dubbed the Seaman Hotel. A subsequent owner, L. W. Spargur, renamed it Spargur House, as shown here in 1909. (Author's collection.)

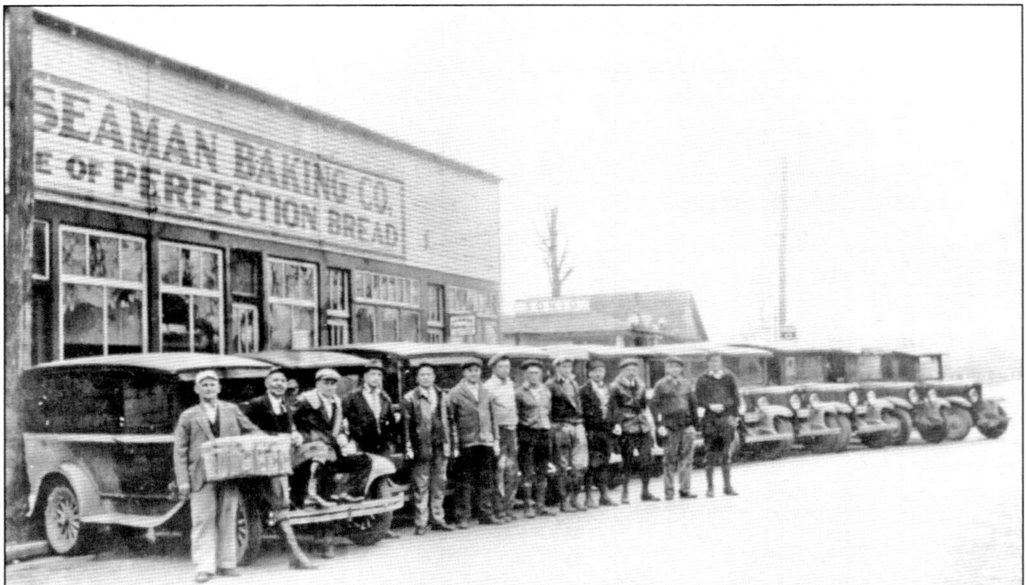

The Seaman Baking Company opened on First Street in 1926. By 1931, there were 20 employees, with 9 truck drivers delivering baked goods to Cincinnati, Portsmouth, Chillicothe, Greenfield, Wilmington, and other communities. Leaving at 5:00 a.m., they would distribute as many as 15,000 loaves of bread each day, as well as sweet rolls, buns, and donuts. Pennington Bread Company bought the business in 1938 and shut the bakery down. (Author's collection.)

The Peebles Roller Mills were built in the summer of 1884 beside the Cincinnati and Eastern Railway in the new village of Peebles. Erected by James and Harriet Rees, they sold the business in 1890 to Jacob, Henry, and William Custer. Operated as a grist- and sawmill, the structure burned to the ground in 1926 and was never rebuilt. This photograph dates to around 1895. (Author's collection.)

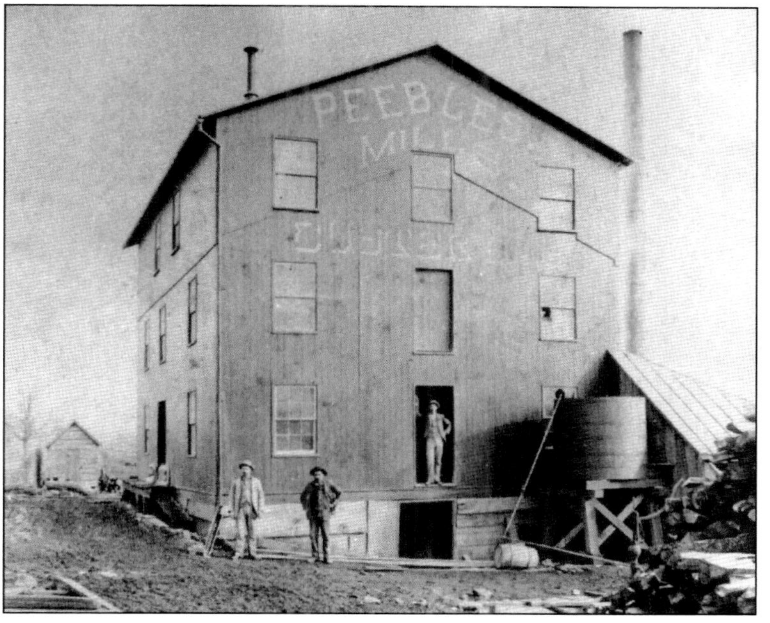

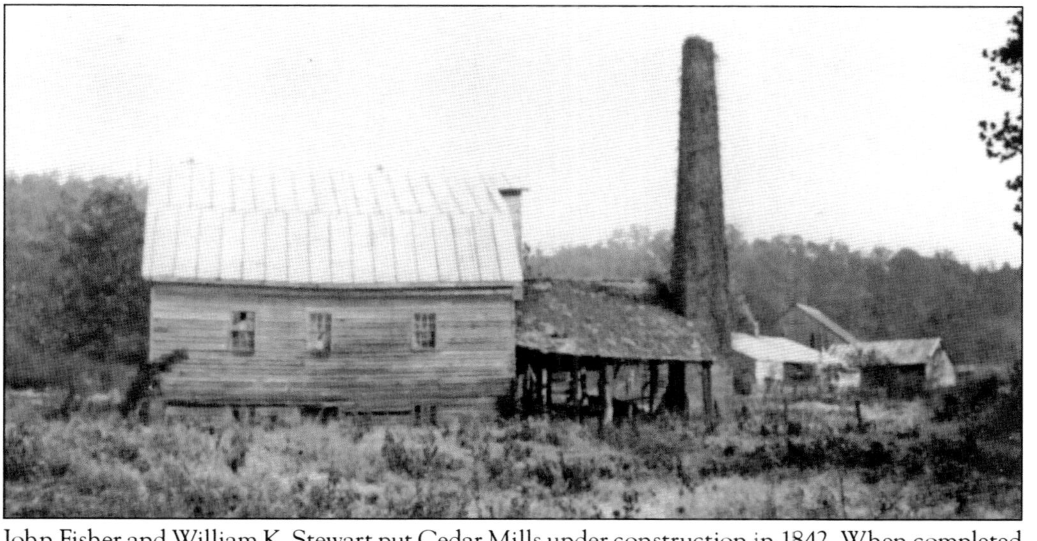

John Fisher and William K. Stewart put Cedar Mills under construction in 1842. When completed in 1844, the mill was powered by water channeled from a dammed-up pond on Cedar Run. Part of the old millrace is still visible today. Dugald Thompson later owned and operated the mill for several years. This picture of Cedar Mills was taken in 1933 by Wilbur Stout. The structure no longer stands. (Courtesy Ohio Historical Society.)

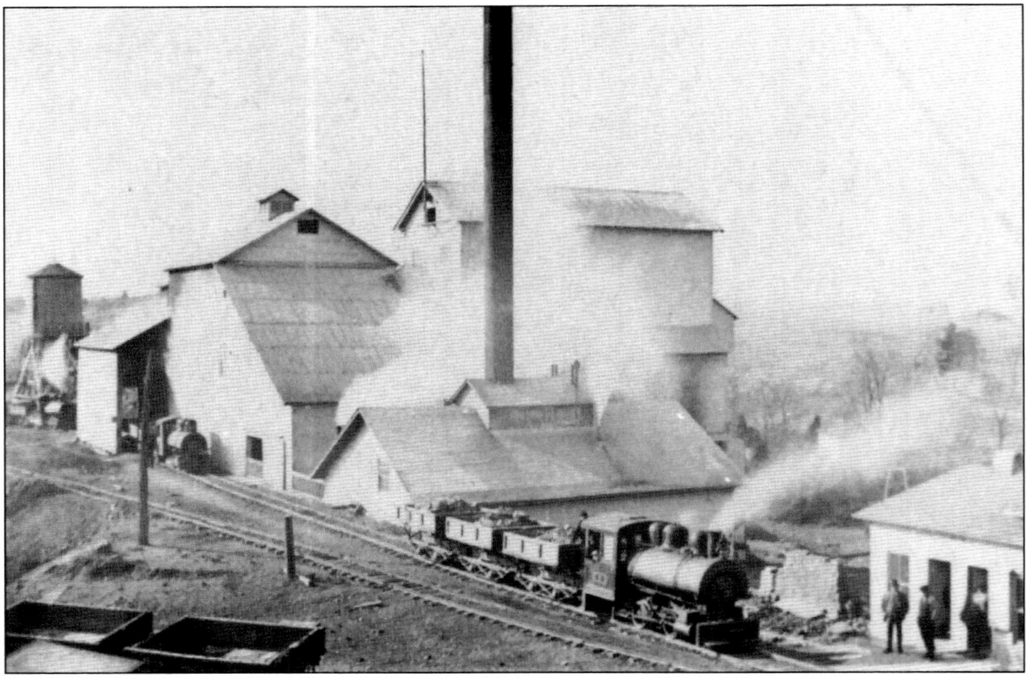

Since the earliest settlement of Adams County, man has utilized the abundance of stone in the area in many ways. This is a *c.* 1920 view of the main facilities at the Plum Run Quarry in Meigs Township. The Basic Dolomite Company of Cleveland, Ohio, then owned the operation. In later years, the New York Coal Sales and Company owned the quarry and operated it as Southern Ohio Quarries Company. (Author's collection.)

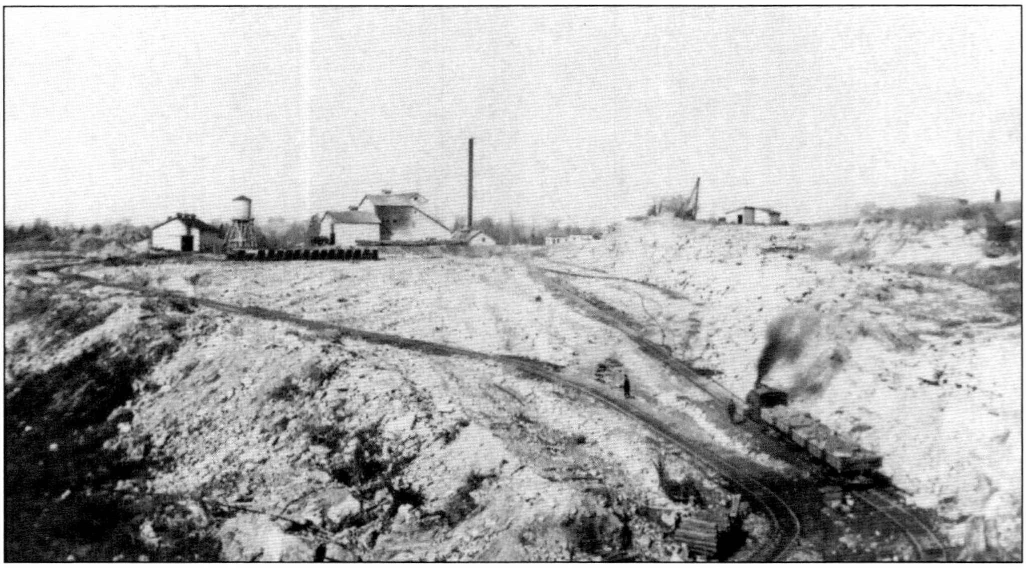

Here is another *c.* 1920 photograph illustrating how large the pit in Plum Run Quarry was in relation to the pulverizing mill in the background. The small locomotives and hopper cars used for hauling the stone out of the pit to the mill were called dinky trains. Dump trucks do the hauling today. (Author's collection.)

A large and powerful steam shovel scoops up the newly blasted stone in the Plum Run Quarry around 1920. On top of the ledge are members of the blasting crew with their tall drill. A series of holes would be drilled in a row, then packed with explosives and detonated to free up more loose rock to be shoveled into the dinky train's hopper cars. (Author's collection.)

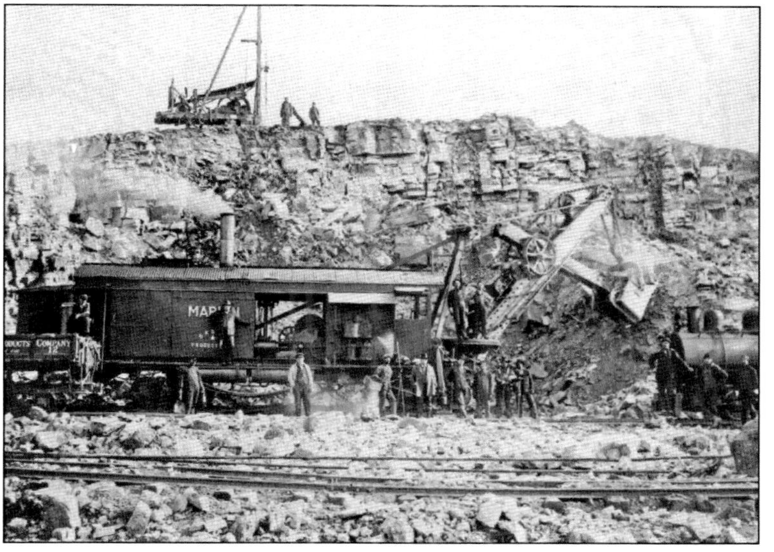

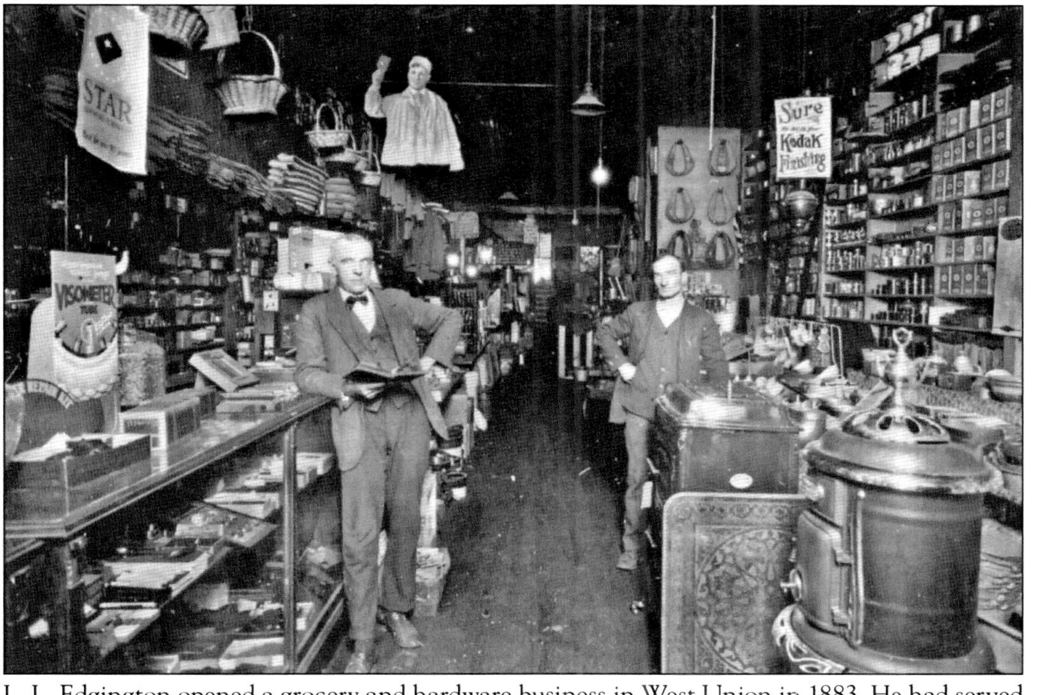

L. L. Edgington opened a grocery and hardware business in West Union in 1883. He had served as a captain in Company B of the 70th Ohio Regiment. His store was on Market Street opposite the courthouse square. His sons, Sherman and Eustace, were taken into the business with him. Here is a c. 1910 photograph of the L. L. Edgington and Sons store with Sherman on the left; the man on the right is thought to be Eustace. (Courtesy Adams County Historical Society.)

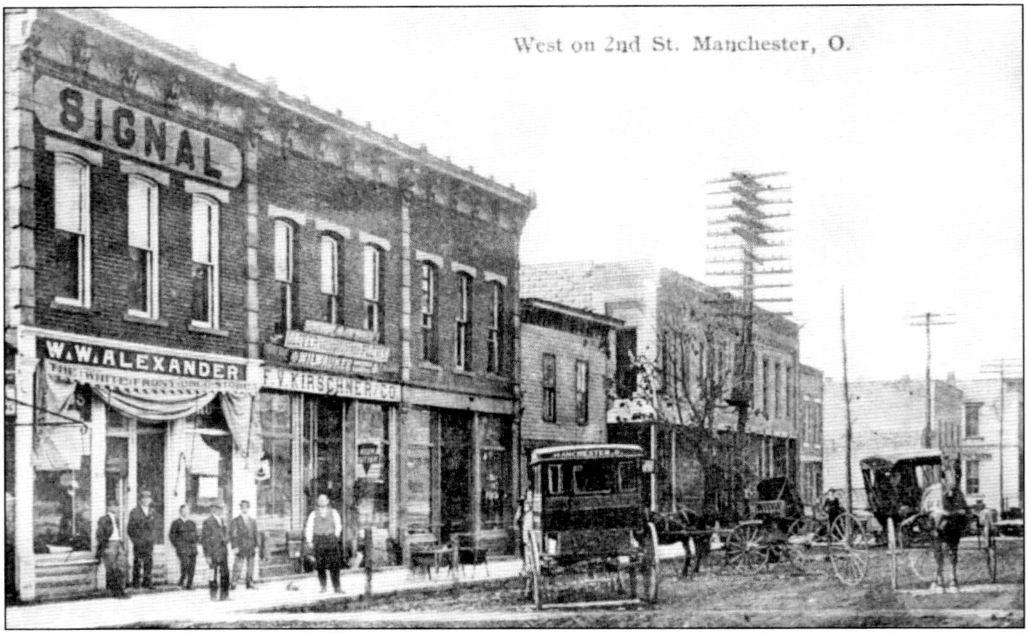

It was a busy day in downtown Manchester when this picture-postcard view was photographed in 1917. The office of the *Manchester Signal* was on the second floor of W. W. Alexander's White Front Drug Store. F. V. Kirschner's farm-implement business was displaying some of its products on the sidewalk. H. C. Brown's hack is parked in front of the stores, perhaps dropping off customers. (Author's collection.)

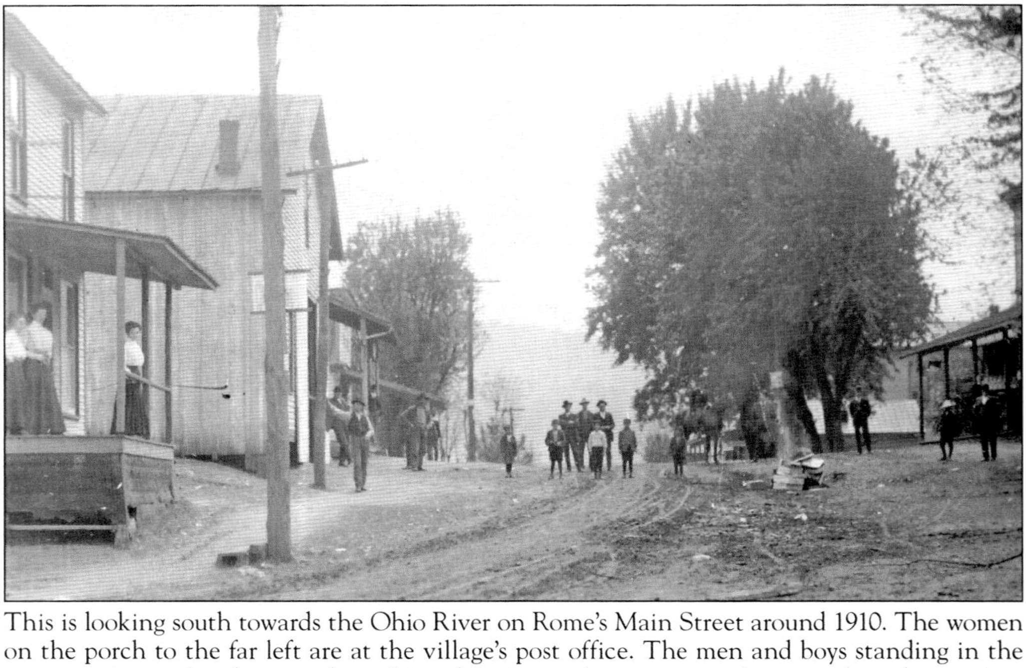

This is looking south towards the Ohio River on Rome's Main Street around 1910. The women on the porch to the far left are at the village's post office. The men and boys standing in the street staring at the photographer taking this picture do not seem to have much to do on a lazy summer day. (Author's collection.)

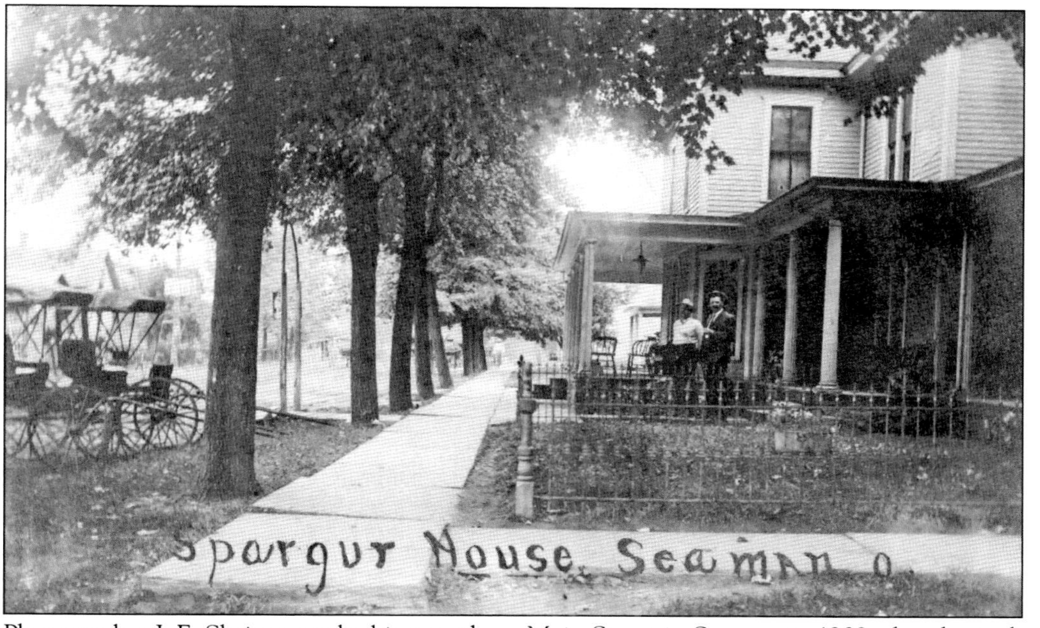

Photographer J. E. Shriver was looking south on Main Street in Seaman in 1909 when he took this photograph. The Spargur House hotel is on the right. (Author's collection.)

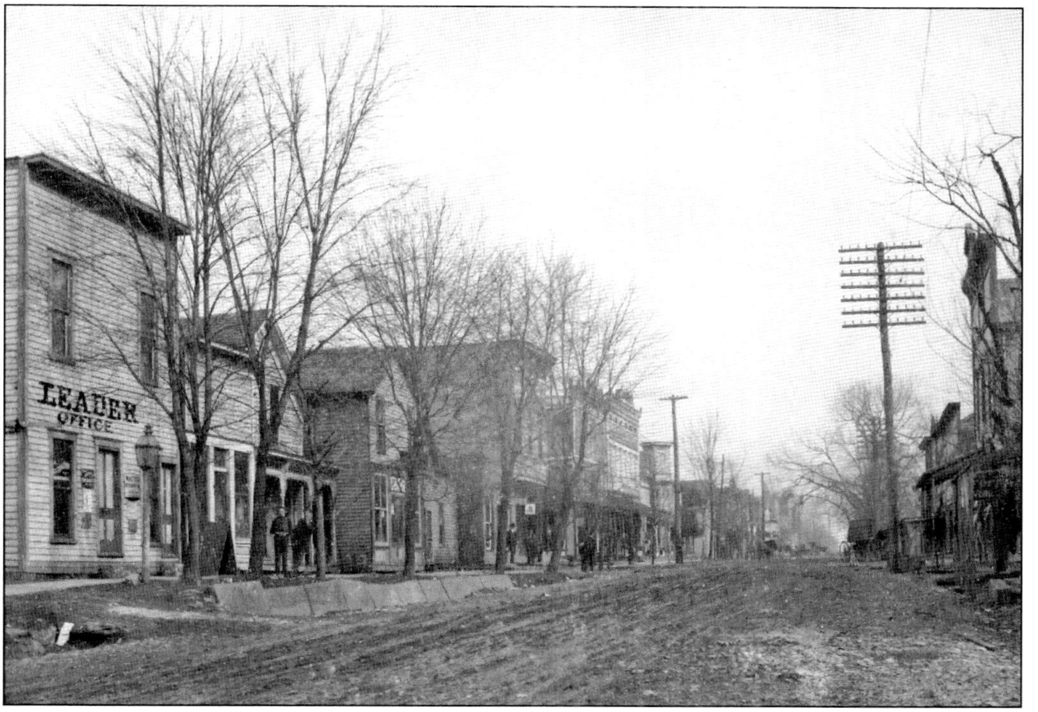

David I. Gardner shot this scene of Main Street in Peebles about 1900. At that time, the growing village had its own weekly newspaper known as the *Leader*. Its office is on the far left. Notice the dirt streets. (Courtesy John and Carol Wickerham.)

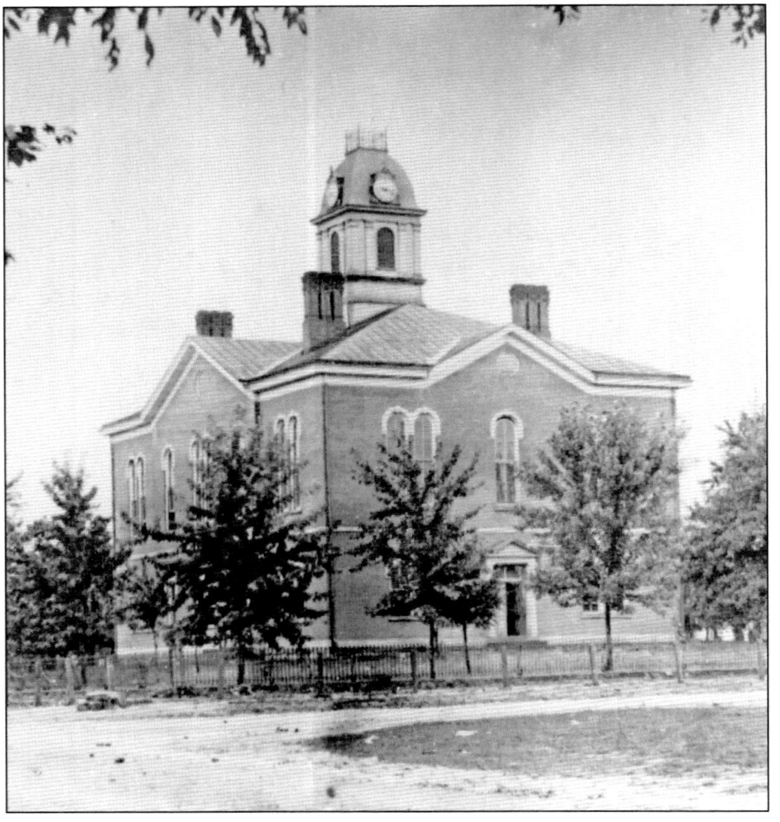

Four courthouses have graced the courthouse square. This is the third structure, photographed about 1885 by David I. Gardner. This Italianate-style brick building was dedicated on July 4, 1876, as part of the nation's centennial celebration that year. This courthouse burned on February 25, 1910, under somewhat dubious circumstances, as the county was then embroiled in a wrenching vote-selling scandal that gained national attention. (Courtesy Adams County Historical Society.)

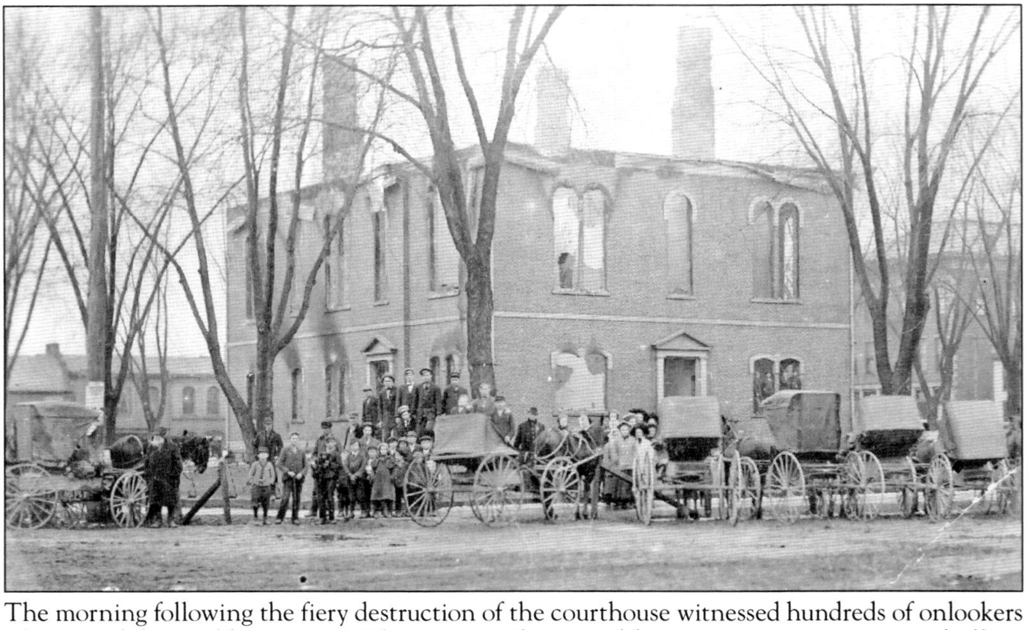

The morning following the fiery destruction of the courthouse witnessed hundreds of onlookers who visited the smoldering ruins. The county jail was used for temporary courtrooms and offices for more than a year until a new courthouse was completed. (Author's collection.)

Nine

Recreation and Celebration

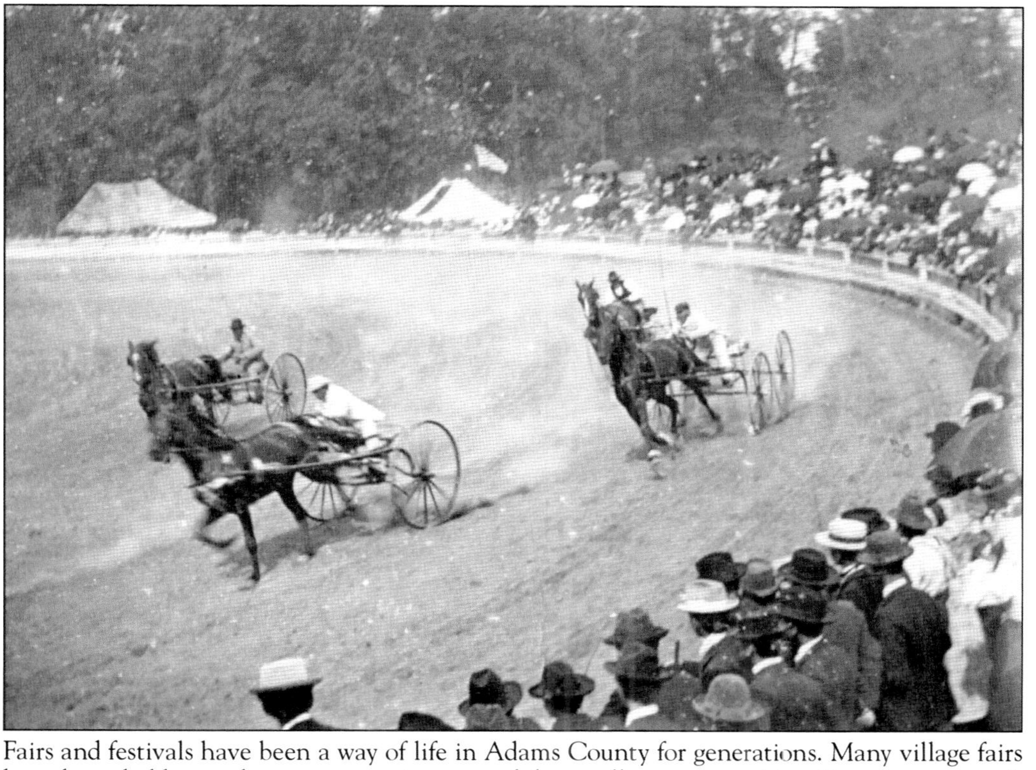

Fairs and festivals have been a way of life in Adams County for generations. Many village fairs have been held over the years, even in some of the smallest communities. Here is a racetrack scene at the Bentonville Fairgrounds taken by Lizzie Treber about 1895. (Courtesy William and Bessie J. Sininger.)

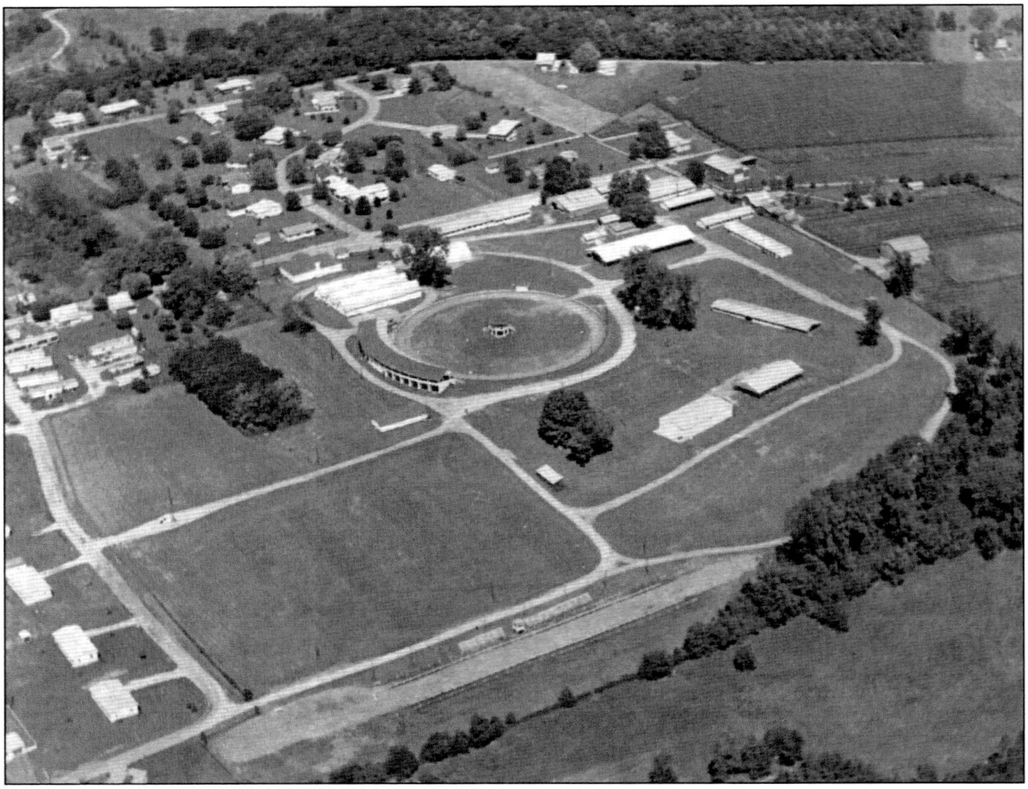

The Adams County Agricultural Society was organized in 1888. Its first annual fair was held that year in West Union. This aerial photograph of the county fairgrounds dates to the mid-1960s. (Author's collection.)

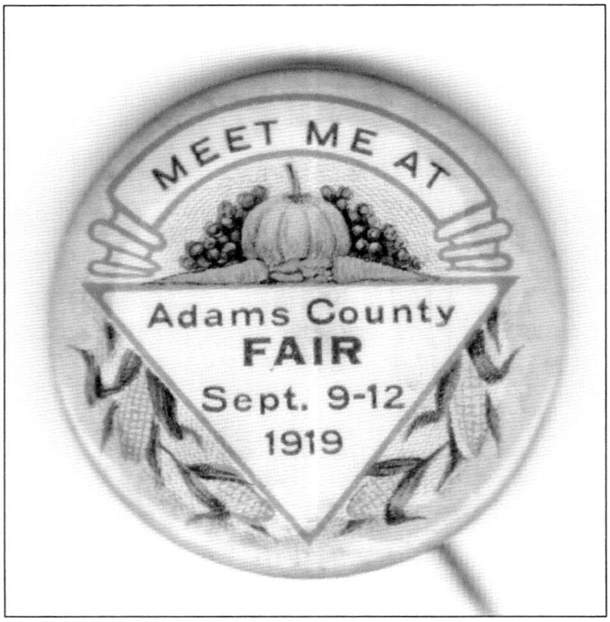

This is a commemorative enameled button that reminded people to attend the 1919 Adams County Fair. (Author's collection.)

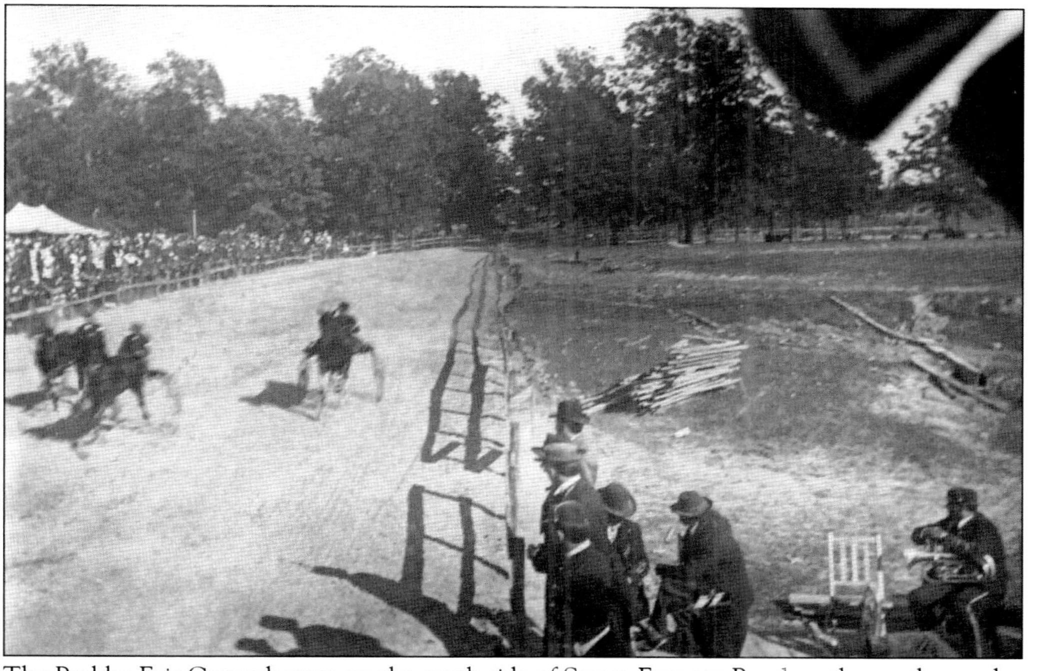

The Peebles Fair Grounds were on the south side of Steam Furnace Road on the southern edge of the village. This view of the racetrack was taken around 1905 by David I. Gardner. (Courtesy John and Carol Wickerham.)

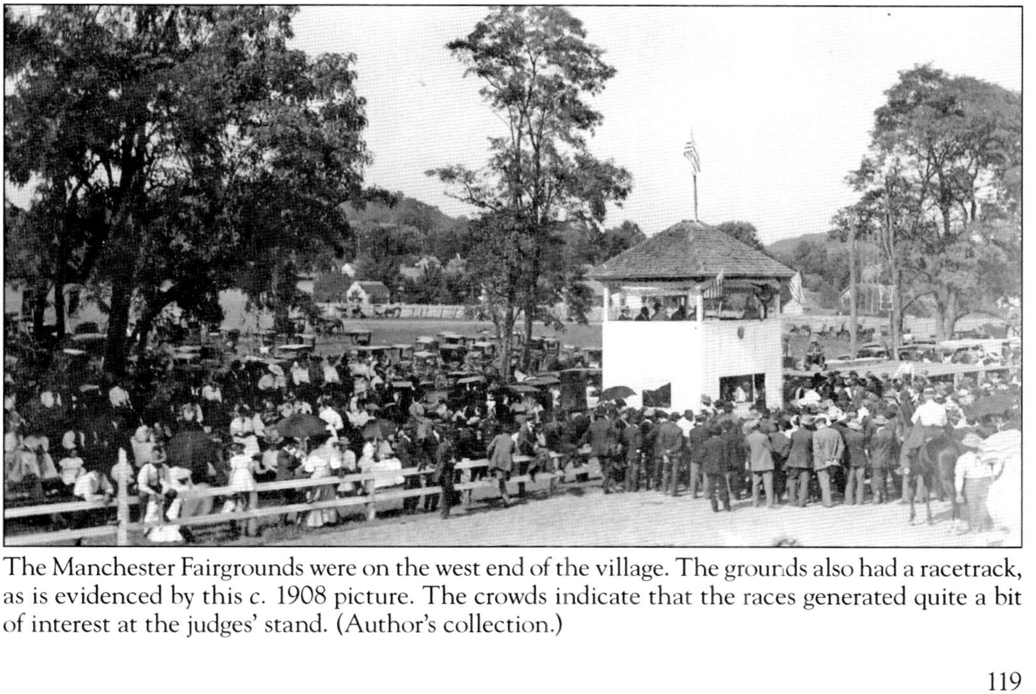

The Manchester Fairgrounds were on the west end of the village. The grounds also had a racetrack, as is evidenced by this *c.* 1908 picture. The crowds indicate that the races generated quite a bit of interest at the judges' stand. (Author's collection.)

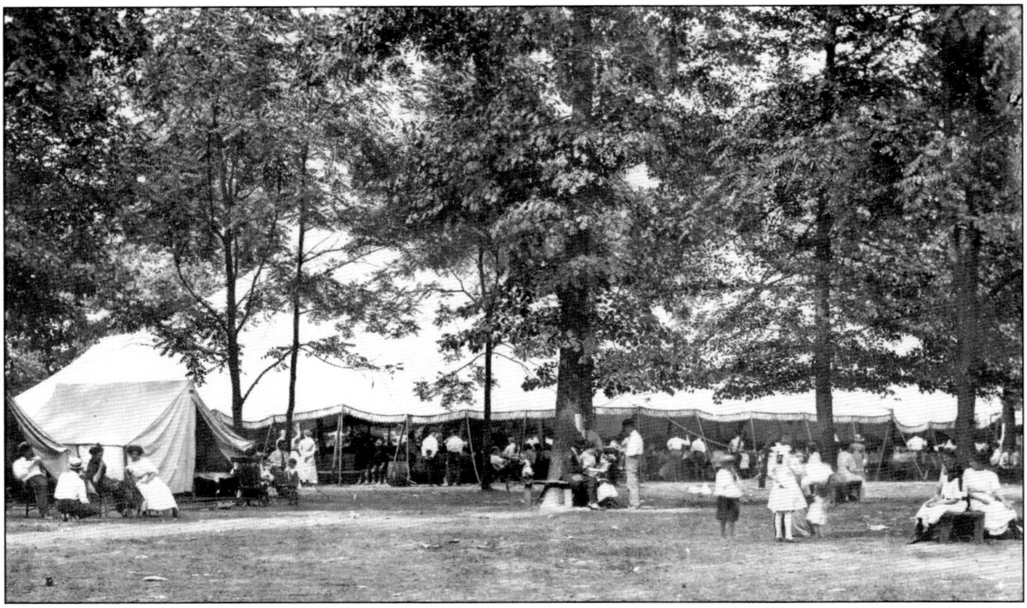

The Chautauqua was an annual event designed to bring learning and culture to rural America. The first Chautauqua held in Adams County was at Peebles in 1906. This is a view of the large auditorium tent where scientific demonstrations, readings, lectures, musical presentations, and such would take place. This photograph was taken about 1910 by David I. Gardner. (Author's collection.)

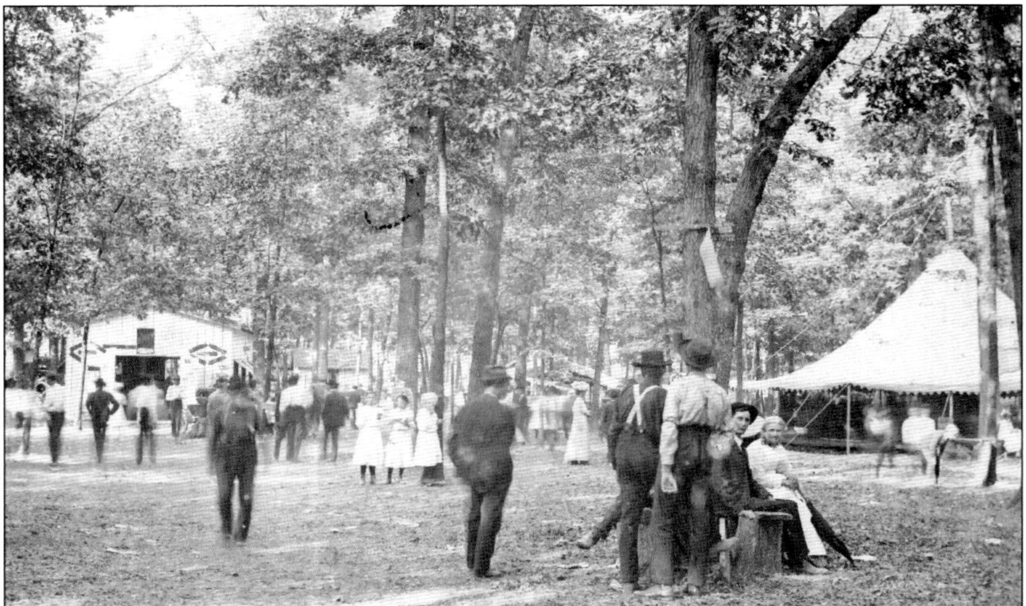

This is a general view of Custer's Grove in Peebles, where the Chautauqua was conducted each year. The large tent to the right is probably the dining tent. The annual Chautauqua became a great place to meet friends and family while experiencing artistic, scientific, and recreational opportunities. Chautauquas were eventually held in West Union, Winchester, and Manchester. (Courtesy John and Carol Wickerham.)

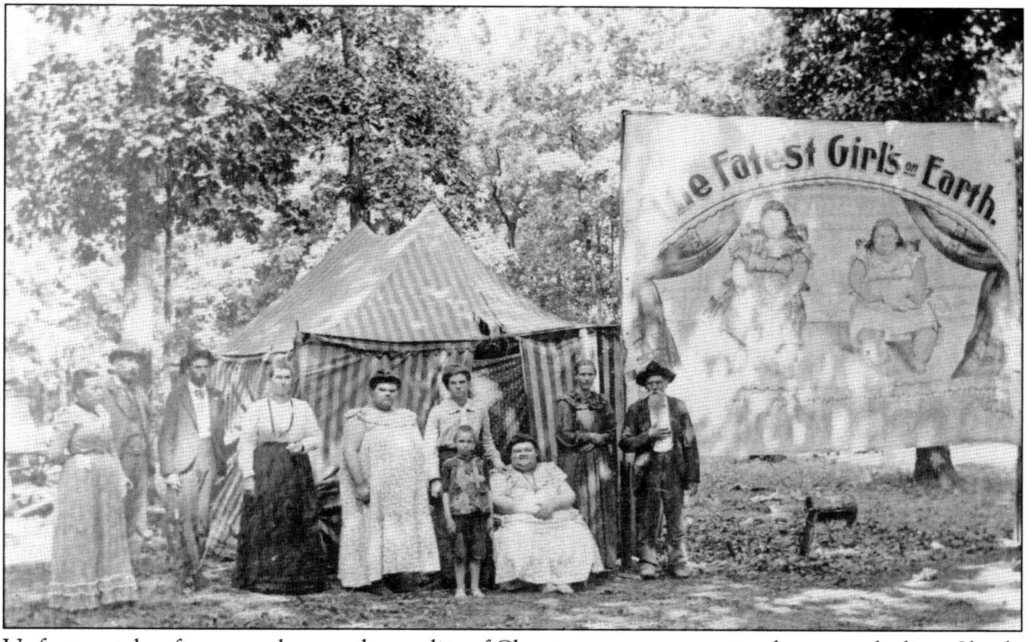

Unfortunately, after several years, the quality of Chautauqua programming began to decline. Slowly the cultural enlightenment of the rural population changed into more of a sideshow or circus. As seen here, more emphasis was being placed on entertainment than education and culture. During the 1920s, the Chautauquas in Adams County passed from the scene. (Author's collection.)

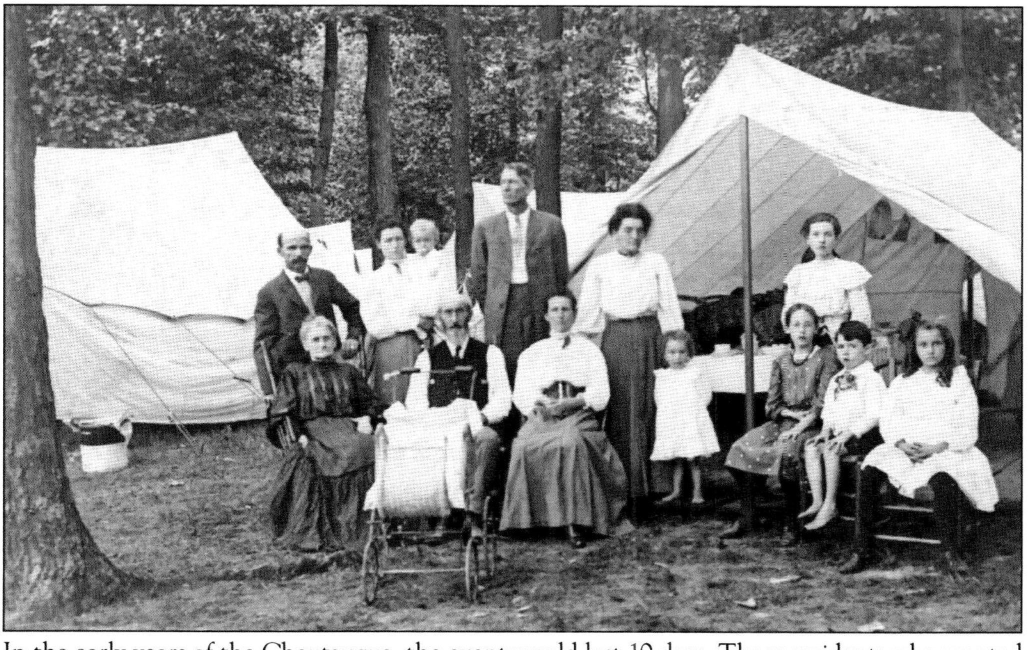

In the early years of the Chautauqua, the event would last 10 days. Those residents who wanted to spend several days at the Chautauqua could rent tents and camping supplies and live on the grounds for as many days as they wished. Here is the David Nixon family posing in front of their tent around 1910. (Courtesy John and Carol Wickerham.)

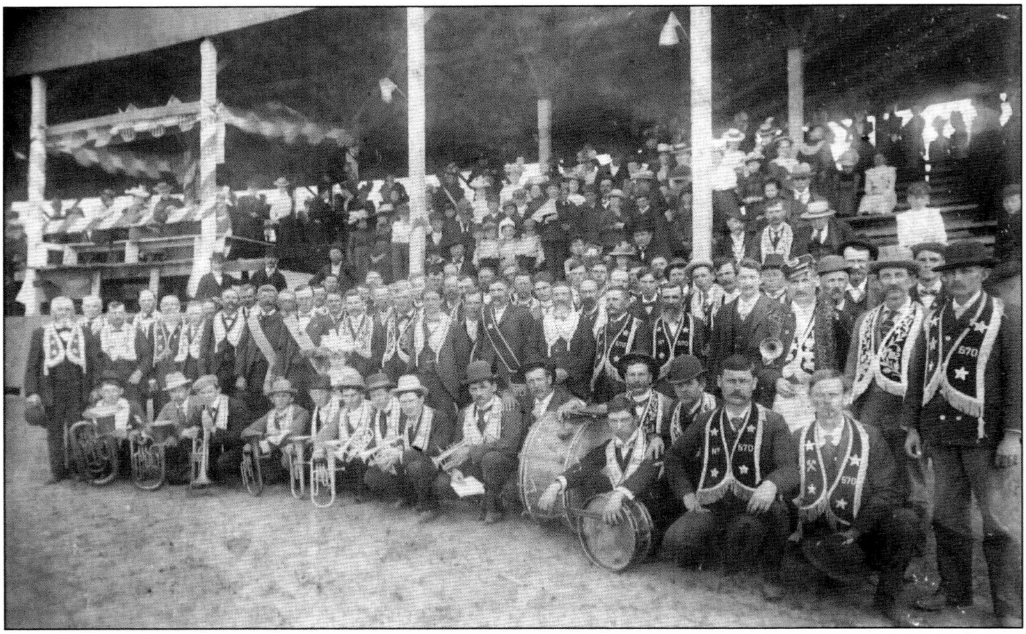

Lodges used to be a major force in the county. The Masonic lodge, Independent Order of Odd Fellows (IOOF), Knights of Pythias, and Improved Order of Red Men were all represented. This is an annual family meeting of the West Union IOOF lodge at the county fairgrounds around 1915. This organization was founded in 1874. (Author's collection.)

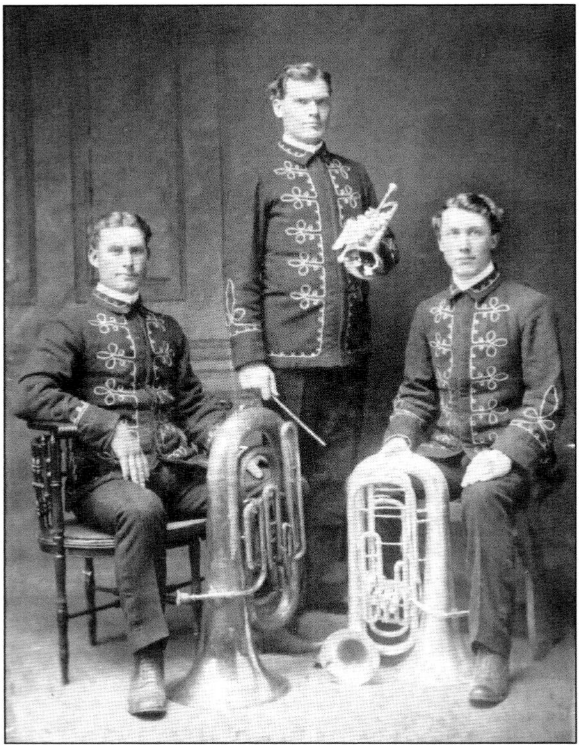

One of the earliest community bands in Adams County was organized in West Union in March 1850. Soon they became the rage all over the county. Certainly one of the foremost musicians who helped the movement to start local bands was Roy Liston of Wamsleyville. Roy, with his brothers James and Floyd, were leaders and motivators of a late-19th-century musical revolution in Adams County. Shown here are, from left to right, James, Roy, and Floyd Liston around 1898. (Author's collection.)

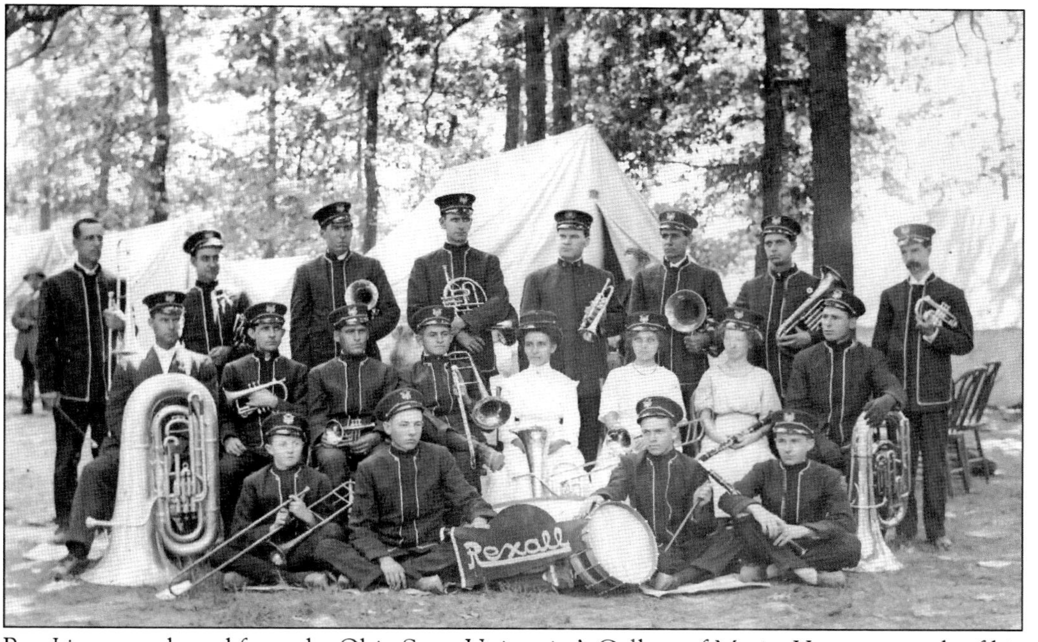

Roy Liston graduated from the Ohio State University's College of Music. He spent much of his time teaching music in public schools, including Manchester and Peebles. He also organized his own community band while living in Peebles. While performing at the Peebles Chautauqua on August 17, 1911, Roy had photographer David I. Gardner take this photograph of the Peebles band. (Courtesy Lester and Jean Wallis.)

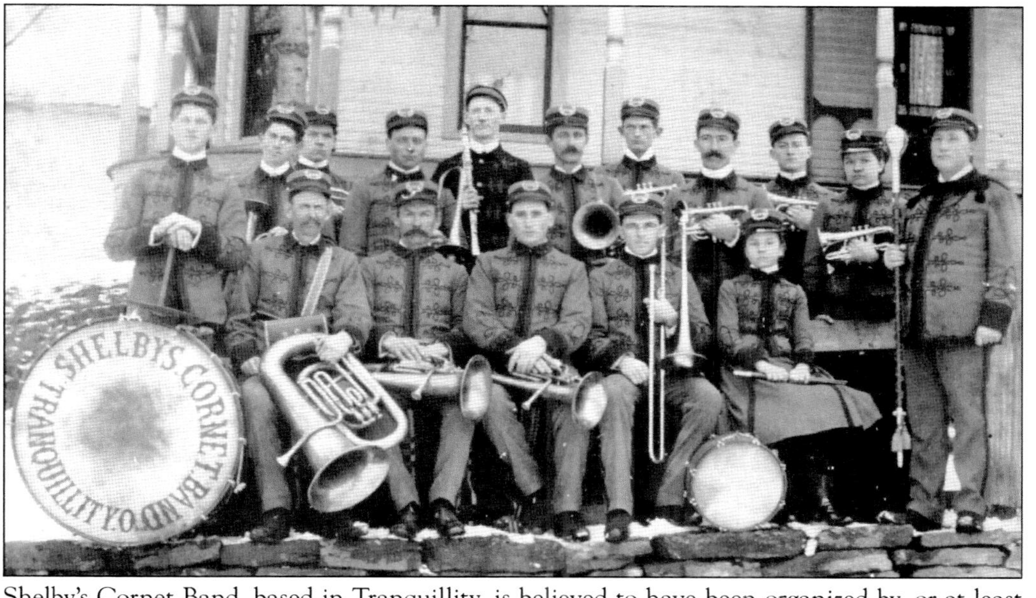

Shelby's Cornet Band, based in Tranquillity, is believed to have been organized by, or at least named in honor of, Ora Dell Shelby. Ora attended the University of Cincinnati College of Music, majoring in piano, but in her obituary in the *Adams County News* she was described as "probably the first girl in this county to play a brass instrument proficiently." This photograph was taken on the porch of Dr. E. M. Gaston's home in Tranquillity around 1912. (Author's collection.)

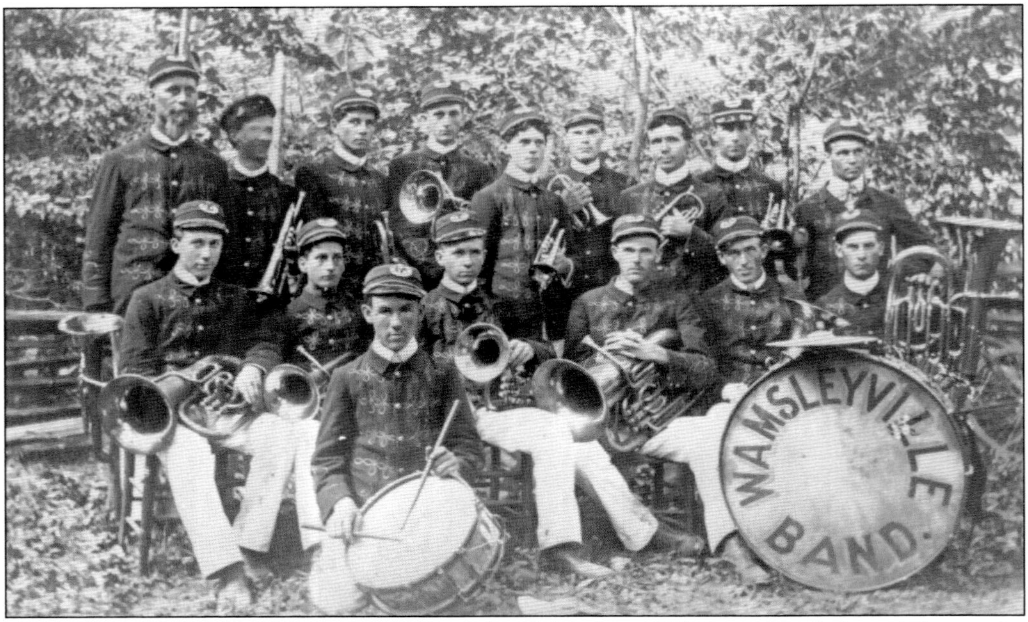

Regardless of how small the community, a local band could be organized there. This is the Wamsleyville Band as photographed in 1900. The only member identified is George Miranda on the snare drum. (Author's collection.)

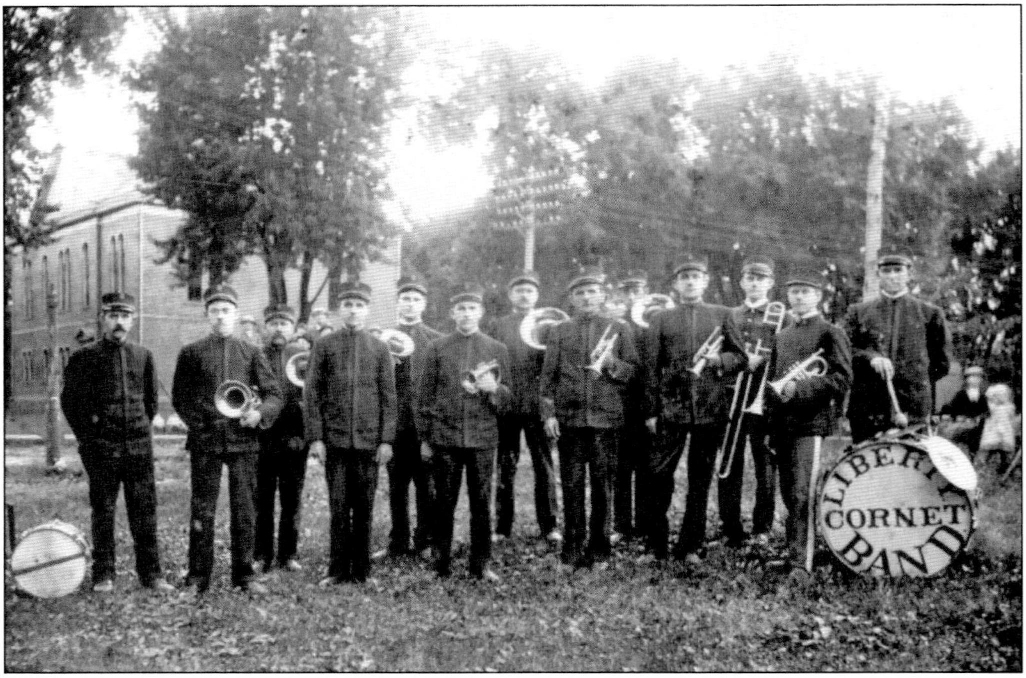

The Liberty Cornet Band is the only community band still playing in Adams County. Organized in 1900 by John Frambes, the band was based in the tiny community of Fairview, Liberty Township, for several decades. It is one of the oldest community bands in Ohio. Here it is on the courthouse lawn about 1907. (Courtesy Adams County Historical Society.)

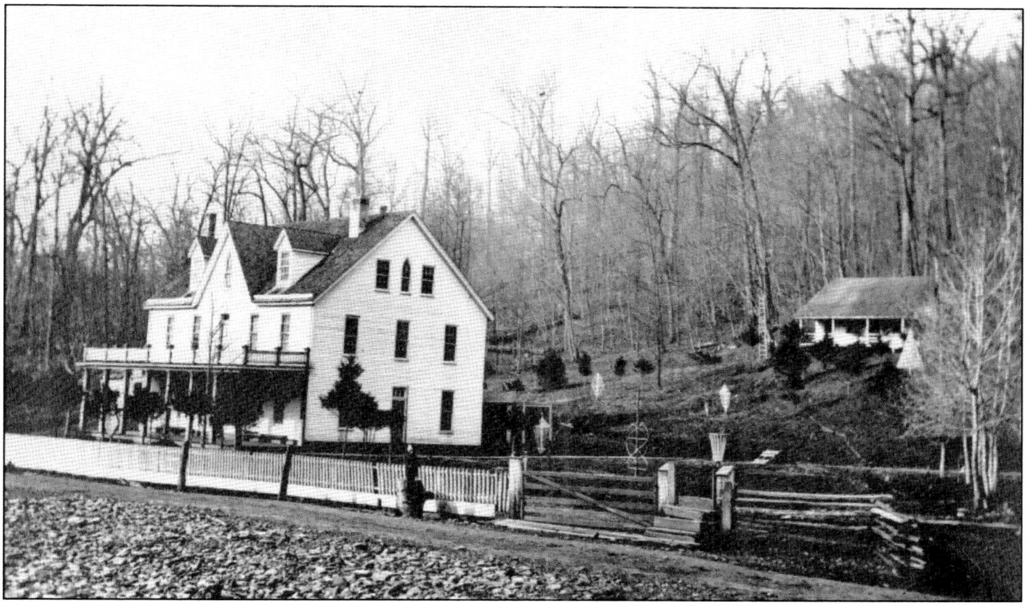

The Adams County Mineral Springs health resort was established in 1864. Over the succeeding 75 years, untold thousands of visitors made their way to the secluded Dry Fork Valley in Meigs Township, where, seeking health and healing, they drank, bathed in, and breathed the vapors of the mineral-laden spring waters. Finley Black took this c. 1870 photograph of the resort's second hotel, which was built in 1867. (Courtesy Lester and Jean Wallis.)

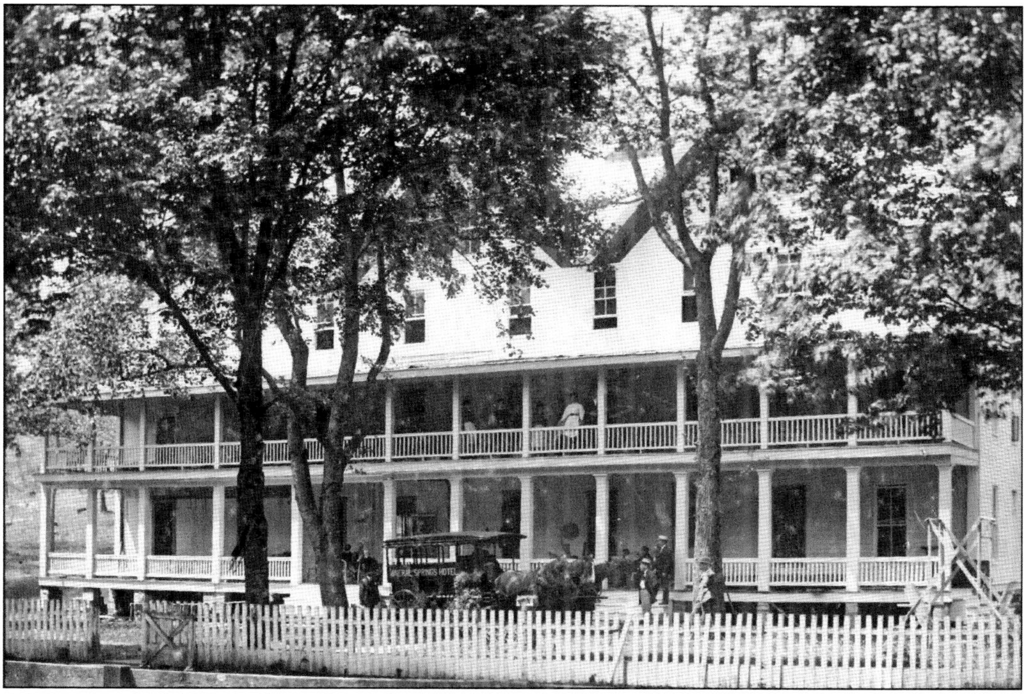

After several additions, this is how the Mineral Springs Hotel appeared in 1908. Workmen were just completing a new third story on the big hotel. (Courtesy John and Carol Wickerham.)

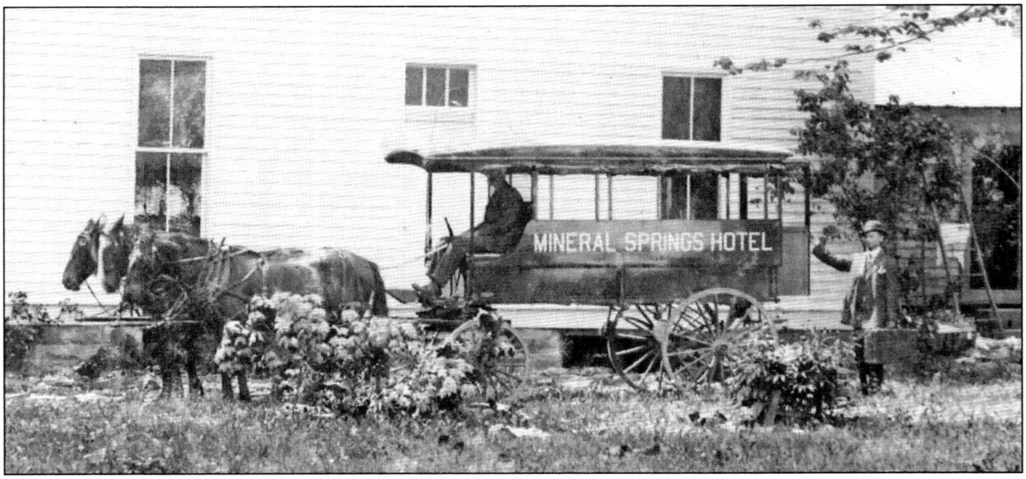

This is the three-horse hack J. W. "Happy Jack" Rogers used at the Mineral Springs Hotel in 1908, when he was the proprietor. The hack was used to convey resort customers to and from the Mineral Springs Railroad Station at the community of Jaybird. To accomplish this, the horses had to pull the hack up and over Peach Mountain, the highest hill in the county. (Courtesy John and Carol Wickerham.)

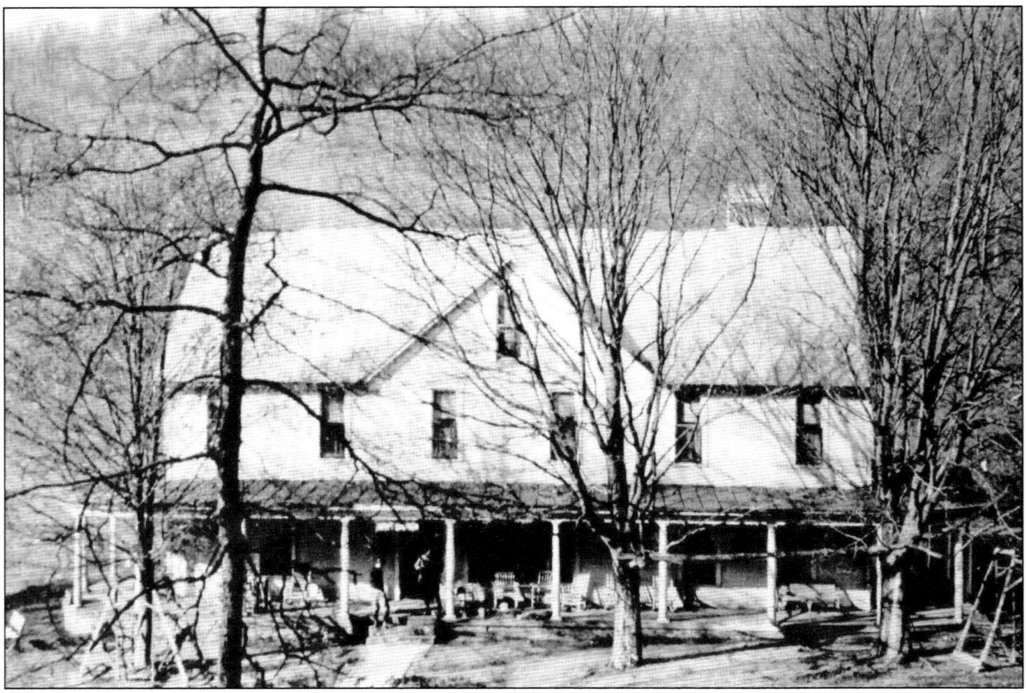

A second hotel was built at Mineral Springs in 1904. Known as the Hotel Baderton and, later, the Hotel Norfolk, it was much smaller in size than the Mineral Springs Hotel. This photograph was taken on May 6, 1928, by hotel guest Dr. E. Lucy Braun, a nationally recognized botanist and geologist who was then studying Adams County's rare plant communities. (Courtesy Cincinnati Museum Center.)

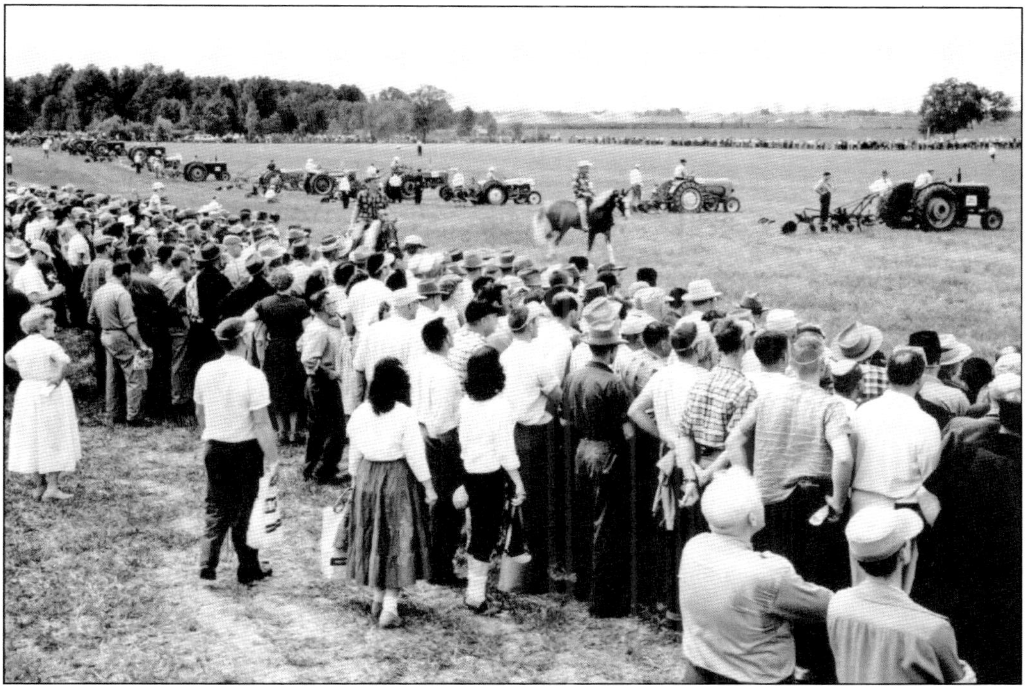

September 1957 witnessed the convergence of an estimated quarter-million visitors upon Adams County as they attended the fifth annual World's Plowing Matches and Conservation Exposition. Fourteen nations participated in various types of plowing skills. Above is a partial view of one of the stubble plowing contests and the large crowds watching. To commemorate the plowing contests, a symbolic Cairn of Peace was dedicated on the site of the contests. Below, the cairn is being unveiled with the Queen of the Furrows, Ann Lane (Schaffer), on the far right witnessing the event. Schaffer returned to Adams County in 2007 to attend the 50th-anniversary celebration of the plowing contests. E. W. Cole of the U.S. Soil Conservation Service was the photographer of both of these views. (Both courtesy Adams County Historical Society.)

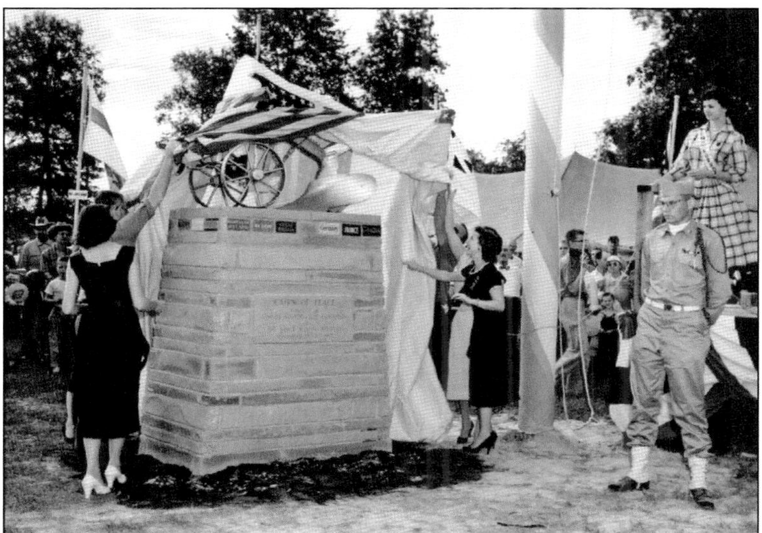